A Poisonous Journey
A LADY EVELYN MYSTERY

Malia Zaidi

For my family.

"All things are in the hand of heaven, and Folly, eldest of Jove's daughters, shuts men's eyes to their destruction. She walks delicately, not on the solid earth, but hovers over the heads of men to make them stumble or to ensnare them."

Homer, The Iliad

"Men are so quick to blame the gods: they say that we devise their misery. But they themselves — in their depravity — design grief greater than the griefs that fate assigns."

Homer, The Odyssey

PROLOGUE

Crete 1908

A chill ran down his spine and goose-bumps prickled his skin as the cold darkness enveloped him, swallowed him, the realm of Hades tormentingly near. He sucked in a breath of the damp air and blinked furiously, anxious to find his bearings, to discern hard rocky wall from empty space. It was his fault, he had dropped the torch and they had no choice but to save the reserve for later. For their destination. He would manage. He knew the way.

"Andros?" The nervous voice caught him almost unaware. Andros, Dros, Dros…the echo bounced off the walls around him and made him feel dizzy for a moment, as though the walls were moving closer and caging him in. He exhaled, trying to steady himself. They just had to follow the plan. He was good at that. Good at being patient, good at doing what he was told, at following directions to the letter.

"It's all right," he tried to sound calm, quelling his fear as it mingled with the excitement that bubbled inside him, ready to explode. They were so close now. He could feel the rhythmic beat of his heart increasing, a nervous echo in his chest. "Stay where you are, your eyes will adjust. Have patience." Listening for a moment, he became aware of the labored breathing of his brother close behind.

He stood still for another moment, no other sounds dared to intrude, eerie silence, thick with mystery, with secrets to be uncovered swathed them in its heavy shroud. The Sirens are calling, only you can hear. Run for safety, or plunge and fall prey to temptation. His eyes began to adjust, slowly deciphering the jagged outline of a rocky outcrop above him. It was close. He could feel it. His muscles tensed, stiff and solid, waves of energy pulsing through him, barely contained anticipation. Despite the cold, he felt beads of sweat dotting his brow and running down his temples.

"Andros? I think I see you. Yes." A few unsure steps followed these words, and he saw the shadowy outline of his younger brother, warily moving toward him.

"Come, but beware your steps, a wrong move could be your last."

Slowly, with his hands carefully outstretched, he felt his way forward. The air was growing stale, thick and cloying with dust and age.

"Are we almost there?"

"Close, very close."

Breath quickening, he shivered. So close now. Everything would change. For a split, indulgent second, he allowed himself a fantasy of the glory that would come, of the life that awaited him. Yes, not much further now. His feet, clad only in his worn leather shoes felt every rock on the uneven ground, a sensation that gave him comfort, a feeling of awareness that had replaced his compromised eyesight and heightened his sense of touch. Hands extended, he reached into the blackness like a blind man. Suddenly they came up against something. Wall. Hard rock wall. The tunnel had come to an abrupt end.

"What is this? Are we lost?"

Andros frowned, small creases folding his forehead, his brother's voice behind him a distracting intrusion. "No," he answered carefully, unconsciously holding his breath. He ran his hands along the roughness of the stony wall, seemingly solid and impenetrable, until… Yes, a smooth oval protrusion in the rock face. Sucking in a nervous lungful of dusty air, he pushed. The oval receded into the wall with neat precision. A momentary silence. Then, as if by some miraculous force, the wall gave way, an ingenious mechanism. A dense cloud of dust and debris rose up, sending both men staggering backward, coughing, and rubbing their stinging eyes. Soon the dust settled and silence was again upon them. Neither spoke, fear and excitement taking hold of them. Andros swallowed. It was all coming together. They were here, finally.

"The torch, now." His voice was almost a whisper, thick with anticipation. A hiss, and a flicker of orange light shot out of the darkness, illuminating his brother's dirty face. Reluctantly the younger man handed it over. No words were exchanged as Andros took the first careful step, holding the glowing light before him. He entered the chamber, eyes wide, barely breathing. He had found it! He wanted to shout out in joy, in relief. He had known all along, he had found it.

"So, this is it."

Andros turned, sensing something strange in his brother's tone. The younger man's face was still cast in shadow, save for the glittering eyes, shining in the gloom like those of an animal.

"Yes, this is it," he turned around again, taking it in, the glory. His glory. A sudden coldness at his neck startled him, a stab of pain. And then the blackness returned. Endless and unrelenting.

CHAPTER 1

London March 1925
Rain and Rain and Rain.

"Ran away from home! And with that man, would you believe it!" Aunt Agnes raises her eyebrows, and I roll my eyes. Her voice drops an octave as she hisses, "Lady Margot told me her parents are threatening to disown her." She nods, her smugness nearly impelling me to get to my feet and leave, slamming the door for good measure, but I restrain myself. There are bigger things to worry about. Frowning, her mouth falls into its natural disapproving position, small lines at the corners crinkling like the tops of my favorite ginger biscuits. Another subtle but firm shake of the head before she busies herself with her embroidery.

Tired, or simply bored silly—I can hardly distinguish the difference—I sink back into the stiff cushioned sofa and glance out of the window facing the empty square. Fat raindrops splatter loudly against the glass, and I barely stifle a sigh. My aunt's ire is fueled by the elopement of my old school friend, Laura Hallan. I secretly wish I could have attended the wedding myself, but it all had to be done very discreetly, and I have little experience in subterfuge, a fact that strikes me as oddly displeasing. There is however, a little nugget of opportunity that has, quite temptingly, been tossed my way; an opportunity that no one in this house could know about, least of all dear Auntie . . . certainly not yet.

I was able to seize the letter before Aunt Agnes had a chance to see the name of the sender and question me. I am a terrible liar, and a lie would have been my only option, if I were to see through the plan that had by now taken firm root in my mind.

I snatched the letter off the silver tray our butler carried into the drawing room. Harris, the butler in question, is fond of me and placed my letter on the top of the pile for me to see, before Aunt Agnes had time to prop her spectacles onto her nose. Feigning a migraine, a favorite malady of many a lady of my acquaintance, I snuck off into my room to devour it. Careful not to tear the lovely blue and white stamp that bore the image of Hermes, the messenger god, I slit the envelope open to find to my delight a letter from my favorite cousin, Briony; Briony being the only daughter of my paternal uncle. As only children and of similar ages, we were always thrown together at the boring adult get-togethers or parties, and our friendship was born.

We kept in touch since she left the country over a year ago with her husband, Jeffrey, to live on Crete of all places! In truth, I am envious, more of Crete than the husband, though Jeffrey is a dear and quite acceptable as far as husbands go. Briony was terribly happy when they were married, and when Jeffrey announced he had been offered a position at the Historical Museum in Heraklion and was going to accept it, she agreed. Jeffrey is a scholar and a good nine years older than my cousin. At first, I was concerned when I learned of their union, but it seems my concern was for nothing.

Briony is a real English rose, all pale curls and pink cheeks, so I was not at all certain this change in scenery would be to her liking, especially as it meant I would have to do without her. I told her as much, though perhaps more subtly, nonetheless she seemed excited at the prospect. Thus, with a heavy heart, I waved goodbye, having extracted her solemn promise to write as often as she could. Well, this letter is a bit different than the stack I keep safe in an old biscuit tin at the bottom of my wardrobe.

A POISONOUS JOURNEY   A LADY EVELYN MYSTERY

March 2, 1925

Miklos, Crete

Dearest Evie,

. Thank you for you last letter. I am afraid the postal service here in my newly adopted country is still rather lagging behind our majesty's royal mail, for it arrived a whole three weeks late! I shudder to think you might have felt neglected. To make amends for this flaw in the system, I am inviting you, dear cousin, to visit Jeffrey and me here at our, finally fully furnished spiti (that means home, see I am learning). The country is beautiful, and I am greeted everywhere with kindness, but I still feel quite a stranger and would so welcome your company. Jeffrey is lovely, but he is at the museum much of the time, so my days have become a little more solitary than I am used to. I know Greek history has always held a certain fascination for you, so if nothing else, perhaps that is incentive enough to convince you to come. I know our darling Aunt Agnes will not gladly suffer your absence, but if you can bear to tear yourself away from the bleakness of English April, please do come. I can promise you the best room in the house and my undying gratitude.

All my love,

Briony

Aunt Agnes is still working away at a maddeningly detailed depiction of a hummingbird, her slender fingers as quick and efficient as ever. I close my eyes sinking deeper into the cushion. Greece—clear skies, olive trees, blue waters, Briony, how could I possibly resist?

Still March, 1925. Still raining. Escape afoot.

It is rather early this Saturday morning. Harris stands waiting at the foot of the stairs, waving at me and opening the front door. A taxi has just pulled up in front of our Belgravia townhouse. It is still dark outside, and for a fleeting moment I wonder whether this is such a good idea after all. I could still go back to my room, slip into bed, and pretend none of this ever happened. Harris wouldn't tell, that much I know. No, now or never, I tell myself, fortifying my resolve. I reach the bottom step. Harris gives me an encouraging nod.

"Ready?"

I nod back at him. "Ready. Thank you Harris. I shall write as soon as I arrive."

"Safe journey, Lady Evelyn." He gives a short bow and turns away, hefting my luggage and carrying it to the cab. As he turns, I catch a shimmering trail on the side of his face and realize it is a tear. I will miss Harris. He, my maid, Milly and our cook, Mrs. Barnaby, are very dear to me and have been bright spots in my life ever since I came to live at Number 12, Eaton Square.

Clutching onto my hat whilst maneuvering an unwieldy hatbox containing the wide-brimmed sunhat I bought for Briony at Selfridges, I slip outside. The cabbie is already back in the driver's seat. I press a kiss onto Harris' cheek, and before I can change my mind, slide into the backseat of the idling motor. Shrouded by the swirling fog of the city, the car drives off, disrupting the peaceful chirping of early birds with its low rumbling engine.

Leaning back against the cool leather seat, I feel a weight falling from my shoulders as I glance back and see the eerie, foggy outlines of my aunt's darkened home disappearing from view. I left her a letter. Cowardly, I know, but at least she will be informed and can make up whatever stories she feels she must to protect my reputation and hers. It is not my proudest moment, sneaking off like this, but it had to be done. I have to get away. Life, whatever it has to offer, is out there, outside the shielding walls of that house, and out of sight of the intrusive and restricting reach of English society.

What harm can it do for me to see more, to do something unexpected? I will return some day. London is home, after all, or at least it carries with it all the familiar attributes that should make it home, but for now ... I let out the breath I did not realized I was holding, for now it is time for something new. As the streets of London pass me by in a gray-misted blur, a prickle of fear and excitement surges through me. When we finally pull up in front of Victoria Station I am slightly giddy and have only one thought coursing through my mind: It is time to make my great escape!

CHAPTER 2

Crete: Warm winds and sunshine . . . mingling with mal-de-mer.

Miklos, the village, is located on the island of Crete off mainland Greece, requiring a short journey from the crowded port. Built around the crumbling ruins of a temple to Dionysus, it maintains an atmosphere of mythological wonder and old-world charm. Or so I am led to believe, if the brief descripton in my guidebook can be trusted.

I will be very frank, the act of arriving here in one piece has been quite an ordeal. The sea voyage from Piraeus on the "tempestuous" Mediterranean was an arduous undertaking, and when I finally glimpsed the craggy gray cliffs, the first sign of land, I breathed a thankful sigh of relief. The thought crosses my mind that I could not now go back England even if I wanted to. Not even Aunt Agnes could drag me back onto that creaking, leaking, quaking contraption of a ship in the near future.

Briony promised to send a driver to pick me up, and I hope my dear but oft-forgetful cousin is true to her word. My knowledge of the Greek language is not impressive, despite my keen interest in the country's rich history and mythology, and I am uncertain whether I could make myself understood, especially as my brain is more than usually shaken from the journey, and I am having trouble stammering in English. Under normal circumstances, I consider myself quite capable when forced to rely upon my own agency, a lifetime of sneaking in and out of Aunt Agnes' house allowed for the cultivation and development of a certain set of skills. Still, I question whether they will come in handy on an island other than good old Britannia.

As I stand here, nervously chewing my lower lip, the ship slowly pulls into Heraklion's harbor, still rocking with a force not befitting the tranquility of my romantic, though clearly uninformed, imagination. In the seaport, I observe a surprising number of other vessels, tied and anchored at the bustling pier. Some are quite small, painted different colors and with names written in angular Greek script upon their sides; others grand, probably yachts for tourists, I observe eagerly as my stomach slowly settles. Most ships are white and blue fishing boats that bob about with their masts tilted in the soft swell of the tide. To one side of the port lies the fortress of Rocca al Mare. It looms large and forboding, walled in a yellow stone that reflects the glow of the sun. The top of the wall is elaborately turreted, like a medieval castle, though the fortress, my trusty guidebook informs me, is Venetian. It is certainly an impressive sight to behold for the visiting traveler, as if to say, "Behave yourself, now!" I will try.

The process of disembarking takes rather a long time as everyone impatiently waits to be ferried off ship and reassigned their respective luggage. My knees still wobbly, I grow impatient, keen to come ashore.

When I finally disembark, I feel a faintly familiar, almost forgotten, tremor of anticipation and glee. I did it! I am here. I ran away from home like a naughty child, but it feels like a triumph! What an adventure alone the journey has been, and what else awaits me now that I have finally arrived?

Again on steady ground, the sea seems much more splendid and far less temperamental than onboard where I felt Poseidon's might, tossed about, stumbling green-faced to the railing. I hold my face towards the sun and bathe in its warm, welcoming embrace. Heavy waves crash forcefully into the wall of the fort, spraying glistening droplets like a crystal shower into the air. The spectacle has something soothing, almost hypnotic, repeating itself over and over again. A calming monotony. I am so entranced by this sight, I barely notice the slim, young man approaching until he is standing right beside me, coughing loudly to catch my attention.

"Oh," I say as I swivel around, a curl of my auburn hair falling out of the pins below my straw cloche and into my face. "Hello."

"Lady Carlisle?" His voice is soft, and his deep-set, watery blue eyes give him the appearance of permanent melancholy. I don't know how I missed catching sight of him earlier. Among the black curls and brown eyes all around me, he stands out like a sore thumb.

"Yes, I am she," smiling most winningly as I answer, I attempt to set the anxious young man at ease. By now I have recovered my composure after the rather miserable betrayal of my body on the ship and experience a burst of eager energy to move on.

"I was sent by Mrs. Farnham to fetch you." He blinks nervously and looks down. I immediately detect a slight Eastern European accent, Russian maybe I muse, though not having ever been there myself, I cannot be certain. Admittedly, I am mostly founding this judgement on the accent of an actor I saw perform a Chekov piece last winter . . . and badly at that! But I digress.

"Oh, she remembered, what a relief! And what, may I ask, is your name?"

"I am Yannick. I am the chauffeur for the Farnhams." Yannick, could be Russian, no? A chauffeur. I smile. So Jeffrey still has not learned how to drive. I happen to be ahead of him on that front. A cousin of mine, Hamish McNally, let me practice with his car, a rusty and rather temperamental old Humber when I was fourteen and in Scotland for a visit with my other aunt. Dear Agnes stayed in London, well away from "our savage sister". I suspected she was describing her own lovely sister, Iris, and not Scotland. Nevertheless, her absence afforded me the opportunity and freedom to expand my horizons in any way I saw fit, ladylike or not. Though, admittedly, there wasn't much to do that would have compromised my virtue. Alas, such is life.

"Very well, perhaps you might help me with my luggage, I fear I rather overpacked." I somewhat indiscriminately took what I could in my great escape, not knowing what would await me here, or when I might return.

He nods, clearly relieved to turn away and push my trolley to the waiting car, a luxurious cream Delage. It is beyond me how Jeffrey resists the urge to drive such a beauty. Perhaps I could convince him or Yannick to let me take it for a spin once I know my way about the place and would not go round a corner and off a cliff.

Yannick opens the backdoor and motions for me to sit and cool off in the shaded automobile, while he busies himself with loading up the various cases I brought along. The inside of the motor is as elegant as I imagined, all toffee-colored leather and shining chrome. Barely conscious of doing so, I turn the slim sapphire ring that once graced my mother's hand on my finger to the left, then to the right. It is precious to me, for so little of my parents remained after the fire. I treasure it and my father's silver fob watch more than any other possessions.

As I sit in the car, clutching a worn leather case, a veil of melancholy suddenly envelops me like an unexpected chill breeze. Twenty years have passed since it happened. I was only four, too young to truly understand, but old enough to sense the sadness, perhaps even to sense that nothing would ever be quite the same again. On that fateful day, I begged to ride my pony and only remember the violent flicker of orange flames as I saw them consuming my home from a great distance. Afterwards, I was whisked away to the houses of various relatives, their gray, miserable faces and red-rimmed eyes telling me that Mama and Papa were taking a long holiday, or some such fantasy one tells children to shield them from the truth, from reality and from pain. No one told me what exactly happened, what caused the inferno, until years later, and even then they used the gentle phrases, "passed on" or "went to a better place" as if saying such things made them any less dead and gone. As if it could make me feel any less alone.

My mother's childless sister Agnes Tremaine and her husband took me in. Her other sister, Iris suffered a breakdown at the terrible news, and could not be granted guardianship of me, despite my mother and her being the closer of the three sisters. Iris lives in a draughty castle on the Scottish border, has been married twice, and given birth to four children, Hamish, my driving instructor, being the eldest of the lot. Poor, dear Hamish. He would be thirty now and might have married some lovely Scottish lass; Iris might have grandchildren to fill the near empty halls of Malmo Manor.

Hamish was listed as missing in action four months after he enlisted. Eight years on Aunt Iris still carries the glimmer of hope that he will one day reappear standing on her doorstep, a crooked grin on his face.

Agnes tried, though she had a different idea of what parenting should be than my real parents. I am grateful to her and always will be, but at twenty-four I am quite old enough to venture into the world unencumbered by her rigid and old-fashioned rules to weigh me down. In less than a year's time I willl come into my inheritance. The only child of Lord and Lady Carlisle, I have been left with hundreds of thousands to my name as well as a large burnt down manor in Somerset that I could bring myself to visit only once in two decades.

My parents were different. Even now people speak of them as rebels of a sort. Both young and wealthy, they traveled for months on end. Even when I was born they took me along for the ride. So often I wonder what my life might have been like with my parents still here to guide and influence. Nevertheless, after the fire I was fortunate to have Aunt Agnes assume responsibility for me, to raise me, send me off to the best schools in Switzerland and France. You mustn't pity yourself, I tell myself, so many people are far less fortunate. Though able to recognize these blessings in my life, I am certain given the chance, I would gladly offer up anything for the company of my parents again. For only a day with them, I—

"Lady Carlisle, we'll go now?" Lost in my melancholy reverie, I barely notice Yannick climbing into the driver's seat beside me and am startled by his low, accented voice, interrupting my thoughts. Still clutching the hat case, I nod at him, and the engine rumbles loudly as the heavy motor sets into motion.

"Yannick," I pause, not wanting to make the young man even more uncomfortable, "please do call me Evelyn." After a moments hesitation he nods once more.

"Yes, Lady Carlisle." I repress a sigh.

It quickly becomes clear that Yannick is a good driver. He elegantly maneuvers the angular, solid vehicle along the curving roads and, at times, shockingly narrow passageways running in a spidery web through the city. And it is a city, not the piddly little town I had, in my ignorance—or, more kindly, innocence—imagined. Alongside us run buildings of pale yellow occasionally interspersed with one rebelliously painted orange or coral façade. Brightly colored shutters flank open windows, and though there is a certain sense of deterioration about parts of the city, it is not the squallid, suffocating kind that one encounters in parts of the East End or Clerkenwell. Children play outside their houses, jumping out of the way when the Delage rolls near. Some point and stare, others run after us as though this strange contraption were a creature of lore. Many people are out on the streets; women and men with tanned skin and dark hair, going about their lives. The women stand in lively huddles chatting and laughing, while a little boy or girl tugs at their hand or skirt. The men seem more inclined to a relaxed pace and move about their business in a manner that suggests they would not be hurried by a fuming bull at their heels.

There is little greenery save for an occasional random tree planted here and there, or the colorful boxes of flowers hanging from many windows. We pass a small square adorned by a large limestone fountain in the center, children splashing around and being, in turn, scolded by their mothers.

The buildings, as far as I am able to judge, appear largely influenced by the Venetian style with elaborate archways, columns, and wrought-iron balconies so small one would have been hard-pressed to install a chair.

After some time, Yannick takes a turn leading up a hill, taking us away from the vibrant port and city scene of Heraklion and away from the tossing waters of the sparkling blue sea. Once the metropolitan area is behind us, we venture into a more barren landscape, dotted here and there with small dark trees I am unable to identify, as well as clusters of thorny bushes and brambles. Then, as if entering another climate entirely, we turn the bend and find a lush and blooming valley before us. Thus the scenery alternates between aridly dry and nearly tropical.

I stare mesmerized out of the window, watching it all drift by, single trees blurred together, a flock of crows screeching, launching themselves into the cloudless blue sky. It is so unlike any place I have ever seen, yet I feel somewhere inside myself a sense of deep familiarity as though I have been here before. This is the land of the stories I gleefully inhaled at school; this the wild sea Odysseus voyaged; the crumbling ruins of ancient temples and theatres for the festivals and plays; the jagged cliffs met by crashing waves, so easily imagined as lairs of the mysterious and terrifying Sirens. Tales of glory, tragedy, and madness permeate this very soil, and I feel a shiver of delight running down my spine, imagining the phantoms of the past swirling in our midst.

The drive might have lasted mere minutes or more than an hour. The hypnotic curves of the road, accompanied by Yannick's pervading silence and the soothing landscape have made me drowsy and distorted the true lapse of time. My head grows light and my eyelids heavy, and I lean back into the soft leather upholstery. It still seems almost a dream, one moment I was sitting on the hard brocade sofa in Aunt Agnes' drawing room, loathingly glaring at the gloomy oil paintings of my ancestors, who just as loathingly glared back at me; and now, now I am hundreds of miles away in a foreign land, chauffered by a strange man, and heading to a place I have never been before. How a situation can change in a matter of days, or mere hours! What a strangely frightening and splendid thing time can be.

Just as this thought crosses my mind the car slows, dry gravel crunching beneath the weight of the tires. I sit up, curious to find us pulling up in front of a cream colored two-story villa. Columns in the Corinthian style I remember from grainy photographs in a library book, with elaborately carved plaster capitals line the front, lending the elegant home an air of ancient mystique. It looks just as I had hoped it would! The gardens are relatively bare, save for a few rows of small, bushy olive trees swaying gently in the breeze. A vivid patch of glowing pink bougainvillea has draped itself from one of the second floor balconies down the left side of the house like a blooming shawl.

Energized by pent up excitement, I open the car door before Yannick is able to help me. I always feel ill at ease with stiff formalities anyway, and here in particular, in this to me still wild and exotic land, they have no place. It is good to stretch out my legs, to feel the hard earth below me, the heat rising through the thin soles of my soft kidskin shoes.

The elevation affords an impressive view of the sparkling blue sea in the distance, the dark color of the water meeting the pale blue of the sky in one delicate horizontal line; the division between the realm of Poseidon and that of his brother, Zeus. Zeus took control of earth and sky, while his brothers, Poseidon and Hades, became rulers of the sea and underworld. For a moment, my mind flickers to an image of the mighty bearded king of the gods I have seen illustrated in one of the books I borrowed from the library. He was depicted reclining on a pillowy cloud, casting his cool, blue-eyed gaze across his dominion, long muscled limbs outstretched. Almost unconsciously I look up. The sky is cloudless and mesmerizingly blue. Where might he be now, I wonder, humoring myself and my illusions, and yet hoping that not all myths are make-believe. It appears to me that Zeus is having a benevolent day, for the sun beams splendidly, and I take off my hat to feel its rays warming the crown of my head.

Suddenly, the door to the villa swings open, and a small, fair-haired woman, wearing a pale blue dress that flutters just below her knees, rushes out, followed very closely by a slightly taller fair-haired man. Seeing my cousin after so many months warms my heart, and an image of her as a child, pigtailed and freckled, running down the drive to meet me at my uncle's house, flickers through my mind.

"Evie, darling! You made it!" Briony takes me by the hands and I obediently lower my head to have my cheeks kissed. "And you look so well! Jeffrey, my dear, doesn't she look well," she asks, Jeffrey, who having followed his wife outside, nods, smiling obligingly.

"Yes, very well." Briony grins approvingly.

"You should have seen me after my first journey here, green as a cucumber!" She laughs. Open and sincere as she is, I cannot help but join in with her cheerfulness. The familiar sound of her laughter makes me feel as though a bond of guilt or anxiety for having run away has been severed, a tension in the back of my neck eased and melted away under the Mediterranean sun.

"It is wonderful to see you in such good spirits, Briony," I smile and turn to Jeffrey, "and you too, of course. What a beautiful spot you have chosen here. Why you may never be rid of me again!" As I say this, I realize I am only half joking. The journey was daunting, but upon setting foot on solid ground I felt immediately lighter than I had in years. It is as though every mile separating me from my old life lifts a weight bearing down on me. Here is no overbearing aunt, no rigid and maddeningly dull social calendar, and most importantly, no crippling memories to burden my mind. The sun shines down on us, and my tired London skin eagerly drinks it up, the sweet warmth spreading through me like honeyed tea, welcome and liberating.

"Yannick, let me help you with those," Jeffrey says with raised eyebrows, indicating my numerous cases stacked beside the car, giving Briony and me the privacy we crave after our long separation.

"So tell me, was dear Auntie Agnes positively murderous when you told her you were leaving?" Briony loops her slender arm through mine, and gently leads me onto a small path toward the garden at the back of the house and away from the driveway. "She was appalled, you know when Jeffrey and I told her of our plans to come here. Truly, I thought I would have to conjure up some smelling salts to pull her from the brink of apoplexy!" I cannot prevent a grin spreading across my lips. It is as though no time had passed, as though we traveled backwards to before she married, before she left. I harbored a niggling fear that our friendship would not be what it once was, that I left England only to feel isolated and alone in a foreign land. A sense of relief washes over me, in discovering these concerns troubled me in vain. In the garden, we sit down on a smooth carved bench of dark olive wood with a view of the strange landscape surrounding us.

"I'm afraid I behaved rather appallingly," I say, looking down at my lap in false remorse, waiting for Briony to respond as I know she will.

"Appallingly! Do tell." Briony's dark blue eyes glitter, and for a moment I am transported back many years; to mischievous times of hiding in the library together in an attempt to avoid Aunt Agnes' reproving gaze; to running away, but only reaching the corner of the park, seduced by the prospect of the freshly baked Victoria sponge we were missing at home. It seems so long ago, but now, sitting here, one dark and one light head leaning together, I cannot help but revel in the happy sense of nostalgia. With some mild embellishment I embark upon the tale of my clandestine getaway and am pleased to put a glow of excited admiration on Briony's face.

"Evie! What an adventure! Well, I shan't let you go back. I have decided," she crosses her arms in determination. "I am simply in dire need of long-term, English company."

"I shall be happy to oblige." This sentiment rings genuine. I believe I could happily stay indefinitely. Perhaps I might marry one of the handsome fishermen I caught sight of at the harbor and buy a little house with colorful shuttered windows overlooking the blue sea in front and the green mountains in the back. Yes, I sigh to myself, such a life would be quite bearable.

Briony sits back, exhaling slowly, the gentle breeze blowing a strand of her curly blonde hair into her face. She brushes it away and turns back to me.

"Mind you," she says impishly, "I haven't told you about our other guests."

"Other guests? Am I a mere one of many!" I shake my head in mock exasperation, curiosity awakening.

"Never, my dear. They are merely invitees of my darling husband. You are solely mine." Saying this, she grasps my hand firmly in hers.

"How glad I am to hear you take such a possessive stance. Now you have intrigued me. Who is this band of men I am to be rooming with?"

Briony throws her head back in delight. "Can you imagine! The scandal, Auntie Agnes would disown you. No, I fear you will be all alone," she grins wickedly. "I suppose how long you remain so will be up to you, my dear. Though of course, I ought to be true to my duty as your watchful chaperone, to protect your sweet innocence and all that." She winks at me, and I roll my eyes. "I've put you in the loveliest room overlooking the garden, or what we call a garden," she gestures at the dry patches of grass and twisted olive trees. "Our other guests are old chums of Jeffrey's. Daniel Harper and Caspar Ballantine. They are charming, handsome, well-spoken and so on and so forth. Caspar is . . . I don't know what, really, and Daniel is a writer. Or so he claims. He is working on a book and won't say much more yet. Daniel comes from a wealthy home, so I suppose it doesn't matter if the book is any good. You'll meet them tonight. They are out sailing now with some people they met at a picnic last weekend. They've been here a while, you see, so they've been busy making friends," she raises her pale eyebrows comically, by which I believed I am meant to infer that these "friends" are of the female variety.

Briony continues, "We're having a few neighbors over. I'm afraid your first evening here will require your social graces. I do hope you're not too tired, but they really all are a friendly bunch, and none too obstinate to tolerate for a few hours."

"Not at all. I look forward to it." I am interested in the company my cousin keeps in her adopted homeland. Briony has written about some of her new acquaintances, most of them expatriots like her, or colleagues of Jeffrey's from the museum. Having created my own images of them in my mind, I am eager to see how well they match up to the person in the flesh.

"That's settled then," Briony smiles, her freckled face still pale with only the slight pink tinge of sunburn on her small upturned nose. Glancing at the house, she observes Yannick closing the empty boot of the car. "The men have done the heavy lifting, shall I give you the grand tour?" Nodding, I hook my arm through hers and follow my cheerfully chattering guide into the cool interior of the villa.

CHAPTER 3

I have truly arrived. It is still hard to believe. I am sitting in my lovely room after Briony's tour of the villa. She proudly showed off her spacious home, narrating all the while with cheerful gestures and well-deserved gratification. It is tastefully furnished with an inviting blend of heavy English pieces of luxuriously polished oak and sumptuous brocade upolstery as well as the lighter, softer fittings of her new surroundings. Woven wicker chairs stand around a small circular table in the conservatory, and everywhere hang vivid watercolors of the sea that she has bought from street vendors in town. Altogether she has created a very pleasing environment for an Englishwoman abroad. Briony has somehow managed to reconcile her old and new home and has created an atmosphere both nostalgic and contemporary.

As we move from the airy conservatory to the modest library, I wonder whether Briony ever intends to return to England. Jeffrey's position at the museum is meant to be for three years, but both he and Briony have made a real home here, and the prospect of leaving it behind in the near future seems a pity.

The house is larger than I had initially presumed, for at the back a further stairway to the servants quarters is located as well as an attic which Briony says she has thus far avoided for fear of exotic creatures lurking in the dust. They keep only a small staff of a cook, maid, and chauffeur. Though Briony is enthusiastic about the house, there is something bothering her, I can tell. As indicated in her letter, she appears to spend much of her day alone, and I am glad now to be here to offer her companionship and support. Wandering around, we come upon one room near Briony and Jeffrey's own bedchamber, painted a pale yellow with a small crib below the window. She quickly closes the door, but not before I notice the flash of sadness flit across her doll-like features. I have the sudden sinking feeling nothing I can do might truly impact the void she feels. My cousin has always had the desire to be a mother, to fill her house with the pitter-patter of children's feet, and it must pain her to have this large house still bare of those sounds she yearns to hear. Perhaps that is why she is so keen to fill it with friends and guests for constant distraction. She has never liked silence.

My room is small, yet in no way lacking in charm. The large window, framed in solid dark wood, opens up to a grand view of the mountainous landscape to one side, while a teasing sliver of the dark blue sea sparkles faintly in the distance. Taking a deep breath, I sigh in contentment. It looks like a postcard. Picture perfect. The sort of image one lingers over longingly and never truly imagines being a part of.

I slip off my shoes, which have begun to pinch. On an impulse, my stockings are discarded as well to enjoy the smooth polished wood cool below my bare feet. Standing here, I am almost in a daze, as though at any moment, Milly, my maid, will gently shake me awake, telling me I am late for tea and Agnes is fuming. Shaking my head, I rid myself of the thought. I am here, and they are there, and that is as it should be as far as I see it.

After showing me the villa, Briony has left me in my room, so she can begin her supervision of the preparations for supper. I am glad to catch a moment to gather my thoughts before the evening of socializing and small talk ahead, and put up no contest.

A breeze sweeps through the window, caressing my face like a gentle hand, and pulling at strands of my bobbed hair, causing them to flutter around my face. For a moment I wonder whether Aunt Agnes will try to contact me, quickly dismissing the thought. As soon as I am settled, I will send a telegraph telling my aunt that I have arrived safely and will remain with my responsible, married, civilized cousin for the forseeable future. I will tell her not to worry, and that I am well looked after. Yes, tomorrow I will ask to borrow the motor, or find some other transport into town and do it. Or maybe the day after . . . No, tomorrow. I nod to myself as if this gesture decides it.

Despite her rigidity, despite the fact that I have never felt she truly wanted me, always a reminder of the sister she lost, or the reality that she herself remained childless, Agnes took me in when I was alone and vulnerable, and for that I will forever be grateful. She has not always had an easy time of it either, and as the years have passed, as I realized what our relationship is and what it never will be, I have come to accept it as such and not to expect more.

Her husband, my uncle, Colonel Brandon Tremaine, died of the Spanish influenza seven years ago, and she has never remarried, nor paid attention to suitors, though there was more than one. His death came as a blow for me, too. With him gone, I felt the loss of yet another father figure. Perhaps my attachment to him caused an even wider rift in my relationship with Agnes. He accepted me as an adoptive daughter, something my aunt never was capable of doing. Upon his death he left me a yearly stipend. This seemed to fuel Aunt Agnes' disdain for me, though she was not cheated, acceding to the ownership of both the Belgravia mansion and a manor in Kent where we hid away during the war. When I was home from school, I joined them there and remember the stories I overheard my uncle tell her before he died; of the battlefields, of the poor young lads, of the damaged lungs, the cut off limbs, the dead, the many dead men who were only boys. He cried then, the only time I ever heard him cry, such a big, strong man, and she whispered to him, words I couldn't hear, the only time her voice resembled the gentle, soothing voice of my mother. Over time, I noticed that the boys in town, boys I played with in the summers when we holidayed there, had disappeared. The only males left were the old or the very young. I was myself too young to be of much use, only sixteen at the end of the war. I felt a gnawing shame everytime I was sent back to the safety and confines of my boardingschool when all around me the world was breaking into jagged pieces. Time has passed, wounds have healed, the dead have been buried, but the black cloud of that tragic past still manages to hover over us even now. Hopefully, this constant, merciless reminder will prevent such a horror from recurring. If I am still haunted, how must those who served, fought, nursed and doctored, suffer?

I frown, willing these thoughts to evaporate, yet they recede only vaguely like phantoms, to the dark shadows of my mind, always threatening to come forth and bring with them the blackness of nightmares. But I am persistent. I am in a new place, soon enough my mind will catch up. Outside my window is the vast canopy of blue, cloudless sky. The demons suffocating me in England must stay there. I want no more grief. No more reminders of loss. Only memories of laughter, smiles, happiness will be allowed to follow the new Evie. Dragging in a deep breath of the scented sea air, I slowly release it, feeling the knot of tension that has crept up on me with the onslought of memories ease away. It will be all right. I will be all right again.

With some difficulty, I pull away from the scene of rugged tranquility outside my window and sink down onto the bed, an elegant four-poster affair with a gauzy mosquito net draped around it. Fit for a princess. The excitement of my arrival and the utter newness of my surroundings have given me a rush of energy, which is now slowly wearing off. I gratefully lean back on the pile of soft, welcoming cushions and fall, almost instantly into a revitalizing slumber, only to be disturbed by the gentle knock of the maid three hours later, arrived to help me get ready for dinner.

Niobe is a slim, dark-haired woman, just as I might have imagined Persephone, though I probably ought not tell her that. She cannot, I muse, be much older than myself. When I think of my dear maid, Milly, now probably being berated by Aunt Agnes, I feel disloyal as though I traded my English rose for this Grecian beauty, whose profile would not have disappointed even the magnificent sculptor Praxiletes.

As it is, the present encounter feels vaguely discomfiting. Niobe barely speaks, and I am apprehensive. The silence takes up all the air in the room. Milly and I always chatted and joked, but now, any attempts at conversation on my part are only granted quick, monosyllabic answers. I know my cousin would not have taken on a maid who cannot speak English. Briony herself considers the Greek language nearly impossible to learn as she has reported in her letters. Maybe Niobe resents the lack of effort made to adapt to this, her native land, by foreigners such as myself? I think, watching her out of the corner of my eye. I suppose I would, too, in spite of Briony and Jeffrey surely being pleasant employers. Just as the thought crosses my mind, I hear an odd thump behind me. I swivel around. Niobe is lying on the ground!

"Oh my!" I can't help but exclaim aloud.

I dash to her side, carefully brushing the thick black curls from the young woman's face.

"Niobe!" My right hand rushes to her neck. The pulse is strong, the skin warm. Just a faint, I think and experience a surge of relief. Having witnessed a fair number of such episodes in my close circle at home, I always managed to stay quite calm. But I will confess, the sight of a person lying unconscious on the ground still has the power to rattle me.

Suddenly, as if on cue, she stirs and opens her eyes a slit. Blinking tentatively, her pupils adjusting again to the light, she looks up at me, a confused expression on her face.

"Oh dear, it's all right. Don't you worry," I try to reassure the girl and help her to sit up, grabbing one of the overstuffed cushions from the bed and propping it underneath her back. Then, reaching for the glass of lukewarm water on my bedside table, I press it to her lips and continue, "You fainted that is all. How do you feel?"

Smiling at Niobe, I attempt to reassure her. Some employers, I know, would consider even such an involuntary show of weakness grounds for a reprimand. Niobe is visibly anxious, though I know Briony would never penalize such vulnerability. Not even Aunt Agnes would be so hard-hearted.

Niobe swallows the water I force on her and takes a deep breath, exhaling slowly. I still sit beside her on the ground. I have never fainted myself, well not really. Everyone does occasionally to get out of some of the more tedious social events and company, but I have simply never considered myself the fainting sort. As my deeply stoic aunt might say, it simply isn't done.

Niobe is starting to improve, her cheeks have regained some color and the dazed look on her face has disappeared. I am relieved, for a moment she had given me quite a fright.

"Are you feeling better?" I ask, smiling what I hope is a heartening smile.

"Yes," Niobe nods. "Yes, I-I think it was the heat. I…this has never happened before." Her voice is soft and slightly accented, her vowels just a little more pronounced, as though they come from somewhere deeper in her throat.

"Yes, I suppose that must be it." I reply, not quite convinced. It has by now cooled down remarkably, and I can see through the open window that the sun has almost entirely fallen into the sea. The darkening sky has become a vast canvas for spectacular streaks of violet, apricot and glowing pink. I offer the young woman another sip of water, watching her as she drinks. As my gaze lingers a moment, I cannot help but notice the vivid blue of her eyes. My mind flashes to the Greek superstition of the blue-eyed charm one wears to ward off bad omens. Oh, I am terrible! I chastise myself. Such pale blue is surely quite unusual in a native of this local, but perhaps I am simply an ignorant fool.

We sit for another moment in silence, save for the rythmic hooting of an owl, somewhere unseen beyond my window. It is Niobe who makes the first move to get up, reaching for one of the beds sturdy wooden posts and pulling herself off the floor, brushing imagined dust from the simple cotton shift she is wearing.

"Niobe, are you certain you are all right? I could tell Briony you feel unwell and need a rest. I'm certain she will understand." I say this as I, too, get up from the hard wood that is, as far as comfort goes, a far cry from the lovely bed I occupied not long ago. "I can certainly get dressed on my own, you need not trouble yourself on that account." There is an ever-present sense of guilt whenever I am allotted another human being to serve my every whim. I grew up with my own maid, nannies, a butler, and though many soon felt like part of the family—often more so than members of my actual kin—I never been at ease with the idea of servitude. Perhaps that is a good thing. I have yearned for independence and getting myself dressed for an evening is a rather pathetic beginning.

Back in the present, I register Niobe shaking her head scattering long dark curls about her shoulders, awakening in me a stab of regret regarding to my own unromantically bobbed cut.

"Thank you, Miss, I am fine. It was just a—" Niobe pauses, searching for the word, "a spell." She smiles, gratified, and returns to my unpacked chest. "I am better now."

"Nonetheless, I truly can get dressed myself." I insist more firmly than intended. Niobe appears nervous, and I fear I have caused offense, so I lamely add, "Perhaps you could help me with the buttons." So much for independence! I open one of the trunks and pick out a pale yellow dress from the top of the heap, holding it up, the row of tiny perl closures shimmering in the low light. "Yes, perhaps you might be so kind. I think my own clumsy hands simply won't meet the challenge."

This has happened to me before. In an attempt to push aside formality, I risk alienating members of the staff who could never see themselves on an equal footing with the people upstairs. I will have to tread more carefully. It is strange how society dictates our behavior. I take one step forward, only to be pushed back as rules of right and wrong bar my way toward progress. Of course I am aware that Niobe, just like our cook and Harris, is performing a job. My problem goes deeper, stemming from the twinge of guilt I carry into every arena of my life. I was born into a completely unmerited existence of wealth and privilege; I was coddled and protected and despite my loss, never abandoned. I swallow, sensing the familiar lump at the back of my throat. That is the problem when I am left to think, my thoughts turn down dark and ugly alleys and do not venture where I want to steer them, onto the better-lit and broader avenues of my mind. Not now, I tell myself, pull yourself together. You must be poised and polished Lady Evelyn Carlisle tonight.

I shrug off my crumpled traveling outfit and slip into the new one. While Niobe buttons up the dress, I try again to make some conversation, eager to ease the unavoidable discomfiture of these encounters. I ask about her family and am told they live in Miklos, not at all far from here, and that she has three elder brothers, upon which I express my only-child jealousy and make Niobe's lips twitch into a smile. Though the young woman is reserved in her replies, I notice that she speaks an almost faultless English with only a pleasantly soft accent.

"If you will pardon my curiosity, where did you learn to speak such excellent English?" I ask as Niobe finishes the last closure.

"Oh, here and there, many on the island speak it well. We had quite a few people coming from England during the war and still. My father," a fractional hesitation before she continues, "he wanted my brothers and me to learn it, to find better work."

There is a firmness to the way she explains, and she lowers her gaze, giving me the strong impression that the subject is a complicated one and therefore is to be closed. Not wishing to cause discomfort to my new acquaintance, I probe no further. Instead, I turn to view myself in the long, carved mirror leaning against the opposite wall, even taller than me.

"Well, I say! I think I am fit to be seen now. Thank you, Niobe."

It is true I am pleased to say, I look half-way presentable. The soft silk of the Patou dress skims my lanky figure rather becomingly, and the intricate beading of the bodice and hem sparkles like a mass of diamonds in the soft light. For a moment I am filled with a sort of giddy excitement, like a girl dressed up in her mother's finest as I did so many years ago, to parade around and imagine myself all grown up. Happy memories are in there, too. I smile at my reflection, wondering whether I resemble my mother when she was my age. I notice Niobe in the reflection behind me. She is watching me, a vaguely curious expression on her pretty face, but she does not ask.

"You look very beautiful, Miss Carlisle." She looks pleased, adding softness to the elegant angularity of her face.

"Please, do call me Evie," then, remembering Yannick's response, "well, at least when it's the two of us." Niobe nods understanding, and I brush down the skirt of my dress and head to the door. "Wish me luck."

CHAPTER 4

The pale yellow silk dress I am wearing, one of the few pieces having survived the journey unrumpled, happens to be one of my favorites. I bought it on a weekend trip to Paris with Briony and her mother shortly before she left and have worn it only twice since! Around my wrist dangles my grandmother's diamond bracelet, one of the few items of jewelry I took with me from London and the only one, aside from my parents' wedding bands, I truly treasure.

As I climb down the broad wooden stairs, I can already hear amplified voices coming from the hall below. Cheerful and masculine. A tiny shiver of excitement mingled with anxiety runs down my spine, and I cling to the solid bannister. It has been a long time since I was at a party of any kind without the watchful eye of my aunt or some other chaperone keeping me perfectly in line. Which is not to say I am white as a bride's veil. There might have been a kiss snuck in, here or there. I am no nun, and this is 1925, after all. One learns to adapt.

My sandals make a light clicking noise as I reach the bottom landing and step into the marble foyer. Following the sounds of chatter and laughter, I make my way in the direction of the main drawing room, a flutter of nerves, the proverbial butterflies busily flitting about in my stomach. Before entering, I carefully smooth the front of my dress and take a deep breath. Shoulders back, I cross the threshold. For a moment, no one notices the addition to their company, and they keep chattering happily. Quickly, I scan the room, taking in the figures of two tall men, one dark the other fair-haired. Jeffrey detects my presence just as I am about to launch into the old, but reliable cough-to-gain-get-attention routine. An inaudible sigh of relief escapes me. I am ususally not the socially awkward type, but I feel a bit out of my depth in this den of testosterone.

"Ah, Evelyn!" He walks towards me, offering a welcoming arm. I could embrace him! "Come and meet the lads." The other men turn around as Jeffrey leads me to them. Briony was right in her assessment. They are handsome. Both look deeply suntanned, presumably from hours aboard a yacht with their new lady-friends. The tone of their skin offers a prominent contrast to the crisp whiteness of their starched shirts. "This is Daniel Harper," Jeffrey gestures at the dark haired man who nods at me and smiles without opening his mouth, "and this scoundrel is Caspar Ballantine. May I present my cousin, Lady Evelyn Carlisle. Evie, I've invited them both to stay for as long as they like, and I do hope they'll behave like gentlemen." As he says this, Jeffrey claps Caspar on the back in a gesture of warning reproach.

"I can assure you, we shall do our best," Caspar replies in a distinctly Etonian drawl as he gives a small bow. Did he just wink at me? His pale hazel eyes sparkle with mischief in the low light. The room is aglow in the light of numerous yellow candles in simple, elegant silver candlesticks. A warm, pleasant radiance illuminates the broad, even panes of Caspars clean-shaven face, only faintly revealing the pale pink line of a scar between his left eyebrow and hairline. His hair tells of long exposure to the sun and gleams the color of honey streaked with paler strands.

I look around, pleased by what I see. Briony has always had good taste, and this house, her new home, has clearly given her an outlet to showcase it. Speak of the devil! Briony glides through the doorway floating in a delicate seafoam green dress that I could swear is this season's Lanvin.

"Evie, darling," She joins our little group arms outstretched, a gesture echoing that of her husband. Pecking my cheek, she turns to the couple that has followed her into the room. Both are fair-haired and tall. On first sight they are, perhaps, no beauties in the traditional sense, but their faces have a pleasent openess worth more than a strong jaw or a high brow.

Briony ushers them forward like a little mother hen, her pink cheeks matching the color of the womans dress. "This is Paul Vanderheyden," she gestures at the man, "and his lovely wife Rosie. Paul, Rosie, my cousin Evelyn Carlisle, and you've met Daniel and Caspar, of course." The men nod at each other, and I offer a modest smile. I am glad she leaves out my title. I do not want everyone here to think of me as English aristocracy. Nor does the new Evie necessarily want to be a lady, come to think of it . . .

Briony places a hand on Paul's arm to draw him and his wife closer to us. "Paul works with Jeffrey for his research at the museum. Imagine they've come all the way from Amsterdam!" She beams brightly, clearly relishing the role of hostess in her own little castle.

Paul holds out a hand and I take it. He has a kind face and a wiry frame. I have a brief flash of what he must have looked like in youth, a very gangly boy, all elbows and knees, and everyone's friend. Behind his thick-rimmed spectacles, I feel the glimmer of intelligent eyes observing me.

"Very nice to meet you, Mr. Vanderheyden, Mrs. Vanderheyden." I reach out my right hand so that I might shake hers, but she doesn't react, standing mutely beside her husband. I pull back my hand, feeling gauche and slightly rejected. Did I do something wrong? Rosie's face is blank. There is a moment's awkward silence until Briony, thank heavens, launches us into conversation.

"Rosie, went to school in England, didn't you, my dear." Briony pats Rosie's shoulder as if she was a child though Briony must be a decade her junior. Still no reaction. Briony chatters on, as a blush creeps up Paul's pale neck. He is clearly feeling uneasy about his wife's behavior. There seems to be something wrong with her. I dare not stare, but cannot keep myself from tossing an occasional glance at her, watching for any signs of reaction or involvement in the conversation. Nothing comes. She smiles benignly at us, yet doesn't utter a word. Caspar and Daniel don't seem to notice anything amiss and wander off to fetch everyone drinks.

Rosie, nearly matching her husband in height, is of a robust build with muscled calves above her sandaled feet, and broad shoulders tinged a painful sunburnt pink. She wears her gleaming daffodil-yellow hair in an unfashionably long braid, which suits her broad face nicely and gives her, in my eyes at least, the distinctive appearance of a Germanic warrior princess. Brunhild, I think, referring to the fierce woman of the Nibelungenlied. Brunhild loses her strength eventually, becoming the humiliated pawn in the games of men. Hmm . . . maybe not Rosie's ideal, then. Paul seems a nice enough fellow, and it should be noted that my imagination can go rampaging down many a wrong path at the best of times. I am eager to know what on earth is the matter with this, to all outward appearances, hale and healthy woman.

We chat for a while longer until the arrival of more guests. Niobe leads he local doctor and his wife, Nikolas and Laria Zarek into the room, brandishing a bottle of ouzo for their hosts. Nikolas is a bit older than his pretty wife—certainly over forty is my guess. Streaks of grey dapple his otherwise thick black hair and the crinkly lines at the corners of his eyes indicate a life lived with laughter, which immediately endears him to me and leads me to believe he will be good company. He is not tall, but well-built with a wide chest and shoulders. He carries himself with a certain self-possessed confidence and natural grace, which surely must have appealed to Laria as might his rather unusual flare for style. Nikolas wears an impeccably tailored jacket with a forest green silk cravat, for my taste a little too much of a good thing.

His young wife is a striking creature, slender and dark, exuding an air of mystery. They make a handsome couple indeed.

Laria tells me, in her low, melodiously accented voice that she, too, has visited London. As she says this, her nose wrinkles. "It was not for me," she comments diplomatically, giving me the clear impression that she has a much less dipolomatic opinion of our capital. "So much cold. So many people. I missed the sea. The river . . ." she grimaces as if the thought of the Thames' murky depths is too much to contemplate, and shakes her head. "No, I was happy when I came back to Crete."

"It certainly is beautiful here, though if you ever go back to England," as I say this, I know she will not, "you might enjoy a trip to the coast. Cornwall is beautiful, and you can walk along the sea for miles."

"Yes," she says, drawing out the last letter, "perhaps I will."

As we continue our conversation, I learn that she studied to be a nurse, in spite of her parent's objections.

"I have my own head, you know, Evelyn?" She taps her temple as if to prove her point. "And that is how I met my husband." Laria beams at him and touches his shoulder.

"My great fortune," he says, dutifully patting her hand, which has come to rest tucked in the crook of his elbow, where it seems to belong like a piece in a puzzle.

The last to arrive is the museum curator, Darius Calandra, a close friend and colleague of both Jeffrey and Paul. He is a small man, especially standing beside the other men of the party, particularly Paul, who dwarfs us all. His neat features and dark hair do little to distinguish him, but there is something about him, something I cannot quite put my finger on, prompting me think one ought not underestimate the man. How does the saying go, don't judge a book by its cover.

Somehow or other, I am left alone with him, Briony having run off to check on the progress in the kitchen and the other men refreshing their drinks. I cannot see either Rosie or Laria, so I assume they must have gone to freshen up themselves. It's all right, I do not mind. For some reason Darius inspires a sense of peace in me, and I feel more at ease than I did in the larger group of strangers a moment ago.

In a soft voice he quickly, though humbly, reveals himself to be a treasure trove of information. He knows everything there is to know about the history of the island and Miklos, his hometown, in particular. All my life I have been drawn to stories, real or fictional, like a moth to a flame. My earliest memories are of my mother's lively voice telling the story of poor Cinderalla, or the cunning Shaherazade, filling my mind with images so vivid I felt certain they were real. I listen now as I did then, welcoming Darius' anecdotes and tales with rapt attention.

Soon the others rejoin us. I am calmer, and even Rosie's blank-eyed stare does not manage to unsettle me. Jeffrey and Darius have been working together for some time now, examining a new excavation site, which has produced the most wonderfully preserved sculptures and relics that have been found in the area in nearly a hundred years. It is a tremendous success for the museum and one of the reasons for Jeffrey's presence here.

Jeffrey took a degree in archaeology at Cambridge before the war and was thrilled to have been offered this position even though Briony, at the time, was less so. As I look at them now, standing side by side, I think the change of scenery has done them good. Briony's cheeks are flushed and Jeffrey appears well rested and content. Now only the sound of children's feet running around in this large house remains sadly absent. But is is early days.

After Niobe returns and whispers discreetly in Briony's ear, we are gently ushered to the beautiful candlelit table and sit down to eat. Hungry now, I am looking forward to the meal, if those delicious smells wafting in from the kitchen are anything to go by.

To my delight, I am seated next to Darius and Daniel, with Briony across from me between Jeffrey and Laria. As Niobe fills our glasses with the palest golden wine, Darius explains that he came here straight from the museum where he had been authenticating a new set of sculptures. He appears a little nervous, but visibly excited, his dark eyes flickering with enthusiasm behind thin-rimmed glasses.

"I now believe," he tells a rapt audience, "we have unearthed an ancient temple site dedicated to the cult of Dionysus. Can you believe it?" He smiles brightly, like a child that has been given a new and shiny toy. "This is most unusual. The temple, it appears, was never finished. In fact," he pauses, perhaps for dramatic effect, "we have found burn marks, and one wall is entirely smashed in. Violently. We believe it was attacked, but not pillaged as so many relics remain. Most fascinating, isn't it?"

"Do you suppose it was damaged two years ago when the Turks were forced to leave?" asks Daniel, leaning forward to better see the man as he replies.

"I don't think so." Darius' brow creases and shakes his head. "The Turks, most of them, were Greek-speakers, you know. Some married native Cretans. There were even Cretans who converted to Islam. The divide was, at least here on our island, not always black and white. I am still in contact with some of my Turko-Cretan friends, who were exchanged in 1924. If they have lived here half their lives, raised their children here, they become your neighbors and friends, not the enemy. Crete is a place many choose as a new home." The words are uttered as simple fact, yet I feel their truth resonating in my own mind. Taking a slow, savoring sip of the cool wine, he continues, "You see, we have many Greek refugees seeking the chance to make new lives here after having been forced out of Asia Minor. That was a terrible business, but we will recover. I am confident of this."

There is a moment of silence as the people seated around the oval table, ruminate upon this. Most of us, I realize, tossing a fleeting look at my fellow diners, in a way are refugees. Naturally, I could not possibly compare my situation to that of the poor and frightened families seeking safety and prosperity here after having lost their homes due to the tribulations of the Balkan Wars. Yet one way or the other, Crete has become our sanctuary, and we must make of that what we can. It is Briony who breaks the uncomfortable silence and asks if anyone is ready for the second course.

We dine wonderfully on fresh fish stuffed with olives and capers, a flaky triangular pastry, spanakopita, filled with spinach and a salty, creamy cheese, thick yoghurt drizzled with honey and sweet little fruits I have never before seen or tasted called kumquats, which have the appearance of tiny oranges with a much sweeter, sugary flavor.

Throughout our meal, Darius patiently answers my questions, not making me feel a fool for my lack of knowledge of the island and its culture, instead happy to share with someone eager to learn.

"Were you born here?" I ask, cutting a piece of my fish.

"Yes, in Miklos where my father was born, and his father before him."

"Where did you get your enthusiasm for archeology?"

"I studied in Athens. Then I joined a dig in Egypt. Most interesting." His eyes seem to glaze over for just a moment as though he is jumping back to a sandy pit in the land of the Pharaohs. "Yes, most fascinating." He smiles ruefully. "I had to return when the independence fights began."

"I have never been to Egypt. I should love to see the pyramids and the sphinx." I reply, reaching for my water.

"Oh, yes, and you must not forget Karnak or Abu Simbel, in my opinion, sites superior even to the Pyramids of Giza." He looks very serious as he explains, and the more I speak with him, the more I see a man who is passionate and devoted to his work and studies, but who seems to neglect an interest in all other aspects of life. He has not, I realize, asked me a single question about myself. Or am I simply envious of his enthusiasm? It would be nice to have something one can be so enthralled with. In time, maybe, I will be as well, I tell myself.

In 1921 I spent two years reading classics at St. Hugh's College in Oxford, one of the few colleges admitting women. I was not awarded a degree as I had to end my studies early to be with Aunt Iris when her husband passed and she was quite unwell. Still, the grand stories of Agamemnon and Odysseus have a hold on me and the enthusiasm Darius feels for his work, exploring the reality behind such mythical tales, is an area I want to hear more about. While he may be absorbed by his own interests, he lacks the overbearing confidence of Caspar Ballantine, who, as the evening progresses and his glass is refilled and drained time and time again, grows ever louder and distinctly unpleasant. I can't help but cringe, observing him from the corner of my eye, dip back his head again, a tiny trickle of ruby liquid dripping from the corner of his full-lipped mouth onto the left breast of his white shirt. I wish Jeffrey or Daniel would discreetly take him aside to put a stop to this before he ruins Briony's lovely party, but neither seems keen to make a move. Unable to do anything, I direct my attention back to Darius.

He is explaining how he and a team of local diggers have found a collection of bronze masks ten miles from the town and are now busily trying to get endorsement to fund a continued excavation. Jeffrey and Paul are assisting him in this matter as well as managing the projects already underway. Much as this is all very interesting, I can't help but allow my mind to wander a bit. I imagine myself, trowel in hand in a sandy pit, a dirty vase with dust-covered black figures pained upon its terracotta surface perched at my booted feet. Or better still, wearing a beautiful pale blue gown, draped across my body as though Michelangelo had painted it onto my form, wandering barefoot through the shallow waters. Or—

My thoughts are interrupted by a wave of laughter all around me. Someone must have made a joke. I join in half-heartedly, aware of a distinct pull in my jaw, indicating my desire to yawn. I clamp it shut and fight the urge.

When Darius and Paul begin discussing a meeting with a potential sponsor, I turn my attentions to my left where I catch Daniel Harper glancing down at his wristwatch.

"Do you have other plans tonight, Mr. Harper?" I cock my head to show my good humor.

"Pardon?" He looks momentarily startled. To his credit, he manages to recover quickly, shaking his head. "Oh, no. Just a habit, I suppose. A rude habit. I apologize, Miss Carlisle."

"No need. And please, do call me Evelyn. If we are to be living together, these formalities only get in the way."

"Absolutely, and I am Daniel as you know" He nods and grins at me. I notice a dimple in his right cheek, which in a very pleasing manner, disrupts the symmetry of his face.

"Well, Daniel. What brings you here? I myself am on the run, fleeing from London authorities of sorts." I lower my head a little closer to him, a move that in hindsight seems more intimate than conspiratorial. Daniel blushes a little, though it would hardly be visible in the low candlelight if I weren't so close to him, and self-consciously I withdraw a little.

"Trouble with the law. Well, I'm afraid I can't top that. I am simply visiting an old friend who has chosen one of the loveliest places to settle down." Daniel takes a sip of his wine, momentarily averting his gaze. His face is angular, less traditionally handsome, perhaps than that of his friend, but no less interesting for it. He has dark eyes, which I first took to be brown and have now observed to be a deep, almost pine green, changing their hue ever so slightly as the light shifts. I swirl the last of my wine in the crystal glass and continue our conversation.

"I can only agree with you on that account. Have you been to Greece before?" I ask him, starting to take an interest in the man behind this handsome veneer.

"No," he shakes his head gently, a lock of hair falling onto his forehead I almost reach out to brush it aside, but thankfully remember decorum. This wine must be getting to my head.

Daniel continues, "I've spent the past year traveling in Cairo and Marrakesh, and before that . . . Well, there was the war of course." Lowering his head for a few seconds, he adds no more, allowing the memories their moment of silence. The war, as it is for so many of us, must be a subject he prefers to avoid. I have found that some people need to speak of it all the time, working it into nearly every conversation, while others cannot bring themselves to say the words aloud for fear of their potency and pain. He looks young, but likely old enough to have been affected by the Military Service act of 1916, which called for the conscription of all eligible men for military duty. He has no visible battle scars, though I can only see his hands and face. Often times, the ones beneath the surface are the most difficult to bear or to comprehend.

Trying to steer the conversation back to safer ground I continue, "Your travels sound fascinating. I'm afraid, I have limited experience in that arena, only Switzerland and France for my schooling." As I say this I suddenly feel very green in the company of all these cultured, well-traveled people. Daniel smiles again.

"Not at all. Contrary to what is expected of a patriotic Englishman, I am very fond of Switzerland myself. I holidayed there many times as a child. Where did you visit?"

With this invitation, and genuine interest emanating from Daniel, I start explaining. I tell him of my time in Zurich, then of Lyon, and later Paris. He counters with stories of his travels to Cairo, the temples, the heat, the souks in Marrakesh, and his arduous sea journey here. It seems he has avoided good old England a number of years.

". . .and the camel simply would not move!" Daniel's eyes grow wide and he gestures with his hands. A sense of pride for what he has seen and experienced in his time emanates from him as he speaks, but it is different from the pride Darius feels. Daniel, as far as I may venture to say, is still looking for something, while Darius has found his vocation long ago and is keen to share it. I can't quite decide which I prefer. Hearing Daniel's stories, I must confess to a distinct pinch of envy.

My adventures until now have never truly gone beyond sneaking out of boarding school lodgings to go dancing in the village. I feel a bit silly exchanging these little stories for his full-fledged escapades, though Daniel never gives the impression of resenting this unbalanced bargain. He asks the right questions, laughs at the right parts, and is overall utterly charming. I must be careful not to fall in love the first night on the island! Yet despite his good humor, there is something underneath the friendly manner, the wit and intelligence. A certain shadow hidden beneath his surface, not fitting into this mold of laissez-faire adventurer he is letting me see. A secret? We all have our little mysteries, I concede in my mind, our little secrets. We all, too, have our battles with that little nagging bane, curiosity.

Before I can allow my imagination to paint some mad picture over Daniel's façade of charm, Jeffrey clangs his dessert-spoon against his glass, a sound I have always found cheering as it reminds me of weddings and other celebrations. Everyone looks up at our host.

"Pardon my interruption, but after a few glasses of Attica's finest, I am compelled to offer the obligatory toast, my friends." A few low laughs ensue, and Jeffrey goes on. "I am tonight very fortunate to be in the company of good friends, family, and with a belly full of this excellent food. To that I raise my glass!"

"Cheers!" Everyone clinks glasses. I take a small sip of what remains in mine, tasting the pleasant coolness of the mildly sweet and fruity wine as it runs down my throat.

"Now," Jeffrey goes on, his brow slightly shiny and his nose slightly pink, "Perhaps you will join me on the veranda. We have a perfect cloudless night, and I have been forbidden by my lovely wife," he smiles obligingly at the glowing face of Briony beside him, "to partake of my après-dîner cigar in the house."

Again laughs bubble up around me. There follow a few moments of mouths being dabbed and forks being set on plates, a cacophony of scraping of chairs and smoothing of crêpe de chine before our little group follows our hosts outside. As I leave the dining room, I catch a glimpse of Niobe, the pretty maid, speaking with Caspar in an alcove leading to another room, a look of petulance marring his handsome face. I have an impulse to approach Niobe and ask whether everything is all right, but decide against it, telling myself it is none of my concern.

We step outside, onto the terracotta-tiled veranda, and I take a deep breath of the fresh, pleasantly warm air. Somewhere nearby, an owl is hooting, a strange, monotonous sound, vaguely ominous and soothing at once. Dry leaves rustle in the trees at the edges of the garden. Nature's music my father called it. I remember the sounds would frighten me as a child, so he began telling me stories of the owl, singing out in owl-language, and the cicadas chatting about their day, and somehow it all became a story and not scary anymore.

There is a cast-iron table with a set of six chairs as well as a beautiful carved wooden bench along one side of the terrace. I have no desire to sit down again, and the question takes care of itself when a few members of the party make themselves comfortable to smoke and chat. There is no space left anyway. I walk across the tiled expanse toward the periphery of the garden. It is fenced off, a wise precaution, I think, daring a glance over the edge. The drop would be a mighty, bone-shattering one and if Jeffrey and Briony throw many such parties where the wine is in generous supply, someone might take a nasty tumble.

Carefully, I step back, dry grass tickling my feet as I gaze up to the sparkling, twinkling lights of countless stars in the blue-black sky. So many, more even than I have seen on my sojourns into the countryside, brilliant and steady. Standing here alone, I suddenly feel very small, a tiny speck in our constantly evolving universe. This is the same sky people on the other side of the world look up to, one true constant in a forever changing world, where nothing is ever quite safe, quite certain. The War provided gruesome evidence of that. We are so fragile, and still oddly resilient. Can we hope for lessons to have been learned? That people might treat one another with the care and respect we require to survive? I have my doubts. Almost without noticing I shake my head, willing the sad thoughts to tumble out, to leave me with the warm feeling of peace and welcome emanating from this very ground.

A cool breeze envelopes me, bringing with it the soothing, earthy scent of camomile and mint. Closing my eyes for a moment, I feel the weight of my tired eyelids. I savor my newfound feeling of freedom, in spite of uncertainty and the newness of it all. A strong desire to lie down on the cool grass, staring up and counting the stars, trying to make out the constellations overwhelms me, but I remind myself that such a course of action might not make the best first impression and may embarass Briony. Another night.

"Quite a view, isn't it?" I turn startled by the voice intruding upon my fantasy, to find Daniel Harper only a few steps away. It takes me a moment to remember that he had gone to fetch us a drink and that the proffered glass containing a finger's measure of clear liquid is for me.

"Yes, it is. Beautiful." There is a moment of silence between us. "You know, I don't believe back at home in London I ever simply stood outside to look at the sky. Probably wouldn't have seen much in the old smoke." I shrug, running a finger along the rim of the glass. "I was thinking how I'd like to lie down here and stare at the sky. I have this idea," I pause, unsure of whether it is wise to explain, but I suppose the desire to say what I am thinking wins over, and I continue," I have this idea that Zeus and Hera and his Olymp are propped up on clouds somewhere up there, and having a jolly old time." I let out a nervous chuckle." My friends, if they could hear me go on like this, would think me a little mad."

"A little madness can be a pleasant retreat sometimes." Daniel says, his voice carrying a trace of melancholy. As he lowers his face, the darkness creates shadows below his cheekbones and his eyes. His statement startles me, a mirror of the workings of his mind. I decide that the new Evelyn is a blunt sort of person and ask the question playing on my mind.

"Did you serve?" A few simple words, but they are loaded with assumption and insinuation, probably unexpected coming from a young and proper English girl, who has been taught not to speak of unpleasant things, especially with men, and never with strangers. If he is shocked or annoyed, to his credit, he does not let it show. He inhales slowly, fresh air perhaps the sustenance his body needs for an unhappy disclosure. For a moment, I experience a flash of shame for my curiosity. I should not have asked, should not force a confession of a man I barely know. Before I can reprimand myself further, Daniel's voice draws me out of my pensiveness.

"Yes, I did," he says, staring straight ahead, a shadowy, unreadable expression on his face. "It was early in 1917. Too young to join earlier. The youngest of three sons." That is all he says. I know the rest of the wretched story. Youngest of three sons. The only one left, I am led to assume by his withdrawn expression and tone of voice. Mentally kicking myself for my carelessness, I cannot think what to say. His story is far from unique, which makes it all the more tragic. A subject of such magnitude can hardly be followed by silly party chatter. Daniel senses the thickening of the atmosphere around us and in a forced jovial tone goes on. "It's all right, you know. One cannot change the past. Let us of think of happier times ahead." He plasters a slim smile across his lips, not fooling me. I resolve not to ask him anything further as I recognize, with a familiar emotion, the effort maintaining his composure requires of him. I will not add to anyone's burden if it can be helped.

Fortunately, at that moment we are joined by Caspar, who, if not outright drunk, is certainly headed down that path. Nevertheless, I am surprisingly glad to see him, his presence shattering the tension that has formed between Daniel and myself.

"Oh, Danny Boy!" He sidles in between us, amber liquid slopping in his half-full glass in one hand, and a rank smelling cigar sending whisps of smoke into the sky in the other. With a loose-limbed gesture sending a spray of his brandy over the garden fence, he waves at the sky in an embarrassingly dramatic manner and grins at us. "What are the words . . . Oh, yes, 'The bright sun was extinguished, and the stars did wander darkling in the eternal space, rayless, and pathless, and the icy earth, swung blind and blackening in the moonless air' . . . can't remember the rest, sorry.'" He beams gleefully and takes a slow drag on his cigar, admiring the thick white plume of smoke he exhales as it drifts into the black night.

"Byron, if I'm not mistaken." An undeniably wry note enters my voice. "Too affected for my taste, I'm afraid." Actually, I like a bit of Byron when the occasion is fitting, but I have taken a slight dislike to Caspar, unfair judgement though it may be. Caspar throws his hands into the air in a gesture of wine-addled exaltation, and I take a tiny step away from him and toward the cliffs edge.

"Affected, no my dear," he drawls, leering down at me from his six inch elevation. "You misunderstand the passion behind his words." Misunderstand the passion? Well, pardon me, please! I happen to have passion in spades! I can see the silver in the moon, the diamond in a dew drop, Poseidon's kiss in a sea breeze. I am tempted to roll my eyes, but restrain myself, not wanting to stir the fire of passion within his flaming bosom. As if on cue, he clutches a hand dramatically to his heart and shakes his head, tossing his pale curls. "Affected indeed. The master speaketh of the driving forces of nature."

"He is, if I am not mistaken," I comment, knowing that I am not, "speaking of desolation and fear. He speaks of the end of days, the end of mankind." At this point I assume I have the upper hand, though I try to hide my smugness, having been taught it does not become a lady. He probably thinks he can impress with the few lines of an arbitrary poem he has memorized to fan the passion of the ladies he wishes to woo. Though, by now, I think, it is quite clear I am not a worthy object for his attentions. He is looking put out, while I continue. "It is rather unromantic, rare as such a poem may be for both Lord Byron, or I venture, for your good self." I say this with a smile, intended to lighten the mood. He has had a fair bit to drink and may be contrite and the sufferer of a thunderous headache by breakfast time. Oh dear, I am sounding like Aunt Agnes!

"Is desolation not fueled by passion?" Caspar raises his eyebrows, not willing to concede. Tiny beads of sweat have formed above his lip, despite the cool breeze, and I wonder whether he might do well to sit down, or better yet, go to bed. Then again, I am no nurse, nor his mother so I will keep my council.

"Perhaps," I shrug noncommitally, slightly taken aback how like Aunt Agnes I was thinking and not wanting to argue with him, especially not in front of Daniel. It has been a long day, and I am not in the best form myself. I ought not be too hard on him, I think, trying to make up for my harsh judgements.

"All is in the eye of the beholder. At that I think we can leave it." Daniel interjects before his friend can add offense. He steadies Caspar, who is looking rather peaky and pale around the gills in the silver light of the moon. Gripping him by the elbow and making an unsuccessful grab for the glass, Daniel pulls Caspar further away from both me, and the fenced edge of the garden. Is this concern for Caspar a result of my sharp tongue, or the threat of sharp cliffs?

"Yes, fine, fine. I shan't argue with you, my friend." Caspar grins, manages to take another puff from his cigar and dawdles off making his slightly curved way towards Darius, who has been standing alone at the edge of the terrace, looking in the other direction at the shadowy hills. Perhaps he is imagining what might be hidden under all of that dry earth, what treasures of the past it may be concealing. I pull my attention away from him and back to the one standing before me, appearing apologetic and a little discomfited.

"I am sorry about him. He's had one or three too many tonight." Daniel murmurs, shrugging his shoulders and raising his eyebrows by way of an excuse. He looks tired, perhaps it is simply a trick of the light, which has dimmed from one moment to the next as a cloud pushes itself across the nearly full moon.

"Quite all right," I smile. "Besides you are hardly responsible for his behavior, are you?" Shaking his head, and without speaking, he takes a few steps to sit down on a small wrought iron bench, nearly concealed by the dipping branches of a gnarled oak, the sole tree of substancial size in the garden. I sit down beside him, once again aware of his closeness, but not intimidated by it. In a strange way, he is more vulnerable at this moment than I.

"You're right," he says, picking up the line of conversation I thought had ended. "Nonetheless, we have been friends for many years, comrades, fellow travelers," he places both hands, palms down, on his thighs, "that establishes a certain sense of responsibility for one another."

"How did you meet?" I whisper, the way we are seated here, playing tricks on my mind. The question has escpaed my mouth before I had a chance to think. In this moment of stillness I worry the answer will inevitably lead back to memories of the trenches, to memories better left untouched. To my surprise, his reply comes with a smile, and I almost sigh in relief.

"He lived on my family's estate. You could say we grew up together. My two older brothers are . . ." he swallows before he goes on. "They were a bit older than me, so Caspar and I got along well. He is an only child, you see. His father manages parts of the estate for me still, and our families were constantly together." I watch Daniel as his eyes glaze over, lost in some other place, some other time, dipping into a pool of bittersweet memories. His obvious show of emotion is unusual to witness in someone I have met only hours ago. All the same, it does not feel unnatural. I try to join him in his reverie, imagining two rambunctious boys running across vast green fields, maybe escaping the consequences of some mischief.

"You must have had a happy childhood." I say before thinking, immediately regretting it, for the moment is over and Daniel's eyes regain their focus, snapping back into the present.

"Yes," he swallows, "yes, I did."

The leaves in the branches above are gently tussled by the wind, and a group of cicadas has begun their ritual humming. Behind our perch, I hear Caspar's voice making a loud joke, and a few half-hearted laughs from his audience.

For a moment, I forget that I have known Daniel just a few hours. We sit here both having escaped something from our past, unwilling to make it real by uttering the words. His friendly manner does little to disguise the discomfort of being trapped in his own skin. I am eager to ask questions, to know more, so my imagination fueled by unsatisfied curiosity will not paint a false picture.

Fortunately, before my tongue betrays my remaining tact, Daniel asks, "Where did you grow up?" It is such an ordinary question, I am snapped out of my spell, feeling a little disappointed.

"Mostly London. My parents liked to travel, though they only took me to France and a few jaunts to Scotland. And you?"

"I lived in Kent growing up," a faint crinkle of a smile appears on the left side of his mouth, and I will it to spread to the right. Smiling faces tend to open up like unfolding maps, allowing an access one did not know existed before. He gives a tiny shake of his head and turns to face me. "You know what happened then." The smile expands, though it seems an odd point in his story for this to occur. "I am sorry, I must have been a terrible party guest tonight. What a miserable impression I am making!" He shakes his head again, letting out a short laugh, neither happy nor sad.

"Not at all," I also smile. "Besides," I cross my legs at the ankles, "I am the one who should apologize, springing myself on you all. Briony sent an invite, though she didn't mention she already had guests." I raise my eyebrows.

"I am quite sure she would have chosen your company over ours. I have the impression," Daniel gestures vaguely behind him where a few of Briony's other guests are mingling, "she quite enjoys a full house." I turn to look around at the veranda a few meters away where I see Rosie staring straight at me, at the same time seeming to see nothing at all, while Paul holds her hand and chats with Jeffrey. The woman unnerves me. Immediately as I allow this thought to pass a wave of shame washes over me, chastizing me for my quick judgement. I turn back to Daniel.

"Yes, I believe you're right. She has always liked being the hostess." A memory flits into my mind."I remember when we were girls she would play the mother at all our tea parties. I am less than three years younger than her, but she would convince me that I must obviously be the child."

I sigh quietly, remembering us sitting in her mother's conservatory, wearing our frilly pastel dresses, our short legs dangling as we sat in the wrought iron chairs, Briony presiding over the tray of pretend-tea and very real strawberry scones we had filched from the kitchen without being caught. While I tell him this little story, the air about him changes. He sinks deeper into the bench looking, if not relaxed, then at least slightly more at ease.

"I can well imagine." The corners of his mouth curve decidedly upward. "You might understand my attachement to Caspar a bit better. We did not play tea-time, but we went fishing and hunting and learned how to ride our first ponies together. People change, but often we remain inextricably bound by happy memories and the people we shared them with."

He is speaking more animatedly than he has all evening, and I am worried I will say the wrong thing and make him retreat back into his shell.

"I understand," I say, meaning it.

"I thought you would." The seconds of silence following are not filled with heavyness or sorrow and when I hear the sound of footsteps on dry grass, I am content to leave our conversation where it is, knowing that the first layer has been peeled back, and we are not strangers anymore.

Briony appears, a pale blue shawl wrapped around her shoulders. Following her are Paul and Rosie. In the cool light of the moon and the wide-casting glow from the torches anchored into the ground on the edges of the veranda, Rosie's yellow hair gleams like a halo. Her face still expressionless, she looks like a statue, hovering over us. I stand up as they approach and feel, rather than see, Daniel lift himself off the bench as well.

"Hello, my dears, Paul and Rosie are leaving." Briony's voice is friendly as always, though I detect a hint of fatigue behind her chipper façade. Shrouded in her shawl she looks smaller even than usual, like a child almost, and I wonder how long she will keep up this mask before she tells me the truth and unburdens herself.

"Yes," Paul confirms as fresh and friendly as at the beginning of the evening, "I'm afraid it's getting rather late. But it was wonderful to meet you, Evelyn, and to see you again, Daniel." He doles out handshakes all around.

Laria and Nikolas approach our little group as Paul is thanking Briony for a "wonderful evening".

"Paul," Nikolas says, his voice deep and slightly raspy, "would you drop Laria and me off at ours? I know you do not drink and I am afraid, I may not be the best driver tonight. "He winks in the direction of Jeffrey, who is talking to Darius a small distance behind us. "Your husband," he smilingly shakes his head at Briony, "has too good a taste in wine. It is a wonder he gets any work done!" He lets out a happy bellow, and Laria squeezes his arm.

"Of course, of course." Paul claps a large hand on the doctor's shoulder. "Come along, the more the merrier." Nikolas shakes hands with Daniel and the other men who have joined our group, and Laria kisses Briony and me on the cheek.

"I was very happy to meet you, Evelyn. We must see each other again soon. I will show you the island." I nod and thank her for her offer, promising to contact her as soon as I have settled in.

After they leave, amid laughter and thanks, Darius takes off as well, smiling shyly as he says goodbye. Standing in the doorway waving goodbye, a wave of tiredness washes over me, and I barely manage to stifle a yawn.

"You take yourself to bed." Jeffrey smiles, seeing through my subtle maneuver. "You must be dead on your feet."

"Yes, of course, darling, you must get some sleep." Briony agrees, looking rather worn out herself.

"All right, but first, can I help you with anything before I slink off? I feel I am abandoning ship."

"No, no, it's all in hand. Nothing to worry about."

"Fine," I turn to face her. "You must promise me you'll sleep soon, too. I hate to say it, but you look all-in." Briony sighs, leans her head against my shoulder for a moment, and I can feel her nodding.

"I promise."

"Good, you see to it that she stays true to her word, Jeffrey," I gently lever my cousin over to her husband, who, with a sleepy, happy look drapes his arm around her.

"Will do."

I say goodnight to Daniel and Caspar, the latter looking rather the worse for wear and climb the stairs to my room. As I near the top, I can barely make out Daniel's voice, low and sharp, "Pull yourself together, man," with a vehemence I had not expected from so quiet a man. He is evidently worried about his friend. I know, put in his position, I would certainly be concerned.

Splashing water from a white china bowl onto my face, I sigh. It was a pleasant evening. Nice people. Good food. I climb out of my dress, leaving it in a yellow mound on the floor, and make for the welcoming refuge of my bed. As I sink into the deliciously soft, smooth linens, I find it almost impossible to fathom all that has happened today. The journey on that awful, shaking boat seems ages ago. It has been such a departure from my perfectly planned and scheduled life under the guardianship of my aunt. Change can be good, I tell myself. As I drift off into a deep slumber, the last image in my mind is the vibrant blue of the endless sea.

CHAPTER 5

I wake as a ray of filtered golden sunlight touches my face. Blinking and rubbing my eyes, I see that the curtain is open just a fingerswidth, enough space for a few slivers of warm brightness to squeeze through. What a pleasant way to start the day; much better than the monotonous thrumming of raindrops against the window as I have grown to expect in England.

Staying in bed for a few more moments, I wonder what today will bring. Yesterday was quite eventful, but I must not expect always to be thus entertained. Perhaps I will be able to make my way into town later. I assume Briony will offer Yannick's services, but I am keen to explore on my own, to make use of the new luxury of unguided freedom.

Reluctantly, I draw back the soft covers of my bed and swing my legs over the edge. I stretch my arms toward the ceiling, already envisioning the blue sky that awaits me, imagining my hands reaching up for it. I stride the few steps over to the window and—in what I will admit is a rather dramatic gesture—throw open the curtains, sending tiny dust motes frantically whirling into the air. I push open the window, happy to allow the breeze to ruffle my sleepcreased hair.

The sky is strikingly blue. Indeed, it is the sort of velvety cloudless blue of mid-morning. A white orb shimmers high above, presaging a warm day. A hand acting to shield my face, I try to catch a glimpse of the strip of dark blue in the distance. The light is glaring, and I blink furiously as it makes my eyes sting, but there it is, a line of azure touching the horizon. If I could only paint! The only Cretan artist I can think of is El Greco, though I cannot recall him having painted such simple beauty, instead preferring, or perhaps simply painting to satisfy demand, religious icons and biblical scenes. This sight calls for the tender, passionate hand of a Claude Monet or Camille Pissaro.

The trees below the window, small and dark, rustle in the wind, their leaves swaying to a gentle rhythm. I wonder what the view from my window at Eaton Square would look like this morning. Almost certainly less inspiring than that which is on offer here. I sigh, feeling like a girl in the pictures. All that is missing is a gruff but handsome fellow, who will save me from all sorts of trouble and with whom I will fall madly in love. And they all lived happily ever after . . . Well, a girl can dream.

Turning away from the glorious sight, I notice the yellow silk heap I had deposited so carelessly on the floor is a heap not more but a lovely dress again, hanging without a crease in the wardrobe. Niobe must have been in earlier without my noticing. I hope I wasn't snoring, I think slightly mortified. I must be sure to thank her later. Slipping out of my nightgown, I carefully drape it over the chair set before my dressing table. I don't want anyone to think of me as some spoilt madam who can't keep her own clothes in order. I am the new Evelyn Carlisle. New, improved and independent. I nod at my satisfied reflection in the dresser table's mirror. Yes, that'll do. Now I only have to tame this birdsnest on my head and get myself dressed, and I will be fit for the queen.

Twenty minutes later, I float downstairs, beckoned by the mouthwatering smell of frying eggs and tomatoes. Briony's cook had to adapt at least the morning meal to good, solid British fare. I can't say I mind starting the day off with a proper English, though I had sworn to fully immerse myself in Greek custom and tradition. My belly grumbles as though warning me off any ideas that might deprive it of a generous portion of whatever is smelling so divine.

Having followed the scent and the muted sound of voices, I find the rest of the household—minus Casper—sitting at a lovely laid out table in the conservatory. From this vantage point, we have a vast view of the mountains in the distance. I marvel to have already seen mountains and the sea before I have even had breakfast.

Amid greetings and wishes of a "good morning", I take a seat at the round table flanked by Briony and Jeffrey. Daniel sits across from me, the plate before him nearly empty. Niobe bustles in, her hair in a long braid coiling down her back, filling my cup with steaming coffee that smells wonderful and so strong I fear it might spoil my taste buds for what is to follow. I take a careful sip, at once invigorated and slightly overwhelmed by the flavor.

"Evie, we were wondering," Briony begins, setting down her fork. "Jeffrey needs to go to town today, to the museum and Daniel will join him to have a look at a new exhibit. I want to ride along and pop into the shops. I have absolutely nothing to wear anymore! You must come and advise me. We'll find no Patou or Lanvin here, I'm afraid, but there are lovely things made by locals. You know, I have been away from the dictates of style for a while, I do not even get Vogue here." Briony raises her pale brows incredulously. No Vogue indeed. I think of the dream in seafoam she wore last night and feel her ability to dress in the latest fashion has not suffered in the least.

"I'd be happy to. I really should find a post office and telegraph Aunt Agnes and Iris." I plunge my fork into a juicy chunk of orange segment.

"Yes, I suppose you should," Briony plants an elbow on the table and rests her chin on her fist.

She looks tired, though her face has acquired a pleasant plumpness that with her rosy cheeks should paint of her the picture of good health. Yet I sense something is not quite as it should be. Perhaps she will tell me later when we have some time alone.

"Did you sleep well, Evelyn?" Jeffrey chimes in, his freshly shaven face showing no signs of yesterday's indulgences.

"Yes," I nod, "yes, wonderfully. And to wake up to this," I gesture at the scenery on view through the large conservatory windows, "is quite something."

"I can second that," Daniel agrees, looking more relaxed this morning in a light blue sweater and gray flannels. "I have traveled a fair bit, but here you have hit upon a true jewel by the sea."

"A jewel by the sea! Do you hear that, darling!" Briony clasps her hands together and tosses her head, spilling blond hair about her face.

"Well, I certainly think so." Jeffrey gives Briony an odd look, just for a second, quickly replaced by his normal, genial expression. He scrapes back his chair and stands up, brushing a few crumbs from his beige trousers. "I have to gather a few papers and such together. There are things, which have gone missing from the recent dig, so I must be well prepared for the meeting to keep the museum's sponsors happy. Shall we leave in," he glances at his wristwatch, "say, thirty minutes, will that do?"

"Fine," Briony replies, not looking up at him. Whatever is going on here? I feel my forehead creasing and throw a glance in Daniel's direction, but he is just nodding at Jeffrey. Men, they have no intuition for domestic matters.

"Good, outside in thirty minutes then." Jeffrey walks away but turns suddenly and adds, "oh, and Evie—"

"Yes?"

"Pay close attention on the drive, and next time I'll let you have a go with the Delage." He winks and turns back towards the door, disappearing into the shadows of the house. I must look delighted, because Briony is rolling her eyes at me, and Daniel is wearing a slightly bemused, if not confused expression.

"Oh dear," Briony sighs. "Put Evie behind the wheels of car and she is Lady Evelyn no more."

True to our word, we manage to get ourselves fed and fashioned in time to climb into the car as agreed. Caspar, I am told by my cousin in a hushed tone, is rather the worse for wear and opted, to my pleasure, to stay at the villa. Yannick is already sitting in the drivers seat, wearing a cap and remaining utterly silent. Jeffrey sits next to him. Leaving Daniel, Briony, and me squeezed, not unlike sardines, into the back row.

The roof has been let down, and we can feel the wind brush over us as the car rolls out of the driveway and onto the road. I hold my straw cloche tightly as we pick up speed, noticing that Briony is wearing the hat I brought her from England. It casts a shadow over her face, and only a few inches of butter-blond hair peak out below the rim. I rest my arm on the doorframe and let my gaze roam across the landscape. Occasionally, we meet another car, heading in the opposite direction. Over the sound of the motor, Daniel tells us about the many small villages along this road, curving sharply and up and down the numerous hills.

The sun is high in the sky now, and I am glad that my skin is not as fair as Briony's, or I would surely burn and blister before we reach town. Thankfully she has her hat. A brillant bit of foresight on my part, was it not?

Within minutes, we reach the low crumbling wall of Miklos, which even by foot would only be a short walk, one I resolve to make in the near future. It seems to be a lively place, with a sign pointing down a lane to the Agora and people going about their lives in the distinctly unhurried manner I had already observed in Heraklion. Women are chatting with their neighbors, leaning out of their ground floor windows or standing on the narrow pavement with their children tugging at their aprons. Men hoist small crates onto handcarts and wheel them down the lanes branching off the road we are traveling. Yes, surely this is a small pocket of Crete worth exploring. As we drive at a slower pace along the main thoroughfare running through the village, the road noticeably narrows by at least half a meter and I cannot imagine what will happen if another motorcar tries to squeeze past us from the other side. To my relief, we pass through without opposing traffic, and I exhale a breath, unaware I had been holding it. Yannick speeds up again, and I once more clutch at my hat.

Heraklion is the capital city of Crete and holds the largest population. That much I know. I flip open the small guidebook Briony gave me and which I wedged into my handbag.

Heraklion is the largest city on the island of Crete. Located in the region of Heraklion, it is the capital and home to Crete's administrative offices. It was named after the Roman port of Heracleum, "the city of

Heracles". Heraklion became the central portal for import and export to and from the island after the Ottoman rule ended, during which the main port of the island was located in the western city, Chania.

The city boasts many cultural and historical assets, among which are the Heraklion Archaeological Museum, offering a rich display of Minoan treasures, the Koule fortress (Rocca al Mare), and the Chanioporta gate, a remnant of the Venetian city walls.

South of the city lies the archeological site, Knossos, offering views and insight into the centre of the Minoan civilization (1900-1400 BC) on Crete.

Further, I am given to understand Crete is divided into four regions. Miklos is in the Heraklion region at the other side of the island nearly ten miles from the capital, in the direction of Messara Bay. Jeffrey is fortunate he must only travel into town about thrice a week. He grew up in the English countryside and would hate the feeling of confined space if forced to live in a large city. Briony, I believe, would benefit from the liveliness of city-life. I suppose she accepted Jeffrey's wishes, believing the big country villa would be livened up by the imminent arrival of their children.

The drive takes us further into the mountains where the wind grows calmer, ceasing its persistent tug. The foothills are surprisingly green, and for a moment I am reminded of my holidays with Aunt Iris is Scotland. Vast hills and emerald peaks dip and dive, and we weave our way around them on the precariously curving road. Yannick is a confident driver. He doesn't swerve or make the tires screech, but takes each winding of the way with knowing calm. The mountains are high and on a clear, sunny day like today, they reach into the vast blue sky, their peaks exposed, with not a cloud in sight.

I recall a story of the god-king Zeus living on Mount Ida as a youth. Nearly shouting, I ask whether these here are the Psiloritis Mountains, the range Mount Ida is a part of. Jeffrey leans back to give me an answer.

"Yes, but these are really just hills. The proper mountains, like Ida, are further west." I nod, vaguely dissapointed, and he turns back to face the road.

The drive through these hills lasts only a few minutes, and soon we are gliding back into a valley. In the distance, I can begin to see the first signs of the city. Oh, and there it is, yes, a wide slice of the sea. I just cannot get enough of that blue!

The motor rolls down the road, and suddenly we have arrived. Yellow and cream colored houses line both sides of the street. The style I can recognize as Venetian, though I am told the longlasting Ottoman ties have also left their mark. Whatever the influence, they look charming. Small and wedged one beside the other, the structures give off a sense of community, a result perhaps of the sheer closeness of living. Interspersing these houseblocks are countless narrow alleys, some dubiously dark, others bright and illuminated by shafts of sunlight creeping in from above. We pass a man sitting at the side of the road overlooking a small square, in front of him a propped up easel. He gives us a nearly toothless grin and I smile back, at once intimidated and exhilarated in the way one feels when about to enter someplace completely unknown. There is an infinite sense of possibility, for good and for bad.

Yannick stops the car in front of the Heraklion Archaeological Museum where Jeffrey and Daniel climb out. The building is quite impressive in size and built of a pale yellow stone, with a wide set of steps leading up to an ornate doorway.

"Here we take our leave." Jeffrey grabs the document case from the floor of the car. "Shall we meet in around," he glances at his watch, "four hours, will that be all right?"

"Four hours is fine, darling," Briony leans forward and gives her husband a quick peck on the cheek.

"Good, well, we will see you then. Have fun, and take care!" Jeffrey claps a hand on the hood of the motorcar, a sign for Yannick to drive on, and Daniel raises a hand in goodbye.

"Girl's time now" Briony turns to me with a twinkle in her eyes, and I let out a girlish giggle. It is just like old times, familiar and fun, full of excitement. She leans forward to give our driver directions. "Yannick, drive as close to the Market Street as you can, please. I want to show Evelyn the Agora."

"Yes, Mrs. Farnham," Yannick nods, while carefully rejoining the main traffic on the busy road.

As we head into the heart of the city, I am again surprised by how large it is. From descriptions in my cousin's letters, I had come to expect a fair-sized town, not this metropolis. All around us people are hustling to and fro, going about their usual routine. I feel small amid all this life, a stranger, ignorant of so much that defines Cretan culture and existence. Still, I am filled with an excited energy and want the car to finally arrive at it's destination, so my feet may touch the ground, and I can walk and explore and observe without the jerked movements of the motor jarring my vision of the surroundings.

The Delage slows and Briony's bright voice announces, "This is us, my dear, time to stretch our legs, and our purse stings!" She climbs out of the car, waving off Yannick's motion that he will get out and open the door for us. "No, no, you stay where you are, we can manage. Would you be a dear, and find us here in a few hours time?"

"Yes, Mrs. Farnham." Yannick is either quite shy or simply unused to the more relaxed attitude of his employers, because he barely dares to glance in our direction as we alight from the vehicle and smooth out our dresses on the pavement.

"Ta-ta!" Briony waves, but is already turning toward a sidestreet, too broad to be called an alley. Other people, mostly women, join us on our route.

"I am going to show you the Agora, Evie darling, I know you must be burning to see an authentic Grecian market, and Agora is one of the few words having thus far wormed its way into my vocabulary, so I rather enjoy visiting it." Briony tucks her hand in the crook of my elbow, leading me along. It is near mid-day and the street is cast in a warm yellow light that pours down on us from the large gaps between the buildings, and the sun is at its zenith. It is not hot, but pleasantly warm, and I enjoy the sensation of sunlight on my sun-starved skin. I hear loud voices up ahead, and though they are unintelligible to me, I know a market vendors call when I hear it. As we round the corner, a strong mixture of heady aromas washes over us like a fragrant wave. The sweet, citrusy tang of lemons and oranges mingles with the sharp scent of cinnamon, thyme, sage and other herbs and spices I cannot identify.

"Here we are. What do you think?" Briony looks at me proudly, and I feel a surge of affection for her.

"It's wonderful!" My eyes drift over the stalls of fruit and olives, jars of honey and oil. There is even a table laden with big white rounds of cheese! I don't know where to begin and need Briony to tug me by the arm, to let other more seasoned shoppers get on their way. We wander over to a stand where a small, stout and heavily bearded fellow is selling plump figs and juicy-looking grapes.

"Good day, my ladies," he addresses us in deeply accented English. "You would like to try my figs? Yes, they are the best figs in all of Heraklion." He takes one from a large pile and slices it in half, offering us the pieces. Obligingly I take mine, sinking my teeth into the sweet, juicy flesh. Briony shakes her head at the vendor, and he raises his eyebrows in slight confusion and pops the other half into his mouth.

"Delicious!" I declare and the man looks delighted.

"You want to buy? I give you very good price, best price in all of Heraklion."

I am about to agree when Briony tugs at my arm.

"Not today, thank you," she tells the man, and before I can protest she pulls me away.

"Why didn't you let me buy some? They were lovely, you should have tried it."

"If you plan on buying something from every stall we pass, we will be here all day. We buy most of our food in Miklos, you know, to endear the villagers to us Brits. I still wanted you to have a look around. It's the largest of the food markets on the island."

"All right," I shrug, already catching sight of a stand of piled nuts. "But I simply must..."

We wander all over the market for a good hour, sampling here, tasting there. As we leave, I clutch a paper bag containing Pistachio nuts I insisted on buying, though Briony couldn't help but roll her eyes. I made the argument that, as a tourist, I must do my bit for the economy of the island. She couldn't argue with that!

We make our way down the lane leading away from the market. People are still hurrying in the opposite direction, though it has calmed down a fair bit, and the sounds from the shouting vendors and haggling customers fade into the distance.

When exiting the narrowing alley at a junction, as luck has it, directly opposite we spy the sign for the post office. I drag Briony and myself across the street to send the obligatory telegram to Agnes and Iris.

To: Agnes Tremaine

Arrived safely. Am well. Staying with Briony.

Will write soon.

Take care.

-Evelyn Carlisle

To: Iris McNally

Dear Iris. Am on Crete with Briony. All is well. Nice holiday.

Will write more soon.

Sending love.

-Evelyn Carlisle

A veritable weight falls from me, having completed the task. Now I can enjoy the rest of the day. We dawdle around the shops, Briony purchasing a ream of a gauzy blue fabric imprinted with a delicate floral pattern. I find an English book in a musty shop, selling second hand texts. It has the intriguing title, Crete, Island of the Gods, and was written by a fellow Englishman called Charles Maypother. Clutching the book in my hands, I rejoin Briony, waiting for me outside, claiming that the dust would give her a migrane. She has become quite a little madam, good old Briony.

"Where are we going next?" I glance across he road at the clocktower. "We still have at least an hour before we are set to meet Yannick."

Briony exhales loudly and lets her shoulders droop. "I could do with something cool and refreshing. Shall we sit in a café for a moment? We can watch the people going by. Do you remember, we used to love doing that in Paris."

I am not at all tired, but notice the weariness in my cousin's manner and nod. "Of course, lead the way!" I would have liked to walk to the harbor, to get a whiff of the salty sea air without having to endure its wild temperament as I did on the ferry, but I plan on staying a while, so it will simply have to wait for another time.

Briony leads me to a small, quaint café with a few round tables set on the narrow sidewalk. There is only one table unoccupied, and we sit down quickly, pleased at our good fortune.

A waiter, no older than us, appears almost immediately and Briony orders two lemonades in an admirable effort, though not quite natural sounding Greek. She looks proud of her accomplishment, and I want to show myself suitably impressed, which I am.

"Very nice. In no time, you will fit in with the locals."

Briony looks suddenly crestfallen. I reach across the table in concern and clasp her hand. "Briony, what on earth is the matter? Have I said something to upset you?"

At this her face crumples further and, to my shock, she is close to tears. "Oh Evie!" She pulls away her hand, holding it up and covering her face. "It is not how I expected it to be at all!" She lowers her hands onto the table, and I see they are shaking.

"I thought everything wasn't quite right, has something happened? Jeffrey appears as devoted as ever. You're not ill are you?" I almost whisper the last sentence, fear momentarily clutching my heart. Briony is like a sister to me, I could never bear anything bad befalling her. Before she can answer and put me out of my misery, the waiter reappears with two sweating glasses of pale yellow lemonade. I thank him, settle up, and he drifts on to another table.

"No, no I am not ill. Well . . ." She lets out a shuddering breath and clutches her glass, not drinking. "I am so lonely here, Evie," it pours out of her. "I try so hard to be a good wife, a good hostess for Jeffrey's friends, but, but—" she breaks off, looking down at the scratched tabletop.

"Why didn't you say something? If you had written earlier I would have come, you know I would have. Briony, you are not telling me everything, are you?" My tone is firmer than I had intended, and I try to soften it with a sympathetic smile. "Please, let me help." Briony shakes her head and a lone, heartbreaking tear tumbles from her eye, dripping into her lemonade with a solitary plop. When she speaks again, her voice is steady but low and cheerless.

"I thought we would have a family by now." Swallowing, she goes on, "I was pregnant, you see." She says it in a flat tone so unfitting to her usully bright and lively self. It startles me.

"But—" I cannot think of what to say. Fortunately, she continues before I get a chance to utter something foolish.

"I lost it. It is quite common apparently, the doctor said. I just . . . Oh Evie, I so wanted it!" Another tear and another.

"Briony, I am so very sorry. But you can try again, surely? It is horrible this happened to you so far from home, too. Still, surely you will have another chance."

"I hope so, but it hasn't happened. Jeffrey and I have been here a year now, married for nearly three, and our loss was seven months ago. Seven months!" Her face crumples and her lip quivers.

"Seven months is not such a long time." I try to sound comforting to mask the fact that I have not the slightest idea what is normal in the realm of conception.

"It is long!" Briony pushes away a tear with an angry gesture. "I want a baby, Evie! When we married I thought I would have a family. I never had any siblings myself as you know, and I want a house full of children. What if it will never happen! What if I am barren? My mother had only me. What if this was my only chance! Am I to throw dinner parties for the rest of my life, while my husband is buried in some sandpit digging up old pottery shards?" She tugs at a curl of her straw-colored hair. Only moments ago she looked the picture of loveliness and now, well, she looks wretched, and I say that with love. A few passersby throw odd glances our way, and I glare right back.

"Briony," I say softly, "whatever happens, you will be a mother. There are options, you know that. And no one says you will not bear a horde of your own children. Or have you spoken to a doctor?"

"Yes, the doctor said there didn't seem to be anything wrong, but who knows!"

"What about your mother? Your parents visited a few months ago, what did she say?" Again Briony shakes her head.

"I couldn't tell her. I couldn't say it. Everyone was so jolly, admiring the house, the home Jeffrey and I created. I just couldn't spoil it by speaking of such ugly things." She looks so vulnerable and small, and I desperately wish I had something of any use to offer, but I don't, so I stay silent, allowing her thoughts to settle.

We sip at our lemonades in this state of quiet restlessness. Slowly, Briony's face, which had taken on a blotchy pink hue, calms and returns to its usual porcelain likeness. When we finish, we rise, gathering our few belongings and head back in the direction of the Agora where Yannick is to meet us.

Walking along, we make an occasional remark on the pretty flowers overflowing their windowboxes, or on the strangeness of the Greek spelling of street names, neither of us mentioning what has been said. There is nothing I can offer, and I am sad and helpless as I see Briony's yearning eyes follow two beautiful, tiny, black-haired children, passing by us in an alley, clinging to their mother's hands. I ache for her, but am hopeful her fears are soon to be allayed.

Yannick is true to his word and meets us at precisely the corner where he dropped us off hours ago. Despite all I saw and the delight I took in it, I feel drained. Briony's troubles have drifted over to me, and I cannot get her tear-stained, desperate face out of my mind.

Daniel and Jeffrey are already waiting as we drive up to the entrance of the museum. They climb into the car, both appearing pleased and relaxed. For a split second, I begrudge Jeffrey his pleasure. Is he struggling, too? Has Briony told him how she feels, what she fears? Am I the only one in her confidence?

"Did you ladies have a nice day?" Jeffrey asks, all innocence as he cranes his head slightly to look at us. Briony's face is once again shaded by the wide-brimmed hat, and I cannot see her reaction.

"Yes," I attempt a light tone, forcing away my worries, "yes, Briony took me to the Agora, and I found this in a little shop." I hold up the small book.

"Oh yes, the Maypother. Quite amusing. He was a raving lunatic, you know." Jeffrey places his arm on the shoulder-rest as he talks to us.

"Why do you say that?"

A knowing smile pulls up the left corner of Jeffrey's mouth. "He was convinced the gods lived here among us. He worried and rather upset a number of his neighbors with his antics, until he was asked to leave. Or so the story goes. In truth, I think he was a lonely man with a wild imagination. It frightened people that he seemed to live more in his mind than in reality. Lonliness can do that to people. He wrote his book, but left shortly after. I don't know what became of him."

"What a sad story." Briony's voice is flat and low, and for a moment I fear a new onslought of tears.

"Yes, I wonder what happened to him." Daniel's tone is subdued as well. Dear me, what have I gotten myself into!

"Well, an active imagination is something to be envied, in my opinion," I announce, trying to bring a sense of lightness back into the car. "It certainly makes for interesting reading."

"Indeed." Jeffrey nods and moves back around to look at the view ahead.

The drive seems shorter than in the morning, and before I can fully relax against the plump upolstery of the seat, the car crunches over the gravel of the villa's driveway. The sun is still glowing white and beaming amid a canvas of blue.

"Let me help you," Daniel offers as I struggle out of the backseat, holding my bag of pistachios in one hand and the book in the other. I let him assist me and hand him the nuts to hold while I disembark.

"Thank you," I say, reclaiming my treat and follow the others to the front door, which is being pulled open by a harried looking Niobe.

"Thank you, Niobe," Jeffrey hands her his hat and briefcase. As she holds out her hand for Daniel's, he declines with a smile.

"Shall we have drinks on the veranda in an hour or so?" Briony asks. She has removed the hat, and her face is again looking rosy, without red-rimmed eyes unveiling her distress.

"Yes, lovely," I nod, "It is so pleasant outside, I might just sit below the great oak and get a start on my book."

"Yes, do, you can tell me what you think at dinner," Jeffrey chimes in.

"I will go to write a few letters, and then I had better see how Casper is faring and let him know we're back." Daniel disappears up the stairs. Jeffrey vanishes into his library, leaving only Briony and me in the hall.

"Briony, you should get an hour's rest. Try to stay optimistic," I reach out and sqeeze her hand. "You will see see, it will all work out as it should." I cannot be at all certain it will, but I am hopeful nonetheless. She smiles halfheartedly.

"You are probably right." She sighs. "I think I will have a little lie down, you don't mind do you?"

"Don't be silly. I have Mr. Maypother for company. Go on."

Nodding, she walks off, and I take myself outside to the garden. To be honest, I am quite happy for a few moments quiet. So much has happened, and I need some time to think. Holding my book, I make my way along the small stone-laid path toward the tree. The wind, at this greater elevation is stronger, but not at all unpleasant, and I take off my hat to let it tease my hair. Is there anything like the warm wind in one's hair? Bliss.

Oh, what is that? I take a few cautious steps toward the tree. Someone has left their shoes lying here. No . . . someone is here. Taking a nap? For a moment, a flash of irritation that someone else has taken my spot stirs in me. It must be Caspar, who else could it be. I step closer, around the tree to the spot where the bench is half hidden beneath embracing branches.

It is Caspar. He is sprawled out on the grassy ground, dead to the world. I sigh with undisguised disappointment. Fine, I will find another place to read. I don't want to wake him and be forced to make polite chit-chat. Just as I am about to turn around and sneak back, I notice the peculiar color of his face. He must have been out here for hours and has become terribly sunburnt. But the oak casts such a shadow . . . How would the blazing rays of the sun have reached him? I take a step closer, thinking now I ought to wake him, to tell him he needs to drink some water and cool himself down. As I bend to tap his shoulder, I cannot help noticing there is something unnatural about the slightly purple tint to his lips. Wine stains? Drinking in the middle of the day and then lying in the sun is certainly not a healthy combination. Shaking my head at his folly, I carefully prod his shoulder. Nothing. I push a little harder.

"Mr. Ballantine? Caspar . . ." Nothing. Oh dear, what if he is ill. Swallowing my growing fear, I press two fingers nervously to his throat. I start to tremble, forcing myself to lean closer. His chest neither rises nor falls. No movement. No breath. No life. As the realization comes to me with alarming force, I shudder. It takes only a moment to find my voice, and I let out a high-pitched scream.

I don't know how long I wait beside the dead body of a man I met less than a day ago. My eyes are still transfixed on his face in mesmerized horror. How could I have been so blind? While I was mentally berating him for drunkenness, he was lying dead at my feet. My whole body is covered in goosebumps, and I wrap my arms around myself, more for comfort than warmth.

Finally, after what seems an age, but in truth has been only one or two minutes, I hear footsteps coming from the house. They are heavy, and I experience a flash of gratitude that it is not Briony. What will this do to her? I turn around, relieved to see Jeffrey approaching.

"What is it? Have you fallen? Are you hurt?" He comes around the bend where I am still sitting on the ground. I force myself to shake my head, to speak.

"J-Jeffrey, he," my voice falters for a moment as I watch him take in the scene, "he is dead!" The last word leaves my throat in a shrill tone, which startles me all over again.

Jeffrey looks at the little tableau in confusion. It takes only a moment for it all to register, and I notice the change in his face as confusion turns to horror. In two swift strides he is at my side, repeating the desperate search for signs of life. He finds no pulse, nor any breath left in the young man's body.

"Good God." He whispers. I can hear another footfall nearing.

"Jeffrey? Did I hear someone scream?" It is Daniel. Oh no, he shouldn't find his childhood friend like this. A tremor of panic flashes through my mind, but I am in no state to prevent the footsteps from drawing closer, keeping Daniel from turning the bend. So I sit as though frozen beside Caspar Ballantine's body as Jeffrey rises, turning towards his friend, beginning to speak, to explain, to soothe. I am deaf to their words, blind to the blue sky, the colorful birds, blooming flowers, numb to the gentle breeze. I hoped I had left death behind. What a fool I was! I saw only the majestic Zeus and powerful Poseidon, forgetting their other brother, dark and dreadful, Hades.

The next hour passes in a blur. At some point Briony is woken and told what has happened. I am pulled off the ground, oblivious to the deep grass stains in my white linen shift. The local police, Inspector Adriano Dymas, arrive with the coroner to pronouce Caspar dead, and take him away. No one is quite certain of what to do. I sit at the small round table on the veranda, unable to peel my eyes from the spot behind the tree where Caspar took his final breath. I barely knew him, of course, but his death has shaken me severely. I thought of this new place as an oasis, a wonderful escape, a chance to start afresh without past wounds being ripped open time and time again. What is it now? The place where I found a dead man in the garden. Everything around that seemed so bright and vibrant, brimming with life, is suddenly dimmed, viewed through a dulling lens.

Briony sits with me as we wait for the police inspector to talk to us. Daniel and Jeffrey are speaking to him in the conservatory. Briony had wanted to take me inside, but I needed air, so she brought a cardigan to drape around my shoulders and two cups of sweet tea. I keep thinking, what happened? What in heavens name caused a young, by all impressions healthy man, to die so suddenly? I am certainly no physician, but as my mind turns to the ghastly image of his face over and over again, I cannot come up with any logical explanation. Did a bee sting him, and he had a shock? Did he drink too much and hit his head? No, there would have been blood, and there was none. Feelings of frustration and utter helplessness mingle inside me.

"Drink up, Evie, it'll do you good." Briony has placed a comforting hand on my forearm, pushing my teacup closer with the other.

Too tired to argue, I take an obliging sip of the syrupy liquid.

"It's vile I know, but it's supposed to help with shock. This is just so awful, Evie! I can't believe it." She shakes her head. Her skin is pale, and she looks as I feel.

"I know." I force down another timid sip. "It is as though we are in some sort of hellish nightmare, but I've pinched myself and it's all still here." Closing my eyes for a moment, I want at once to rest and to run away.

"Daniel must feel utterly wretched. They were quite close, I think. Almost like us." I shudder involuntarily. "Sorry."

"No, you're right. They grew up together. Caspar is . . .was his best friend. He was a decent fellow as far as I knew him, which wasn't very far at all. Although he had been at the booze a bit much lately."

"Poor man. That poor, poor man. He was so young." I am cold now. The sun has begun its descent, moving on to warm others far away. Still, I cannot bring myself to move. I want the wind, which has grown colder and sharper, to sweep over me, to make me shiver, to fill my lungs with life giving force, to make me feel I am still here. The thought brings on a strange wave of guilt. I am alive and Caspar is dead.

Before I can sink deeper into despair, I hear the door behind us opening. The Inspector, a man perhaps seven years my senior steps onto the tiled veranda, Jeffrey in his wake.

"Hello, I am Detective Inspector Adriano Dymas." He gives us a curt nod, then turns to look directly at me. His gaze is focused and not unkind. "I must ask you a few questions, if you don't mind. I believe it was you who found the body of Mr. Ballantine."

"Yes." I swallow, experiencing a tinge of anxiety, though of course I have done nothing wrong. For a moment no one moves, then Briony, as if awakening, gets up with a start.

"Oh, yes. I am sorry. You want to speak to her alone." She is clearly reluctant to leave and lingers by my side, a hand on my shoulder, a protective hovering presence. "Perhaps, I could stay. I won't interrupt, I—"

"It's all right," I pat her hand. "Truly. Make youself a proper cup of tea." Hesitating a few seconds, she finally pulls away, disappearing into the villa with Jeffrey's hand on her back.

The inspector takes a seat in the small chair Briony has vacated. His frame is too large for the delicate, wrought-iron furniture, all broad shoulders and long, solid limbs.

"Lady Carlisle," he pauses, a crease forming between his generous eyebrows, "I am sorry you had to be the one to find the body. A very bad business." Resting his hands on the table, he appears completely at ease, despite the circumstances of our meeting.

"Yes, terrible." I stammer, unsure of what else to say, though my feeble "terrible" doesn't desciribe the tragedy by half.

"You must understand, Lady Carlisle—"

"Evelyn, please, or Miss Calisle, if you prefer." I interject, wanting him to appreciate I am no uppity miss he has to humor with false deference.

"Miss Carlisle, then. I would like you to tell me exactly what you saw. I know this is unpleasant, but it will be of great use in our investigation."

"Investigation? Wasn't it, I mean, it was an accident . . ." I let the last word trail into the air between us, waiting for him to agree. Please, please don't make it even worse than it already is, I beg inside my head.

"No, Miss Carlisle. I am sorry to say, your friend, Mr. Ballantine, was the victim of a crime."

I gasp, too startled to speak and he waits a moment before continuing, "The coronor could not give me a definite answer, but was almost certain that strychnine was used on the victim."

"Strychnine? You mean rat poison? Who would do such a thing?" The questions bubble out of me in a confused stream. The news has taken me aback. I pull the cardigan tighter about me, knowing it will do nothing to drive away the fierce chill creeping into my bones.

"Yes. Strychnine is used commonly as a rat poison, thus it is readily available. Please, Miss Carlisle, if you will tell me what you saw, you can go and rest. You have had a bad shock."

Trying to breathe evenly and keep the quivering out of my voice, I retrace my steps for him. He listens calmly, nodding occasionally for me to go on when I begin to falter.

"And that is all really. Then Jeffrey must have called you. I truly do not know any more." Replaying the scene in my mind has exhausted me. I only want to fall into bed and disappear beneath the covers.

"You do not remember seeing anyone near the house as you arrived? Someone might have climbed the fence, it is quite low after all, and gained access to the garden. We found a wine glass that had rolled to the side. He would likely have known the killer if he was drinking with him, though a second glass has not yet been discovered."

I tense as he mentions this. Someone he knew, someone he might have shared a glass of wine with killed him, coldly took his life. I clasp my hands together so tightly I can feel my nails digging into the tender flesh of my palm.

"I do not know. I didn't notice anyone." Shaking my head, I emphasize the fact that I am as lost as he.

Probably realizing that I truly have nothing else to add, Inspector Dymas rises, which I take as a sign that I, too, may go. Pushing back my chair, I pull myself up, steadying my jellied legs by holding on to the edge of the table. I follow his gaze to my white-knuckled grip, and the expression on his sun-tanned face softens.

"Thank you for your time, Miss Carlisle. You are not well as would be expected after such an event. Shall I call your cousin to help you inside, or will you take my arm?" Letting out a slow breath, I try for an appreciative smile.

"No, you are very kind, but I can manage. Thank you." I turn to the doorway and hear him follow. We walk to the entrance hall.

"I will take my leave now. I have spoken to the other members of the household already. Please do not leave the island. We will have to be in further contact with you. Also, do not touch anything in his room, we will need to search it and confiscate anything that may be of value in this investigation."

"Can you search for fingerprints?"

"We have only rudimenatry equipment, this is not London, Miss Carlisle. You may trust we will do our best." His tone is kind, not mocking, and I simply nod.

"I understand." As he turns to leave, a question drops into my mind, and I take a small step toward his retreating figure. "Oh, inspector!" He turns back to face me, an expression of puzzled curiosity drawn across his features. "What will happen to his body?" As I ask the question, I cannot understand why I feel the need to know. What business is it of mine? I suppose Daniel will deal with all of that.

"Well, once the coroner has made his examination, it will be released for burial."

"I see. Thank you." He gives a quick nod of his head and exits. As the door falls on its hinges, I drag myself up the stairs and to my room.

Once in the room, I am suddenly unable to lie down and close my eyes. The house is silent. Everyone is probably wondering what to do with themselves. Briony will be thinking whether is it appropriate to serve dinner? Jeffrey will be trying to distract himself with work and Daniel . . . I do not know. I wonder whether I should look for him. He must be feeling acutely alone. Maybe Jeffrey is with him. They both knew Caspar far better than Briony or me, and will have more to talk about, more to mourn.

Feeling suddenly stifled, I step onto the balcony, overlooking the hills and the strip of deep blue in the distance. The air is cool, and the branches of small olive trees in the garden below are still swaying as peacefully in the gentle breeze as they did this morning when everything was different.

I inhale slowly. How strange it is that air and breathing are so vital to life. It is the simplest of actions, but then . . . Caspar will never breathe again, never laugh again, never cry; there is nothing left for him in this world now. Nothing to enjoy or to despise. What a frighteningly fragile thing life is. In the blink of an eye it can be over. A chill runs down my spine like winter's icy breath, and I close my eyes. I haven't cried. A man is dead, a man I barely knew, a man who, hours earlier I spoke to. I try to remember his voice, slightly tinged with arrogance, clean Etonian English. A cool man, yes that is the best way to describe him. Distantly suave. How strange and unfathomable it is that he should be gone from one moment to the next without a goodbye. Has he left an imprint on the world, an impression that he was here, that he lived and died? I catch myself asking the same questions regarding my own existence. If I disappeared at this very moment, what would remain? Exhaling a gust of air I've been holding, I open my eyes stunned by the brightness. No, this is no way to be thinking now. I suck in another breath like an addict before retiring into my room.

As I am resting in the solitary coolness of my bed, I cannot bring myself to close my eyes. They are heavy and tired and beginning to ache, yet each time I allow them a moment's respite, the ghost appears. Caspar's face, pink and purple. It was a mercy his eyes were closed. I catch myself drifting off again, sleep trying hard to overwhelm me. Maybe I can bear it for a moment, a few minutes. I allow my eyes to close, determined to wrench them open before the nightmares begin. As I try to clear my mind and to imagine the blue sky, the azure sea, white fluffy clouds, the faces of my parents, smiling and cheerful, drift into my head. Oh, how I yearn for them in a moment such as this. Moments where I feel so small and alone, and the world seems so unyieldingly harsh. I am grateful to be near Briony and Jeffrey, but they are struggling with their own problems. Lying very still, I force their faces to stay with me, to keep smiling at me. I want to climb into the memories, to be there and not here. To be a child, coddled and protected, naive, and loved. Despite my attempts to resist its relentless pull, the need for sleep overwhelms me. In my last moments of semi-lucid consciousness, I hear my voice, sounding like a far away whisper, "don't go." As if they hear me, they do not disappear. The nightmares never come, and for a few hours I turn back the years to a time where life was still simple and pure.

CHAPTER 6

The sun is shining brightly the next morning. I let the rays, streaming through the window, wash over me, relishing the warmth. About to climb out of bed the memory of yesterday's horror comes back to me like an ache one has reawakend with a wrong movement. I sit frozen for a few seconds, unsure of myself, unsure of whether to get up and go downstairs, or hide here under the covers for the rest of the day. How will we all face one another? What will we say, sitting together at the breakfast table? I cringe at the thought of Daniel's face, a face I last saw ashen and defeated. Though he was vague when telling me his life's story, I got the sense he has seen more than his share of tragedy, but has not come away from it a hardened man.

Perhaps he would be glad of company. I would welcome some distraction, or at least some comiseration. I know, of course, that Caspar Ballantine was a relative stranger to me and one I hadn't even particularly taken to. Yet he was so young and so alive in those few hours I had known him, and seeing his body . . .

The words of the police inspector, Adriano Dymas come back to me. Mr. Ballantine wass the victim of a crime. So he had at least one enemy.

Climbing out of bed, I walk to the window. Yesterday this scene made me feel like the heroine in a film. Outside nothing has changed. The sky is still a dazzling blue, even clearer than yesterday morning, and the line marking the dark sea appears nearer.

When the war began, when I became more and more aware of all the grief we humans cause and bear, I developed an interest in the pagan gods and gods of the Olymp. They do not pretend to love man, they meddle, confuse, upset. They protect nature, make trees grow, rivers run, flowers bloom. They wreak havok, often with terrible consequences. This I can believe. I can no longer place faith or trust in a benevolent god.

Looking out at the beauty before me, feeling the heaviness in my heart, I wonder whether there is a god protecting the natural world, keeping the sea blue, the valleys lush and green, following the cirlce of life that keeps the animal kingdom sustained. But is there a god protecting us? Or has He given up on the human race when we began destroying one another?

Washing and getting dressed, I take my time, in no rush to go downstairs. As I run a comb through my hair, I catch my reflection in the oval mirror set into the vanity. I don't look any different than I always have. I almost expected my outward appearance to show similar signs of transformation as my inner being. My elation and sense of freedom is now at odds with the shattering reality of Caspar's death. I came here with the thought of starting afresh. I am young, but I have lived twenty-four years on this earth. There is no such thing as a mid-life rebirth for me, only an attempt to become more like the person I want be, past included. My reflection gives a tiny nod, and I am reassured.

I wear an unadorned navy dress, slightly longer than the current fashion, with a simple dropped waist and kick pleats. My sandals are flat and plain, making barely a sound as I descend the stairs. It is quiet, and as I reach the bottom I have the urge to climb back up again. Forcing my reluctant feet, I walk toward the conservatory where we had breakfast yesterday and which is Briony's favorite room in the house.

Relief mingles with nerves as I hear low voices. As I step into the doorway, I observe only Briony and Jeffrey, their heads together, sitting at the table. I feel like an intruder, but cannot back out now. Briony notices me and straightens in her seat, not looking at all upset at my interruption, thereby loosening the knot of tension at the nape of my neck.

"Evie, sit down," She points to the empty chair beside her. An unused plate, cup, and set of fork and knive are laid out in front of it. I nod and sit down. "You must be hungry," Briony continues. "I am a terrible host,

I didn't even ask whether you wanted to eat last night. It was just—" she breaks off, gives a sad little shake of her head and frowns.

"Don't be silly. I do not think any one of us could have mustered much of an appetite." I pour myself some coffee and half-heartedly look at the breakfast spread. "I am still not particularly hungry, but I wanted to see how you were." Looking at Jeffrey I ask, "How is Daniel coping?"

Jeffrey sighs and wipes his mouth with one of the ivory linen napkins before finding his voice. "He is completely shocked. As we all are, of course. They grew up together, you know, so it's like losing another brother for him."

"Another brother? His others were lost in the war, weren't they?" Jeffrey nods solemnly. "I had thought so."

"I don't know what to say to him. They came here for a holiday, and now this!" In a rare show of passion Jeffrey throws up his arms, looking helpless and frustrated.

"It is good he has a friend like you, Jeffrey." I try to make my voice stronger than I feel. "And you are a good friend. Just listen to him, try to make it somehow easier to bear. That is all any of us can do."

"You're right, of course. Still it is a terrible blow." We sit for a moment in silence, lowering our gazes, staring at nothing.

"Evie, were you told how it happened?" Briony swallows nervously, crumbling a piece of toast onto her plate. "I mean, how he died?" There, now we can say what is on our minds. It is almost a relief.

"Inspector Dymas said it was poison."

"Strychnine," Jeffrey chimes in.

"Ordinary rat poison." Briony drops the toast and folds her trembling hands together in an attempt to steady them.

"Yes, I still can't believe it." I say, knowing how banal it sounds. None of us truly understands or believes it yet. However, despite any wishing or hoping, it is true and it happened and it cannot be reversed. I am glad I am with friends, with people who love me, and whom I love. Sitting here with them makes me feel I am not alone. We share the confusion, anger, and sadness and don't have to pretend and put on masks at a time when caring and truth are most vital.

"I keep thinking," Jeffrey leans his elbows on the table, manners fogotten, "who would possibly do such a thing?" A flicker of miserable confusion appears on his open face. "I know Caspar wasn't without faults, but he wasn't a bad person. Careless at times, but—oh."

Oh indeed, at the moment Jeffrey utters these words, Daniel walks through the door. We all freeze and observe a pained expression dance across his face.

"Oh, Daniel. There I go putting my foot in my mouth, I only meant—" Jeffrey tries, making to get up. Daniel raises his hand.

"No, please stay." Jeffrey hovers for a moment, then obeys and sits back down. Looking pale, Daniel sinks into the empty seat beside me. I am in the awkward position of wanting both to embrace him and to run away. Before I get the chance to do either and confuse the poor man even more, he resumes speaking. "Don't look at me like that, Jeffrey. It's all right. I know who Caspar was. I had my own difficulties with him on more than a few occasions, but—" he takes a deep breath, "he was my friend. Even if that friendship wasn't what it once had been."

"Of course." Jeffrey replies somberly, and Briony, desperate for her nervous hands to do something pours Daniel coffee, spilling a fair bit onto the saucer in the process.

"I assume the police told you what happened?" Daniel asks, shooting a little smile at Briony who is loading his plate with slices of toast and thick rashers of bacon. She seems intent on making him physically ill too.

"Yes, Inspector Dymas told us. I still cannot believe it was murder." Jeffrey utters the last, ugly word in a low voice, creases of concern lining his forehead. He appears older today. The crime committed in his garden has aged him, and Briony looks particularly young beside him, her face tired but unlined.

"Can't you?" Daniel's voice is sharp. He hesitates, a pained expression crosses his even features. "I am sorry. I only meant, we need not paint a false picture of Caspar. He chose to live life a certain way, without regard, without care, there were times in our travels, well . . ." he allows his gaze to sweep to the far reaches of the garden behind us. I cringe inwardly as my mind's eye brings forth the image of the body I found there only hours ago.

"He was no saint. None of us are." Jeffrey's voice brings Daniel back to us, and his eyes glint in the warm light streaming through the windows.

"You're right. None of us are."

Briony and I follow the awkward exchange in silence. I clearly sense her deep unease. She thrives on being good in social situations, aways saying the right thing, the perfect hostess. It unsettles her, as I see in her wide-eyed stare, to be able to do nothing to make this moment any more pleasant. I feel the urge to get her away from this scene, and myself as well.

"Briony," I start, my voice much too loud as I shatter the thickening silence, "would you help me, I cannot find my passport and travel papers. I must have mislaid them somewhere. Inspector Dymas wanted to see them when next we met."

A look of relief comes over my cousin, and she all but jumps from her seat as though she had been sitting on hot coals. "Yes, of course. He might be back today. You'll excuse us." She is talking quickly, and Daniel and Jeffrey look almost amused at my transparent attempt to extricate my cousin and myself, all the while giving them the privacy they probably desire.

"Of course. Good luck with your search." I can hardly believe it, but I almost detect the hint of a smile on Daniel's lips. Now I wish I wasn't leaving and could follow the continuing discussion. I take some comfort in the assumption that Briony will wheedle it out of her husband and relay anything interesting to me.

"Yes, in fact," Jeffrey adds as Briony and I are almost at the door, smelling sweet freedom, "Inspector Dymas said he would come by later with the—" he pauses, shooting a nervous glance at Daniel. "Well, to tell us whether the doctor has been able to find anything more. You see, since

Caspar was a British tourist the authorities will be keen to solve this quickly. Any dragged out business may create scandals."

"Oh!" Is all I manage, before noticing a tug at my sleeve and following Briony into the interior of the villa.

I actually have to tell Briony that it was a ruse, my travel documents are safe and secure in my mother's hatbox. I am either a good liar, or she is quite innocently gullible. In all probablility the latter is true.

"Oh well," she says as we find ourselves climbing the stairs to my room, "we need to have a chat and some privacy anyway."

I close the door after we enter my bedchamber, more out of habits formed at Aunt Agnes' house than for fear of being spied on. Briony sits down on the small chair in front of my vanity table, and I drop myself onto one of the closed trunks.

"Oh, Evie, what a terrible mess!" In a frustrated gesture, she drops her hands into her lap and immediately begins fiddling with the hem of her skirt.

"Daniel seems oddly calm about it all, don't you think." My brow creases as I air my confusion. "How was Jeffrey last night?"

"Oh, you know. Upset, of course, but to be honest," a guilty expression comes into her open face, and she lowers her voice, "Jeffrey never much liked Caspar. He knew Daniel's family quite well, went to school with one of his older brothers, so inevitably he met Caspar too."

"He knew Daniel's brothers?" I cannot keep the curiosity out of my voice.

"Well, he met them years ago, yes. They died, you know." Briony looks down at her hands. I suspected as much. Hearing her confirming such a tragedy still manages to strike at my heart.

"How terrible." My voice comes out in a whisper.

"It was. They had enlisted together. Daniel was too young at first and in school. His parents begged him, all three of them, not to go. Of course they would have had to join eventually when conscription began in '16." As she speaks, I see in my minds eye, the eager faces of young men, proudly showing off their khakis, not understanding what it all meant, not understanding their own mortality.

"And Daniel?" I know he fought as well, but Briony needs to talk, and I want to hear whatever she knows.

"It was a very bad business." She shakes her head sadly, hesitating a moment before finding her voice and continuing in a soft, melancholy tone. "While he was still at home, being the youngest, he got news of both his brothers, killed at the Somme. He was so infuriated that, in some misguided rebellion, he joined up as soon as he could. Three days after his eighteenth. Apparently, his parents pleaded with him not to. Told him they could get him away, he wouldn't be drafted. This was before conscription, you see. But he wouldn't listen. Stubborn bitter youth, I suppose. Couldn't see his parent's fear beyond his own anger."

I swallow, but the hard lump in my throat won't be moved. So much suffering. I want to tell her to stop now. I want to climb under those lovely soft blankets on my bed and hide away until I am old and all of this is so far in the past I can hardly remember it. That is impossible, of course.

Memory must act as our restraint. It must hold the evil, the carelessness, the greed at bay. We call it the Great War, why I have wondered many times. It bestows upon it an ill-deserved aura of glory when it was only horror, and all that remains of it is pain.

"His mother turned very fragile after they heard news of the of the tragedy that befell her eldest sons. She became ill, couldn't eat or sleep, and passed away after only a few months. The father was desolate, inconsolable. He shot himself two days later. Daniel was already in France at the time and didn't hear the news until weeks after it happened. I cannot imagine how he coped. Jeffrey said he might have found brotherhood in the army, people who looked out for him. I cannot really understand it. He was only a boy. He only went back to visit their graves. Since then he's been traveling far away from home. No one really knows what he does, though he says he writes travel books. He has the funds, so nobody questions him."

I listen in silence to Briony's narrative, distraught at the thought of the immense burden of grief this man must carry with him every waking hour. I wonder how many mornings he has to do battle with himself to find the will to start a new day. Another orphan, does not the world have enough? I cannot help the strange sensation that we both belong to some deranged, melancholy club. I know the sort of grief that can be so overwhelming it is like a virus clawing its way into my body.

Briony and I sigh almost in unison. I have been gripping the edge of the trunk I am sitting on, and my knuckles have gone stiff and white from the tension. Releasing my hold, then not knowing what to do with my hands, I fold them in my lap.

"And Caspar?" I finally manage to say.

"They enlisted together. Caspar was part of the family. I don't know how his parents reacted, surely much the same way any would. They were just boys." Briony's eyes are gleaming, but she does not cry. The stories have been told a hundred times, we know them well.

"Stubborn boys. Oh, Briony, how often can one wish the past undone." It is not a question, simply a statement every human being must arrive at at some point or another.

"They were in France for a long time, almost until the end."

"That might explain why he seems so closed off."

"He has had more than his fair share of suffering." Briony pauses and gives me an odd glance.

"What is it?"

"I don't know if I should say—"

"Say what?" I hear the hint of irritation in my voice. This is one of Briony's few bad habits, she loves a good baiting, even if she isn't aware of doing so.

"Well..." Another drawn out moment until I widen my eyes in exasperation. "Oh, fine. Daniel might be a bit more closed off with women as, even in that realm, fate spared him no heartbreak."

"What happened?"

"He was engaged."

"Engaged!" I cannot hide my surprise. "He was?"

Briony nods, and I get the sneaking impression she is taking a little pleasure in having such juicy gossip. By her manner, I can at least assume his wife-to-be has not died.

"I only know this from Jeffrey, who swore me to silence." She wavers only a second before continuing, "I am quite certain he wouldn't be angry if I told you. He likes you." Pleased as I am that Jeffrey likes me, I am keen to know more about Daniel's romantic past.

"Go on, then!" I find myself leaning forward. Feeling the hint of a blush creep up my neck, I lean back again.

"Before he went off to France, he got himself engaged to local girl. I don't know her name, they had been sweethearts awhile, and he wanted to marry her. Then he got shipped out before they could make it legal. Apparently, she wrote to him when he was away. You remember how the soldiers could receive mail and little packages to keep their spirits up? Well, he thought everything was fine, that they would truly get married once he arrived home, something to live for, I suppose. Then, 1918 rolled around and he was released from duty, only to find his fiancée got married a year earlier!"

"No!"

"Yes! In a way she did the decent thing in continuing to write to him as if everything was as he imagined, so he wouldn't give himself up completely. In truth, she fell for some flat-footed boy at home and married him instead. It was a terrible blow. He was shocked and angry, and who could blame him?"

"Indeed."

"He went a bit wild, did some foolish things, that was when Jeffrey met him again." As Briony explains, my attention is immediately caught on foolish things. Before I can inquire as to their nature, she continues her narrative.

"Jeffrey was injured so early in the war, he never really saw much battle. He and Daniel bonded over other matters and Jeffrey," her face takes on an expression of loving pride, "helped him recover again."

"Jeffrey is a kind man. I am sure he was a good friend to Daniel then, and will be now." It seems such a silly thing to say, but I am all out of wisdom. I knew Daniel had tragedy in his past, but to this degree . . . No, I would never have imagined. It would not be wished on one's worst enemy. It will be strange facing him in a little while, pretending not to know, yet desperate to make him realize he is not alone. A small flicker of shame runs through me. Perhaps Briony should not have told me this. I know it would disturb me to find others discussing my own past behind my back.

"What are you thinking?" Briony is staring at me, the light shining through the open window setting her golden hair aglow, a halo around her face.

"I don't know," I wipe my eyes. "I suppose I just feel so helpless."

"And hopeless?" I hear the fear in her voice and look up to meet her eye.

"Do not be afraid for me." I get up and walk over to her perch on the edge of the chair. "I am out of the blackness. I carry memories everywhere I go and many are good. I have you and Jeffrey, Iris, and even Aunt Agnes. I know I am not alone and neither are you, and neither is Daniel."

Briony gets up and gives me a quick hug. "I'd best get myself together if the Inspector is coming soon." She walks to the door. Opening it, she turns back, a small smile tugging at the corners of her mouth, then she is gone. The light tapping of her heels on the wooden floor echoes faintly in the silence.

For another moment I stand frozen to the spot, allowing the impact of her words to settle. How I sometimes wish the past did not have such mighty power to hold us in its talons! But then I remember laughter and cheer and try to let those happier memories overwhelm the desperation that awakens when I realize I will never hear it again.

CHAPTER 7

Detective Inspector Adriano Dymas arrives less than an hour later. He has come alone, leaving his constable to work on other matters at the station in Miklos. Briony guides us into the sitting room, which I have thus far only seen in passing. It is a long room with high white ceilings and a comfortably elegant set of sofas and armchairs. Most importantly, there is enough space for all of us as even Niobe, Yannick, and the cook, (whose name I do not even know!) have been called to congregate here.

I am seated beside Briony and the inspector on one of the long low-backed sofas, upholstered in a pale green fleur-de-lis pattern. Jeffrey sits beside his wife and Daniel on a chair next to him. The household staff has huddled together on the opposite setee.

"I wanted all members of the household present when I gave you the news." Dymas looks around, just as I imagine a detective in one of my novels might do. He gives each of us a glance, though I catch only a moment of his searching black-brown eyes as we are seated close to each other and I am at the edge of his periphery.

"What news? Has the doctor finished his report already?" Jeffrey is on the edge of his seat, and I notice the taut muscles and the throbbing of a vein in his neck.

"Yes. It was as he suspected." Dymas pauses, presumably for dramatic effect, though I cannot imagine why. All of us have reached the apex of tension and curiosity by this stage. "It was strychnine, or as you may know it, rat poison. We found remnants in the glass we discovered near his body. He ingested the poison, likely through wine."

"Good heavens!" Briony gasps, though this is no real surprise, but then she did not see the body. Exhaling slowly, I wish we were outside. I suddenly feel very closed in. So many people, and me squashed between them all. I fight the urge to dash out of the room, remembering with startling slowness that I am in the middle of a murder investigation. Suspicious behavior would be noticed. I push away my anxiety as best I can and sit up a little straighter.

"Could it have been an accident?" Daniel asks, sounding neither hopeful nor convinced of such a possibility, and I wonder what motives for Caspar's murder he might be aware of, or what enemies he might suspect for that matter.

Dymas shakes his head. "I very much doubt it, Mr. Harper. The amount found in his stomach was not insignificant. He might have been saved if it had only been a small, accidental measure, though as I understand, no one but him was at the house for most of the day, is that not correct?"

Everyone nods dumbly, and I wonder where Niobe and the cook were? Yannick drove us into town. He could easily have come back here in the four hours between the time he dropped us off and picked us up again, but I am sure the inspector will have asked him about that.

"Yes, we were in town, Daniel and I at the museum, and my wife and her cousin were together at the market." Jeffrey answers as representative of this household. "Niobe was visiting her mother, and our cook had the day off and was in Klima to be with her daughter." Niobe and the cook, whose real name I must discover at the nearest convenient time, nod their heads in unison, saying nothing.

"Hm . . . yes, so you told me yesterday." Dymas doesn't sound entirely convinced, and I wonder whether he already has suspicions. I cannot imagine anyone here . . . Someone in this room could be a murderer! No, no, we all have alibis. I shake my head and catch Briony giving me a strange look.

"Did he suffer?" We turn to look at Daniel, whose calm face belies the fact that he must be aching with emotion.

I catch the policeman glancing quickly at his large, brown hands lying folded in his lap before he meets the grieving man's eyes.

"I am sorry to say, it was not an easy death." He looks apologetically at the faces around him, and I can only sympathize with him. What a miserable task it must be to have to tell people such dreadful news; to watch the sadness and agony and anger written across their faces and be unable to offer any true comfort. I do not think I could do it.

"Can you be any clearer?" Daniel is forcing the words from his mouth, and I feel the urge to get up and fetch him a glass of water, but find myself frozen in my seat, eagerness and dread mingling in my mind as I await the inspector's answer.

"This will not be easy to hear."

I respect him for not saying it will upset the ladies, but shrink from what he will say all the more.

"Go on."

Dymas inhales and does as he is asked. "Strychine ingested causes spasms of the head and neck. These occur repeatedly and result in paralysis of the airways. The victim dies of asphyxiation two or three hours after ingestion."

The silence between us lasts a few seconds as we take in the horrible fact. The tiny hairs on the back of my neck stand up. Without noticing I reach for my throat, but lower my hand quickly so no one else will notice either.

"Do you know when it was taken?" Daniel's questions are clear and logical. I cannot imagine how he can think sensibly enough to articulate them. Perhaps he wrote them down last night. I doubt he slept, if the rings beneath his eyes are anything to go by.

"The doctor's report states the poison would have been consumed around noontime. You arrived at the villa at four, or thereabouts, I believe," Dymas waits for a nod from Daniel, "and Miss Carlisle discovered the body near that time. This is all correct, is it not?"

I shiver as the image of the poor man's body pushes itself into my mind. I can almost feel his flesh, recalling the sensation of my fingers searching for a pulse on his still warm neck.

Daniel is starting to lose his composure just a bit. "So, he would have only been dead an hour, two at most?"

"Yes," Dymas nods gravely.

"If we had come back sooner!" Briony whispers what we are all thinking. There is a sorrowful desperation in her voice, and I am grateful to see Jeffrey clutching her hand.

"I am afraid, Mrs. Farnham, it would have been too late. The poison was taken with a large amount of wine and some olives. No other food. We have examined his room, and any open wine bottles on the premises and have not been able to find anything with traces of the poison. Nor was a bottle found near his body. The murderer must have taken it, and possibly his or her own glass away as he or she left. Mr. Ballantaine would have, in all likelihood, been suffering the effects quickly, judging from the amound in his system. We are still considering the idea that he may have been somewhat inebriated before ingesting it. Strychnine, as you may be aware, has a very bitter taste, so the amount of alcohol in his stomach would explain why he might not have had the . . ." his voice trails off as he searches for the word.

"The sense to taste it?" Daniel interjects. Dymas looks, if not pleased, at least appreciative of this assistance.

"Yes, thank you Mr. Harper. Depending on how much he had drunk, his senses would be dulled. When he swallowed the poison, only noting a bitter aftertaste, it would already have been too late. A sober man might have made himself sick to expunge it . . ." again his voice drifts off to let us find our own conclusions.

It seems Caspar was rather fond of drink. I thought it had been only at the party where everyone was jolly, but to be so beyond sense at twelve o'clock, strongly hinted at a deeper problem, which makes the situation all the more disturbing.

"Further, we have noted a small bruise on the side of his face. Not strong enough a blow to have knocked a tall man like him down, but it may be related. Unless he acquired it before?" He looks at us and we shake our heads.

"No, not to my recollection." Jeffrey adds.

"I shouldn't have left him alone." Daniel closes his eyes for a moment, breathes deeply, opens them and gets to his feet. "Excuse me." He runs a visibly trembling hand through his dark hair and in long strides steps from the room. On impulse I stand up, notice everyone staring, and sit down again. What use would I be to him? He surely wants to be alone in his grief. From what I know now of his and Caspar's relationship, they were almost like Briony and me. I banish the thought of anything happening to her from my mind, terrified of even allowing the possibility to exist.

"I am investigating this murder. I will be asking questions and require your absolute cooperation so we can discover what happened and give your friend peace." This last statement takes me by surprise, and I turn to look at him. He meets my gaze, only smiling sadly, and gets up. Everyone else rises as if by command, and we follow the inspector to the door.

"I will talk to the list of people who were at your dinner party last night," Dymas looks at Jeffrey. "At the moment, we have no leads as to who might have done this, therefore we must consider all the people Mr. Ballantine was in contact with. Again," now his gaze sweeps over the rest of us, still huddled around him in the hall, "if you can think of anything at all, any enemies or problems he may have had, let me know. You have my card, and you can contact me at the Miklos police station. I will leave now, but will be back when I have further questions or if new developments arise." He puts the hat he has been handed by Niobe on his head, covering his thick black curls, and disappears. Moments later, I hear the low rumbling of a motorcar.

For a moment all of us stand there, a forever-bonded little group. Then, as if a spell has been lifted, Niobe and the teary-eyed cook, a small plump woman with a kindly face, take off to their allotted domains. Jeffrey, Briony and I, as if by some unsaid agreement, head toward the conservatory.

Once we are comfortably seated, we begin to talk all at once. After some, "no, you go", and "please, go on" being politely offered, I begin.

"I only arrived yesterday, so I didn't know him well at all, but was Caspar in the habit to drink in excess on a regular basis?" I put this as diplomatically as I can, not wanting to ask outright whether he was a habitual drunk.

"He was rather fond of the stuff," Jeffrey shakes his head and sighs. "But that it should come to this?"

"Was it commonly known?" I hesitate, trying to formulate the question without sounding harsh. "Did your acquaintances or people you met know of his problem? That it was his weakness? If so, someone might have seen an easy way to . . . to take his life." I finish feebly. I cannot bring myself to say "murder him." It is too fresh still and, for that matter, may always be.

"Surely you can't think any of our friends would do such a thing!" Briony sounds shocked, though not as defensive as she might.

"I am only saying, if it was common knowledge that he liked to drink more than average, someone, some enemy—" I speculate, feeling a bit melodramatic, but finding no other word for it, "some enemy might have thought it would be the easiest way to, well, you know."

"I cannot imagine who—" Briony begins, more for the sake of speaking than real conviction.

Her husband interrupts her. "Caspar was not a bad man. He had problems, yes, but murder? To murder him, what motive could there be?"

"They say poison is a woman's game."

Daniel's voice startles us, and we swivel around to face him. He does not look angry or offended, which lets me exhale the nervous breath I am holding.

"Sit down, Daniel," Jeffrey motions to an empty chair. Daniel hesitates for a moment, then steps out of the doorframe, sitting in one of the light rattan armchairs.

"I am sorry. I shouldn't have said that."

He looks contrite, though there is no need. We all sympathize and would tolerate a more impassioned outburst just as easily. having only known Daniel for a single day, I nonetheless feel as though we have been acquainted for years. This tragedy has brought us together, our little clan.

"Tell me if you'd like me to ease off the topic, but do you have any idea who might have wanted Caspar . . .?" Even Jeffrey is unable to say it.

"Dead?" Daniel rubs chis chin and rests his elbow on the narrow arm of the chair. "No. I have thought about it all night, and I just don't know."

"He might have offended some native Cretans. I'm afraid when I took him to market last week," Briony volunteers meekly, "he . . . he was a bit unsteady and might have made a grab for one or two of the women. I got him away before anything too upsetting happened."

"Murder for an inebriated grope sounds a bit far-fetched, Briony, though I suppose one never knows what goes on in people's minds." Jeffrey raises an eyebrow and takes off his specs to pinch the bridge of his nose.

"You are probably right. Yet I wonder whether he ever . . ." I hesitate, suddenly awkward.

"He ever what?" Briony asks and everyone's eyes are on me.

"Whether it ever went further than a harmless scuffle."

There, out it was. "Love and greed are so often at the root of any action. Of course, in this case it would be very drastic indeed."

"People here are tradition bound," Jeffrey begins, and I have to think of my aunt and the confines of tradition I tried to escape by coming here. "They are protective of family honor. If Caspar had . . . interfered with that, there would be repercussions. Usually it would involve a mean thumping, and that would settle it."

"I don't believe it was a man. Men fight it out to defend their pride. It would not satisfy a spurned husband to quietly poison his rival." I look at both men present and detect the hint of a smile as I see Briony's face from the corner of my eye.

"This is probably true. Although, if it was not the motive, then I cannot think of one at all. Caspar was, shall we say, not above an affair. Whether any husband knew of it, I cannot say." Daniel lifts his hands, palms out in a defeated gesture before he lets them drop limply onto his lap.

"The police will have a better idea of how to catch the guilty party." Briony concludes the conversation. She stands up, "I am sorry, but I must call Laria and tell her what has happened. She called earlier and left a message with Niobe. Please excuse me."

I wonder whether she is really calling Laria, or simply escaping to avoid having to hear further speculation on this ghastly matter. I wouldn't blame her. Much as we are alike, we were raised very differently. Briony was protected by her parents like a fragile porcelain doll. During the war, they tried to hide newspapers and radios from her for fear of her hearing what might upset her. She is a gentle soul, and while I am not what one might call hardened, I believe she is still shielded as if by an armor from certain miseries that come with reality. I hope she will forever remain protected the way she has always been. A cynical Briony would be a loss of light in the world.

"I am sorry this is causing you all such distress," Daniel says, while we know his suffering must be far greater than our own.

Jeffrey waves a hand and shakes his head. "Please, Daniel. I will not hear of you blaming yourself for any of this. What happened is one person's fault, and whoever it is will be found, of that I am confident."

"I wish I shared your confidence," a sad smile plays with the edges of Daniel's mouth. "I do not know where to begin. On the one hand, Caspar lacks . . . lacked both tact and gentility, and on the other he could charm an ogre. I do not know whom he offended to such a degree." He lets out a breath. "It is all so unbelievable."

Unbelievable is truly the best word to describe the situation. Yet believe it we must.

"Inspector Dymas seems a competent man. Do you not think so?" I try to bring a degree of confidence into my tone.

"Yes, good man, Dymas." Jeffrey nods, clapping his thigh in one of those self-assured, meaningless gestures I have only ever seen men make.

"And he said he would keep us informed, which is all we can ask of him at this stage."

Daniel creases his brow. "I suspect he is being so agreeable largely because Caspar was a tourist. An Englishman dies on his patch, and he has the miserable task of having to investigate thoroughly. Otherwise, it will undoubtedly cast a shadow over Crete."

"Oh yes, they will be worried. I can see the newspaper headline once this gets out, 'Englishman Victim of Cretans' or 'Crete: the Den of Cretins'. They will be doing what they can to resolve this and pronto!" Jeffrey waves a pointed finger.

As I open my mouth to reply, Niobe appears in the doorway. The men, not facing her, do not notice, so I smile and beckon her forward.

"Niobe," I wave a hand. She seems reluctant, her left hand holding the wooden pane as she hovers for another moment in the frame, looking like a painting.

"Niobe, is everything all right?" The men have turned toward the young woman, and Jeffrey looks up at her as he speaks.

"I do not know, Mr. Farnham. There is a man on the telephone. He wants to speak to you. He would not tell me his name."

"Not someone from the museum, then? Hm . . . right, lead on." Jeffrey gets up, gives Daniel and me an apologetic little grin and follows Niobe back into the main house.

For a moment, there is silence, and my mind returns to the last conversation we had with one another. The night of the dinner party. The night Caspar was still alive. Yesterday. As my mind flashes back to the scene, I remember a vague glimpse of him talking to the young maid before we left the house to go outside. Could he have acosted Niobe? I hope not. She appears to be a kind, if slightly melancholy young woman. I supress a shiver considering the chilling possibility of someone in this household being in any way involved in the whole ugly business. We were in town, which leaves the staff. The inspector apparently accepted their alibis. Still, I now wonder what Caspar said to make Niobe so ill at ease?

Daniel's voice pushes my thoughts aside, and I avert my gaze, away from the fauna beyond the windows and back to his weary face.

"I must tell Caspar's father before any outside news reaches him. Ballantine is not a common name, should it appear in a paper." Daniel rubs his temple, "I tried calling this morning, but missed him. He is in Brighton, visiting his sister and he won't be back until the weekend. I will have to send a telegraph."

"Were they very close?" I lean forward a little in my chair, placing my hands on the table. My uncle Brendan once told me, people are more likely to trust you when they see your hands. Could be a load of hogwash, it was said after a few glasses of brandy after all, but worth a try.

"No, not really. It will be a terrible blow for him still. Caspar was his only child, his wife died in childbirth . . ."

"I see." I cannot think of what else to say.

"I grew up with him always around. He taught Caspar and me how to fish. It will be very difficult to tell him what has happened."

His words fill the space between us. Daniel needs to talk and, given the chance, I believe he will. His green eyes fix mine as if he is trying to assess whether I am worthy of his trust.

"Shall we take a walk?"

His suggestion surprises me, and I nod and get up. He leads me into the house and toward the front door. I couldn't bear to walk the garden, passing the forever-branded spot. Surely Daniel feels the same. As we make for the door, Jeffrey comes back into view.

"Everything all right?"

"Yes, we are going for a walk. I can't sit here all day wondering. Some movement will be good."

"Yes, yes," Jeffrey nods somewhat absentmindedly. I wonder who called him? "Good idea. You won't be upset if I don't join you? I have a mountain of work to look at."

"No, not at all," Daniel replies. "Where is Briony?"

"She is discussing something with the cook. To be honest," Jeffrey lowers his voice, "she is much more upset by all this than she lets on."

"Then maybe I should look after her?" My forehead tenses in concern.

"No, I will send her off to bed. You go for a walk. Take the road to Miklos. Daniel knows the way. It might be a nice distraction." As he says it, he knows it won't be. Nevertheless, it is a kind thought and, I offer him a smile and pat his arm.

"We'll do that." Almost as an afterthought I add, "I hope your mystery caller didn't add any more to your work load."

Jeffrey goes very pale. "No, not really. It wasn't a colleague, you see." He looks nervously from Daniel to me. "It was a man from the local newspaper, actually. A Davros Kanansakis, if I got that right. He, well he . . ." He stumbles over his words, and Daniel jumps in.

"He wanted to get the story?"

"I'm afraid so," Jeffrey does a nervous shuffle, shifting his weight from one leg to the other. It's making me jittery just watching him.

"What did you tell him?"

"Nothing!" Jeffrey's eyes grow wide and he stops his little dance.

"It's all right, Jeffrey. I knew the vultures would smell a good story. I just don't understand how they found out so quickly."

"News travels fast here. Someone at the Miklos police station might have told his wife, and she told her neighbor, and on and on the chain goes until everyone knows and the story is so wildly exaggerated, they might as well be recounting a fairy-tale."

"The nature of gossip." The fact that reporters are beginning to hound us already sets me on edge.

"You two go for your walk. I will check on Briony and get some of my work done." Jeffrey bestows a fatherly smile on us.

"Right, then. We will see you in a while."

CHAPTER 8

Daniel and I leave, making our way along the gravel driveway and toward the road. I am glad I remembered to grab my hat from the hallway stand as the sun is high and bright. We walk in silence, the gravel underfoot crunching beneath the weight of our steps.

Upon reaching the road to the village leaving the house behind, a strange lightness comes over me as though a load bearing down on me is lifted the more we distance ourselves from the villa. From the scene of the crime. I look at Daniel, who straightens, and wonder whether it feels the same for him.

"Do you know many people on the island? You've been here how long now, a few months?" I watch his profile from below the brim of my straw hat. The sun has dappled his hair with streaks of amber and his skin, outside the house, has lost some of its pallor.

"Just a few locals. People we went sailing with, fishermen and Jeffrey and Briony's friends you met at the dinner party." His mind must be drifting back to the night when, under the star-speckled sky, everything was peaceful and pleasant. I try to move our conversation onto a lighter path.

"Sailing? After the voyage on that ferry the Sirens themselves couldn't coax me onto a boat. Don't you find the sea terribly rough?" I watch with pleasure as a smile creeps into his face.

"Yes, it can be quite severe, but once you are in calmer waters, it is like nothing else in the world. The fishermen I have gone out with know exactly where the sea is peaceful and where the fish like to gather."

"I must admit, I haven't been on many sea-vessels. I'm a city girl, though I did go punting at Oxford a few times. I suppose it is hardly comparable."

He turns slightly and gives me a curious glance."You studied there." It is not a question, which somehow pleases me.

"Yes, at St. Hugh's. Not many of the colleges accept women, of course. St. Hugh's always has. I read classics."

"Ah, so Greece must be a dream come true. Have you been here before?"

"Never, sadly. I really ought to brush up on my Greek skills. I am embarassed to admit, I am by no means fluent."

"That's all right. So many of the islanders I have met have been very patient and try to speak English. Some speak it as well as you and I."

"I noticed that. Niobe, for one, speaks perfectly. She said her father wanted her to learn."

"I am sure it helps with employment nowadays."

"I should very much like to see the Acropolis some time and Knossos ,which is so close. I was hoping Jeffrey might take us one day," I say as we round a bend and see the low walls of Miklos village in the near distance.

"Yes, you must. It is quite a site. I went there when we first arrived." I was hoping he would offer to accompany me, but perhaps that is too much to ask, his mind being occupied with other matters. A car, a standard black model, drives from the village gate toward us, slowing on its approach.

"Lady Evelyn, Daniel, what a coincidence!" It is Darius, the museum curator and Jeffrey's colleague. He pulls over to our side of the road, leaving barely enough space for a bicycle to pass by. We move further to the side, and Darius pokes his head out of the window. He is wearing his small round specs and a mournful expression.

"I am so terribly grieved by what has happened. I called Jeffrey earlier this morning, and he told me. What a waste, what a tragic waste." He shakes his head and sighs. Daniel and I do not quite know what to say and simply nod along somberly.

"Are you driving to the villa, Mr. Calandra?" I aim to steer the subject from Caspar's death.

"Oh yes. Darius, please call me Darius."

"Then you must call me Evelyn."

"Very good. I wanted to see how you all are managing. I don't want to impose, Jeffrey is a good friend and if there is anything I can do to help . . ."

"Actually," Daniel's voice surprises me, "you might be contacted by the police. Inspector Dymas is in charge of the case."

A look of surprise plays across Darius' face before he answers. "Dymas, I know him. He is a good man. Why would he want to speak to me?" He raises his shoulders slighty. "I will do what I can, of course, but I do not see what he could ask of me?"

"It is probably routine. Do not worry. He wants to speak to all the people at the dinner, because we were among the last to be in his company — " he falters, swallows, and adds, "when he was alive."

"Yes, I understand," he says slowly.

"Well, we don't want to keep you." Daniel forces a smile, and I follow suit. A rickety looking delivery truck laden with crates slowly approaches, but cannot possibly sqeeze through the narrow gap between the fenced edge of the road and Darius' motorcar.

"I should go." Darius casts a fleeting glance at the truck, and the driver makes an impatient gesture. Daniel and I step back to allow Darius to move without compromising our feet.

"Goodbye." We wave, and Darius offers a small nod and drives off. The truck rattling after him sends up a cloud of dust. Daniel and I stand by the roadside a moment longer, coughing and rubbing our eyes before continuing our walk toward the village gate.

As we pass the wall, we pass under the remnants of a stone arch. Once in the village, we stroll comfortably, side by side on the pavement. There are few people about. Mostly women carrying baskets of fruit, vegetables, packets wrapped in brown butcher's paper and oval loaves of bread.

When Daniel leads me around a corner and down a sunlit alley, a small child, a girl of perhaps three or four, collides with us. She is running, her expression not concealing naughty glee, her dark curly hair bouncing on her narrow shoulders.

"Hello, young lady!" Daniel catches her as she pummels against him. She looks up at him, her impossibly dark eyes curious and not in the least intimidated.

"I know you." She says this in Greek, which I am thrilled to be able to understand. Still, I am not quite confident enough to venture a reply, even to a child.

"Yes, we've met before, haven't we? You're Kaia Zarek. Where are your parents?" Before the girl can answer, we hear a relieved cry and Laria Zarek, the doctor's wife comes rushing around the corner, albeit in a much more dignified manner than her daughter, who is still glaring at us in the open, inquisitive way only a child dares.

"Kaia! There you are!" Only now does she register us, and expressions of confusion and then recognition flash in succession across her face. "Oh, hello." She smiles and shakes her head as she grabs the squirming child's hand.

"Hello Laria, you remember Evelyn."

"Of course I do, Daniel." Laria smiles warmly in greeting.

"This is your daughter? She's a beauty. Kaia is such a lovely name." Laria looks suitably pleased at my observation and pats Kaia's head.

"Thank you. Kaia was my grandmother's name. Where are you off to?" From Laria's easy manner, I gather she has not been told of the murder, and thus did not call Briony this morning. I must remember to ask about it.

"We wanted to take a stroll around the village. You haven't heard it then?"

"Haven't heard what?" She raises her eyebrows and turns her head, a very faint line appears questioningly on her forehead. Daniel glances at the little girl, who is twisting in her mother's grip and will soon have freed herself.

Laria notices his gaze, looks down and then at us again, her expression tightening. "Has something happened? Is Briony all right?"

"Briony is fine . . ." Daniel trails off pressing his lips together.

"You have time for a coffee?" Laria doesn't wait for a response. "I will drop Kaia off at my mother's house. She lives five minutes from here. Then we can talk."

"In ten minutes at Hector's café?" Daniel asks, and Laria nods.

In a light voice she adds to her daughter, "Say bye-bye to Daniel and Evelyn."

"Bye-bye," the girl dutifully imitates her mother's English words and waves a small hand as Laria pulls her in the opposite direction.

Daniel and I find "Hector's Café", which is really just a tiny room, with three round tables packed onto the pavement in front of it. We sit down at one and the proprietor, whose name is not Hector but Daion, comes to greet us.

"Mr. Daniel and beautiful lady!" He claps a large hand on Daniel's shoulder and smiles jovially, displaying a gleaming row of three gold teeth.

"Daion, good to see you. This is Miss Evelyn Carlisle. She is visiting from England."

"Ah, wonderful, wonderful!" He smiles happily.

"How are your children and your wife?"

"Very good, all are very good. You are good to ask. I will bring you some wine?" He raises one caterpillar of an eyebrow.

"Three coffees for now, or would you prefer a glass of wine, Evelyn?"

"No, coffee is good." I am quite off wine for the forseeable future. Daion waggles his head and rushes off.

"You have settled here rather well. You already have a local." I try to lighten the mood. After all, in a few moments he will have to tell Laria that his best friend has just been murdered. Before he can respond, she appears at the entrance to the alley. She spots us and waves.

"Hello, again. Thank you," she smiles, and Daniel pulls out a chair for her. "That's better. I have been running after that child all day. There must be a storm coming, she always get's partuculary energetic when a storm is coming, strange isn't it?"

"Laria," Daniel is noticeably struggling to turn the subject from her lively child to his dead friend. He moves uncomfortably in his chair, almost squirming.

"Laria, we have bad news." I interject and look in Daniel's direction. He gives me a tiny, almost imperceptible nod of approval.

"What is it? What has happened? You are so serious." Laria looks from me to Daniel and back again. "Out with it then."

"There is really no easy way to put this. Caspar —" I falter. I thought it would be easier for me, but I hate these words. I hate them, and what they mean and their ugly hopeless finality.

"He died yesterday." Daniel's voice is very quiet, and his face frozen as though he can hardly believe he said what he said. Laria's eyebrows knit together in an expression of puzzlement and disbelief.

"I don't understand, he died?" Her tone carries an unmistakable note of bewilderment. "What do you mean? We just saw him. He was fine! I don't understand." The skin around her nose and cheeks has turned pale.

"Laria," I reach across the table and gently place a comforting hand on hers, "he was poisoned. It is being investigated by the police."

"Oh God, oh God," she mutters and stares at me, a wild expression in her eyes. As fate would have it, Daion chooses this moment to appear at our table with the coffees and a small basket filled with small round biscuits. To my great relief, he evidently senses something amiss and leaves without a word. I push a cup of steaming coffee across the table at her.

"Drink some of this, it will help." A lie, of course. What use is coffee in a situation like this? I must admit, I am somewhat surprised at her strong reaction. She looks positively ill. At the party I did not get the impression she particularly liked him. In fact, I remember her looking distinctly annoyed with Caspar and his antics over the course of the evening. Perhaps she feels guilty?

"Yes, thank you." Holding the little cup, she takes a careless sip, surely scalding her tongue, but not even flinching.

"I am sorry to have distressed you, we— " I gesture at Daniel, "didn't want to leave you ignorant, only to find out through gossip or exaggerated tales."

Laria nods, sips again and sets the cup down, clattering on its saucer. Black-brown liquid slops over the sides and into the shallow little plate.

"Shall we walk you home? This was a shock." Daniel is already pulling his wallet from an inside pocket of his beige linen jacket and placing what I take to be a generous sum on the table.

We get up and lead Laria back the way we came. I assume Daniel knows the way to her home, because Laria doesn't utter another word. I catch him occasionally glancing over at me, perhaps to make sure I am keeping up. I am surprised he is coping well enough to lend support to someone else. Maybe it helps to be useful, to be active in some way. If one can be find use for oneself, be helpful even, one can probably pull through the day. And the next, and the next, until one day the grief is only a dull pain one has grown used to and barely notices anymore. It will take time, but we can be a resilient lot.

Laria's house, a smaller, no less elegant villa than that of Briony and Jeffrey, is located a few minutes from the village gate. Nicolas has his medical practice in a separate building off the main road and is not home when we arrive. Fortunately, her mother, a small, elegant woman, who, despite her stature, carries herself with the distinct air of one-who-will-take-charge, is home to do just that.

Daniel quickly explains the situation, and she responds in heavily accented English, "I am very sorry for your loss." Glancing at her still ashen-faced daughter, she adds, "You will excuse me, I must take care of her now."

"Of course. We will see ourselves out."

"Goodbye. Laria, I hope you will feel better soon." A silly thing to say, but one tends to say silly things in situations that are quite the opposite.

Daniel and I make our way back. The street we follow is almost deserted, and there is more space between individual houses, some even have small gardens. Clearly, this is a more affluent neighborhood. Eventually, we near the main road again. The buildings are squeezed closer together once more and people going about their daily routine walk past us. Some give us an interested glance, and some smile and nod, most don't bother with any sort of acknowledgement.

"I didn't expect Laria to react so strongly. Was she well acquainted with Caspar?"

Daniel rubs his chin and gives me an odd look.

"What is it?"

"I might as well tell you. I think you will understand." He hesitates another moment, and the tiny ball of curiosity that has been building inside me since I saw Laria's shocked, ashen face swells tenfold.

"Yes?" I try not to sound too interested. Bad manners, Aunt Agnes would chide.

"Laria and Caspar had a little affair. A dalliance."

"A dalliance!" I burst out, unable to suppress my surprise. Despite my desire to stand still and hear more, Daniel pulls me along in the direction of the village gate from where we are, once again, on the road back to the villa.

"Now," he slows his pace, "I don't want anyone to hear about this. It could get Laria into deep trouble, or at the very least embarass her and Nikolas, and I don't want that."

"How do you know? Did he tell you?" Daniel is wearing a vaguely bemused expression at my undisguised incredulity.

"Yes, he told me. He wasn't the most subtle." He flinches slightly as he uses the past tense. The sun is warmer now, and he slips off his jacket and slings it over his shoulder, before continuing. "Maybe I should have said so to Dymas, but I wasn't thinking. In any case, it didn't last. As you know, we haven't been here long, so . . ." He narrows his eyes, whether in question or as a reaction to the bright light I don't know.

"It was over? They weren't still . . . " I trail off, hoping he will simply pick up from there.

"Lovers?" Daniel startles me with his candor, but I try not to let it show, lest he think of me a prude, which, perhaps, I am . . . He goes on, "Yes, it was over. They were reasonably friendly, but as you might have noticed at the dinner party, there was no love lost between them anymore."

"I see."

"I hope I haven't scandalized you? I shouldn't have come out with it like that. You have only just arrived, and—"

"No, not at all," I lie. "It is simply . . . unexpected, though it explains her reaction. Poor Laria. I wonder whether her husband has any idea. If not, she will have to pull herself together before he meets her."

"I am sure her mother will see to that. Caspar called her a 'dragon', so yes, poor Laria." We are silent for a few steps, and I let this new information sink in. If Laria was suitably angry . . . no, her reaction couldn't be faked, unless she is a superb actress.

"What if Nikolas found out? Daniel, you might have to tell the police. He could have had a perfect motive!" I am stunned at the words I have just uttered. Nikolas Zarek seemed a very amiable, confident man when I met him. And now, by a small twist of fate, he is turning into a murder suspect in my mind. I look at Daniel. Staring ahead at the road, half his face is turned away, the other bathed in yellow light turning his skin golden. From the side he looks older, the angles of his cheekbones sharper, the line of his jaw more distinct. From this angle, the tired sadness in his eyes, giving him the appearance of being very young and a little lost, is hidden from view.

"No, I can't believe that." He sucks in a breath of warm air and shakes his head, turning slightly to face me, while maintaining his stride. "I can't tell the police. It would humiliate Laria, and she doesn't deserve that. She ended it, you know. The bitterness should be on Caspar's part. I doubt very much Nikolas knew anything about it."

"Maybe, but you can't be certain, can you? Daniel, you must tell Inspector Dymas. I know you like the doctor, but he might have had a motive. Jealousy is as strong a drive for such impassioned action as any." I fall silent, allowing my words to take root. Foolish, terrible, irreperable things have been done in the name of love. Murder not excluded.

"If I don't tell him, will you?" There is tension in his questioning tone, but his expression has remained mild.

"I would be duty-bound, Daniel. You probably view me as an outsider. But now you have told me of this, a confidence I do not want you to regret, but one I cannot forget either. I owe these people nothing, so it would be easier for me to tell the police than you. I have only been here two days. All the same, the police will ask how I found out about this, and then what could I say? It will be better coming from you." I add in a low, placating tone, "Dymas is an understanding man. You could surely tell him in confidence without feeling like a gossip?"

"You are probably right, though I am certain neither Laria nor her husband had anything to do with any of this."

"The truth about their affair may come out one way or another. Dymas wanted to question everyone who was at the party, and if Laria has a similar reaction as she did with us, he might put two and two together."

"I might as well save the man some time and effort." Daniel sounds almost relieved now. Sometimes people already know what is right, what must be done, they just need a little push towards it.

"I think that would be wise. You of all people will want this resolved as quickly as possible, I am sure." For a second I think I have overstepped the mark, but after a moment's hesitation he nods in agreement.

"I will call him once we are back at the house."

"Good." We round a bend, and I glimpse the creamy façade of the villa in the distance. "Daniel," I slightly slow my pace, and he matches it instantly.

"Yes?"

"Thank you."

"For what?" He wrinkles his brow.

"For trusting me. You are not a gossip, and wouldn't tell someone's secrets easily, so I appreciate it." The words hang between us for a moment, until he breaks into a tiny smile.

"You're welcome. Selfishly I confess, I am happy to have someone to listen."

"My pleasure."

The house is very near now and keen to lighten the mood before we reach it, and before miserable memories overwhelm us, I begin chatting about the village, about the pretty houses, Hector's café, the sharpness of his coffee. Daniel understands what I am doing, for he joins in without batting an eyelid and we stroll through the gates nearly at ease. Yannick is in the drive, shirtsleeves rolled up to his elbows, white-blond hair tousled by the gentle wind. He is washing the motor, running a large, soapy sponge along the dripping sides. He nods at us as we approach. Daniel excuses himself to call the inspector. I feel mildly guilty for pushing him into doing it, but it would be wrong to ignore any sort of clue, even if it is far off the mark, and I am almost certain that it is. As he disappears indoors, I linger for a moment, delayed by the desire to talk to the chauffeur who appears to exist almost as a spirit, always around, yet never really there.

I saunter over to the spot where the Delage is parked. Yannick notices and straightens, like a soldier.

"Miss Carlisle, good day."

"Thank you, Yannick. How are you today? Such a terrible thing happened yesterday. I wanted to know how you are. I didn't notice you this morning when Inspector Dymas was here."

"Ah, yes. I spoke to the inspector yesterday already. I had to change one of the tires this morning, so . . ." he gives me a smile, but I can see muscles of his bare forearms and in his neck tensing and his grip around the sponge tightening, sudsy water dripping from his fingers. He may just be uneasy. He clearly doesn't like to chat, and knowing a man has been murdered in the vicinity is something that might set the noblest man on edge.

Nonetheless, I have the eerie feeling there is something not quite right. A I have noted before, my imagination is not of the idle sort.

"I am ever so relieved we all," I emphasize this, "have alibis. It would be terrible if the police were to suspect any one of us living here." A look of panic enters his eyes, and though he quickly tries to appear normal, I am certain I saw it. It makes me nervous, and I have to steel myself not to take a step away.

"Yes, yes. Very good." He looks at the car and the sponge, clenched in his fist dripping onto the gravel, turning it stormcloud gray.

"Well, I shan't take up any more of your time. Goodbye then."

"Goodbye, Miss Carlisle."

As I turn to walk to the house, I feel his eyes following me, boring into the back of my head. Inside again, I quickly close the door, a sense of relief mingling with growing anxiety. There is something left unsaid bothering me. Yet who am I to interfere, to meddle? Only the unfortunate soul who found the body. I sigh and remove my hat, patting down the stray hairs.

I glance at the hallway clock, and I find we have been away almost two hours. As if on cue, my stomach grumbles, reminding me that lunch is overdue. I am surprised to have any appetite at all!

"Evie! Oh good, you made it back safely." Briony rushes at me from the direction of the kitchen. Though she is smiling, I perceive tension in her face.

"Yes, everything was fine. Are you all right? You look a bit pale."

Briony, to my surprise, glances around furtively, then grabs me by the hand and pulls me into a small sitting room.

"What is it? Why are you being so secretive?" I follow along willingly. The room is cool and smells mildly of something floral. I sink into the floral silk settee and become aware of my tired feet still encased in "sensible", low-heeled shoes.

"Evie, Laria called. She was in such a state!"

"She called again? Twice in one morning?" Childish, I know, but I can't resist. Briony doesn't even blush.

"Oh, well, you caught me. I wasn't feeling up to company this morning, so I told a little lie. I am sorry. I shouldn't have left you alone with the men. You're not angry, are you?" She blinks a few times very rapidly, and I shake my head. I recognize the first signs of imminent tears and certainly don't want to be the cause.

"No, not at all. Just teasing. Go on."

"Right. Well, she called, whispering hysterically. She said you and Daniel told her about what happened. Oh, you should have heard her. You won't believe this!" Briony's eyes are wide with barely supressed amazement. I can imagine what she will say and refrain from interjecting, not wanting to spill out the truth in case Laria's affair isn't actually the subject she is so desperate to confess.

"Well?"

"You mustn't tell anyone about this, but she told me she and Caspar had an affair! She assured me it was all over by now. I think she merely needed to tell someone. Laria seems to think my morals on these matters are much looser than those of her other friends," she furrows her brow, momentarily displeased.

"Nonsense, she trusts you, that is why she told you. You are her friend." This buoys her spirits and she straightens.

"Well, I did tell her I was quite shocked. Which is the truth. Laria and Caspar! It doesn't seem . . . well, right. Nikolas is lovely and their daughter, you should see her, such a beautiful child." Briony's eyes glaze over with a faraway look.

"Maybe Laria was unhappy? Maybe it was simply a foolish mistake. Either way—"

"That's where you're wrong, Evie, I think she loved him," she interjects.

"Why would you believe that? Their affair was over, wasn't it?"

"Yes, yes," Briony waves this off as inconsequential. "It was the way she spoke, the grief. I tell you, I could almost feel her tears through the telephone receiver! She loved him. I am sure of it. Maybe she still does."

If Laria's relationship with Caspar was more serious, it could prove an even greater motive for her husband to be connected to his death. If Nikolas found out, or if she confessed and told him she loved another man, or even that she wanted to leave him . . . But then why break it off? I have to find out when they ended their liaison.

"Did Laria tell you how long this relationship went on and when it ended?" I try to sound only innocently curious as the wheels spin in my mind.

"Not long. Only two months. It started almost as soon as Caspar got here and ended a few weeks ago."

"Hm . . . so quickly? She might have felt guilty. Her husband appears to be a kind sort of fellow, and at the party, I thought she doted on him."

"I thought so, too, how deceptive people can be," she shakes her head in confusion.

I wonder whether I should air my suspicions to Briony, experiencing a tiny stab of guilt for pretending this information is entirely new to me. What if Nikolas knew nothing of the affair? I only hope Dymas speaks to Laria first, and that he understands such delicate matters must be touched with kid gloves.

"Briony," I finally begin, "I shouldn't say this, but after I saw Laria's reaction to Caspar's death I was confused, and Daniel confessed he was aware of the affair. Now that you also know, we can talk about it without betraying anyone's trust." Pronouncing this with emphasis as though it is something to be glad about, I wait a moment for the news to sink in. The expression on her open face remains composed.

"Go on."

"If her husband knew of the affair, he would has the perfect motive for the murder." Out it is. Briony opens her mouth, then closes it again and shakes her head.

"No Evie, no, this cannot be. I know them."

But do you? I want to ask, finding myself hoping her faith in humanity won't be badly shaken once this is all over. Briony has maintained much of the innocent optimism of her childhood, a precious attitude I hope will remain as long as it can in a world such as this.

"I am not saying anything is certain, of course. It is only speculation."

"Why did you have to put such an awful idea into my head, Evie?"

"Do you not think you might have come to the same conclusion? Besides, even Daniel, who has a good deal of respect for the doctor, agrees it might be possible."

"Daniel? You said this to Daniel?" Her voice rises, a sign of her distress.

"You have no need to get so upset. It may be nothing at all—"

"But if it is true, it will ruin their marriage!" Her outburst stuns me for a brief moment, before I can find the words to reply without causing further distress.

"Ruin their marriage? If her husband is a murderer, I would say they are already on shaky ground. She had an affair, it must have been less than rosy for some time."

"They have a child, Evelyn," she narrows her eyes, looking at me in an unfamiliar way. Perhaps I was wrong about her lingering naïveté after all.

"Briony," I aim to sound calm, though I feel my heart pounding against my chest as I continue, "please, this isn't my fault. Do you think I want him to be guilty?"

She shudders and closes her eyes for a moment. When she opens them, they are glistening. "No, of course not. I'm sorry I got so upset."

I put an arm around her shoulder, very much the big sister, though in fact I am a few years younger than her, though five inches taller, it should be noted.

"I do understand. Maybe it's nothing, but I cannot get the image out of my mind. Until there is resolution . . . Oh, I don't know." I brush a strand of hair from my face.

"This is all too much!" A teardrop splatters onto her salmon linen shift, coloring it crimson.

"Don't cry." I soothe, placing a hand on hers. "It will work itself out. You are not at fault in any of this. None of us can control what other people do. It is a horrible, horrible thing, but Briony, you cannot blame yourself! It is not your fault by any measure."

"I know." Her voice is small, almost a whisper. "Some days it is as if nothing can motivate me to even get out of bed. And now this has happened and—" her shoulders rise slightly as she takes a deep breath, "and I just can't . . . I just can't . . ." She doesn't finish her thought.

I have been aware that there are problems, still this admission frightens me. I know Briony as a happy person. Smiling, making people laugh, caring and fussing, and being the life and soul anywhere she goes. Looking at her now, mistress of her own home, wife, grown woman, her familar brightness has been dimmed and diluted.

"It will be all right" I mutter the necessary words of reassurance, feeling I must say something, lest she regret having confided in me. "I am here now. And Jeffrey loves you. You are not alone, and as long as you want me to, I will stay."

"We're sisters, aren't we." Her voice is thick with uncried tears, nonetheless I have to smile. We're sisters. As children we would introduce ourselves as such. Sisters.

"Yes, always."

CHAPTER 9

Twenty minutes later, I have sent Briony to rest. Her frame of mind worries me. Should I talk to Jeffrey? I don't want to betray her trust. Surely he must know she is not happy? Still in the sitting room, I lean back on the soft cushions of the armchair. I have borrowed a well-thumbed copy of *Emma*, and am about to settle in for a nice hour or so of lighthearted reading when I hear someone enter the room. Turning around, craning my neck to arched doorway, I spot Niobe, carrying a tray.

"Hello." I smile at her. She looks nervous, my company clearly unwelcome.

"Mr. Farnham said I should bring you some lunch." She approaches slowly and sets the tray on the low table in front of me.

"Thank you. How kind." I lean forward, hungrily eyeing the small plates of olives, triangular pastries and shards of cheese. "This looks wonderful. Is Mr. Farnham not eating?"

"He ate when you and Mr. Harper were out."

"And Daniel, Mr. Harper?"

"I will bring him a tray as well."

"Perhaps he will join me. Do you know where he is?"

"In the conservatory, Miss."

"Thank you, Niobe." As I look at her before she turns to leave, I notice the pale red rims around her eyes and the dark shadows below them. An instant stab of guilt grips me. I completely forgot to ask after her. The poor girl must be as shocked as any of us. "Niobe?"

"Yes? Can I get you something else?"

"No, no, this is perfect," I gesture at the tray. "I was wondering how you are? This has all been a terrible shock, and you knew Mr. Ballantine longer than I did. Are you all right?" It takes her a moment to answer as she stands awkwardly beside the table.

"I am fine. I did not really know him."

"Still, it must have been a bad shock." The word hangs in the air, and I wonder at this young woman's composure. Suddenly, the image of Caspar and her talking away from the group at the dinner party flashes across my mind. She seemed uneasy then, harassed even. Was it simply the old case of upstairs getting too friendly with downstairs, or something more?

"Is there anything else I can help you with?" There is a hint of impatience her voice.

"No, thank you for the meal, it looks lovely."

Niobe nods, turns and hurries from the room. Strange. Of course, she may simply feel disinclined to unburden herself to me, a relative stranger, but I get the sense there is something I cannot place a finger on, that is just not right.

Sighing, I lift a pastry from the tray, lean back in the chair, and take a satisfying bite. As the savory flavors of spinach, cheese and buttery crust melt in my mouth, I push suspicions from my mind, open my book and wonder if men like Mr. Knightley are merely rare or complete fantasy.

Briony wakes after her rest looking much better and informs us that we will eat together tonight. These household plans and orchestrations give her something to distract herself, something to make her feel capable. I am now in my room, shedding the wrinkled dress I wore all day, and slipping into a pair of wide navy trousers and a boat-neck blouse. Looking into the mirror, I am quite pleased with my efforts. I run my ebony handled comb through my hair a few times, until it falls in auburn waves an inch or so above my shoulder. Yes, that should do.

On the landing to the first floor, I momentarily wonder whether I ought to have worn black. As I stand there wavering, a door at the end of the hallway opens, and out comes Daniel in a pale gray suit.

"Good evening."

"Good evening. The house smells wonderful, I can only imagine what the cook is going to spirit onto the table for us tonight."

We descend the stairs in step. "In the time I have been here, the one thing that we could always depend on was good food."

Apparently this standard will hold, no matter the circumstance. Entering the dining room, we spy a lovely array of small bowls filled with delicacies already on offer. Briony and Jeffrey emerge from the library at that moment.

"Oh, good, you're here," Briony leads us to our seats. "I told the cook to prepare something light." It all looks wonderful. The table is too large for the four of us, and we are clustered together at one end, leaving the other half bare and uninhabited tonight.

"It smells delicious, Briony," Daniel smiles, and Briony looks gratified by his praise. I glance at Jeffrey, he only nods and tucks his specs into the front pocket of his jacket.

"Right, I thought we could be informal. You don't mind, do you?"

"Of course not."

"Niobe wasn't well, and I thought we should let her get some rest. We can serve ourselves."

"Niobe is ill?' I ask, thinking of her fainting episode right before the last dinner we ate here together. "I spoke with her this afternoon, and she was well."

"I don't know. She's such a quiet one. She was rather pale, and I had the impression she was exhausted, so I sent her to bed."

"That was kind of you, dear. Now, would you pass me that plate of Keftedes?" Jeffrey sounds weary and slightly impatient.

Briony places a few of the fried meatballs onto his plate. I wonder whether his tension is due to the crime committed in his garden, his marriage, work anxiety or a combination of the above? Briony appears to be better now, and the soft radiance of the candlelight casts a gentle glow over her.

"Mm . . . this is wonderful. I must compliment the cook." I say, between bites of a smooth and spicy eggplant dish, moussaka. As we eat, we talk about mundane things. Despite this, I cannot help but wonder whether our minds are not all circling around the same matter. How can any of us sit here and truly enjoy the food, carefree and happy when the table should have been set for five? Caspar's seat is empty, and as my eyes wander to it, my appetite disappears. I become suddenly aware that we are all looking at the chair in unified dismay. Almost as one, we set our forks and knives down.

"I should have known this was a bad idea," Briony looks down at her plate.

"No Briony, this was a kind thought," Daniel interjects before I think of the right words. "We have to eat, after all." As our attention is on my cousin, Jeffrey's low voice almost makes me start.

"We should be honest."

"What do you mean?" Briony stares at him with wide eyes.

"We are all thinking it. Let us say it. The air is so thick with unsaid words I can hardly breathe, and I see in your faces you feel no differently." The words are hard; his tone is not. He is right. We all look at one another with Jeffrey's words still ringing in our ears.

"All right, Jeffrey," Daniel swallows, a flash of anger in his deep green eyes, "you begin, then. Why don't you tell us what you think?"

"Daniel, I don't—" I start, fearing an escalation where there should only be comfort and care.

"Evie, he is right," Jeffrey looks straight at Daniel, the flame of a candle in one of the silver stands flickering, so the space below his eyes and cheekbones looks hollow and dark. "I didn't think much of him. He was not the kind of man I would typically associate with."

"Jeffrey! Please, let us eat and go to bed. There is no need to—"

"Let him speak." Daniel is sitting rigidly in his chair. "I want to hear what he has to say."

"I don't want to speak ill of the dead—"

"Then don't!" My pleading tones fall on deaf ears, and Jeffrey is already drawing breath to continue.

"He was a cad and a user and you knew it!"

"He was my friend!" Daniel's voice is brimming with anger.

I wish I could do something to stop this. They are friends. They should not quarrel at a time like this. While these thoughs course through my anxious mind, I manage only to sit here, my eyes running back and forth between the two men, always sweeping over poor Briony's worried expression seated between them.

"Friend! He was using you! Always tagging along, allowing you to pay for a lifestyle he could not sustain, too lazy to—"

"Enough!" Briony stands up and rushes from the room.

Silence. I scrape my chair back and follow. The men are glued to their seats. How could Jeffrey behave like this, surely knowing his wife is barely coping, and his friend has lost nearly everyone who mattered to him? What on earth is happening here?

"Briony wait!" I call as I follow her small figure onto the veranda. Briony has stopped at the edge of the tiled area, wrapping her arms around herself. "Briony." She turns around, her face cast in shadow. "Come back inside, they were just being foolish."

"I wish I could make all of this undone."

"We all do. Daniel and Jeffrey are frustrated and grieving. Let's go back inside and finish dinner as best we can. Your cook has made such an effort. Come now," I hold out my hand, and after a moment's hesitation, she nods and takes it as I lead her back into the house.

We enter the dining room for the seccond time that evening, and both men rise, looking suitably contrite.

"Briony, I am sorry. I behaved badly, please forgive me." Daniel is the first to speak.

"Yes, I apologize, darling. Come, sit down, let us enjoy our meal and raise a glass to Caspar, all right?" Jeffrey holds out her chair. I, too, find my seat and we all raise our glasses.

"To Caspar, may he rest in peace." Jeffrey says, but before he takes a sip, Daniel interrupts.

"No, peace wouldn't suit him. May he live on in our memory." A moment of silence follows, and we all clink our glasses together.

"To Caspar."

"To Caspar!"

The rest of the evening passes peacefully, and we eat and chat about banal, soothing things like the weather and the food. All the while, our minds are still only on one topic. After the earlier outburst, none of us dares to mention the dead man's name.

To end dinner, the cook, whose name I have finally discovered is Eleni, brings out a plate of soft white cheese and dried apricots. Tired and sated, we bid each other goodnight.

In my room again, I drag the small chair to the open window and let the breeze, cool though it is, ruffle my hair. Slipping off my shoes, I rest my bare feet on the low windowsill.

Was it wise of me to come here? I wonder, not for the first time. In all likelihood, Caspar would still have met the same fate. Nevertheless, if I hadn't been here, we might not have stayed in town so long, and . . . Oh, I don't know. Such pointless speculation will get me nowhere. It happened, I cannot make it undone.

I am curious whether Inspector Dymas has already spoken to Nikolas. I wanted to ask Daniel how he had reacted to the news. Everytime I thought I might ask, someone interrupted, and I couldn't possibly bring it up at dinner. I assume Briony will tell Jeffrey about Laria, Caspar and of my far-fetched suspicions.

What was that? A knock at the door. I lower my cold feet and stand up, walking over to the closed door.

"Yes?"

"It's Daniel."

This is unexpected. I run a hand through my hair and open the door.

"I am sorry to disturb you, but I thought you have probably been waiting to know about my conversation with the police."

"Oh . . . yes," I stammer. "What did he say?"

"Dymas didn't sound as shocked as you did, that much I could ascertain. Still, I don't think he knew about it."

"What will he do now?" I lower my voice. "Will he arrest Nikolas?"

"I think he wants to speak to Laria first, though he wouldn't tell me outright what his plans entailed. He should probably find out whether she told her husband anything, before he asks the doctor point-blank whether he knew of the affair his wife was having with that English lothario." There is a sharpness to his tone as he utters the last word.

"Jeffrey didn't mean to upset you. He is overwhelmed."

Daniel gives a bitter laugh. "He wasn't very wrong. Jeffrey has always been a good judge of character, though he should not have said what he said. If only for the sake of Briony's nerves."

"Oh, I—"

"I am sorry, I have shocked you. Please understand I will miss Caspar dearly. He was my friend, though he had his own unique understanding of the meaning of the word. He was no saint, and he would not have claimed to be one. He knew who he was, and I did, too. Maybe he used me, but when I felt more alone in the world than you might imagine, he did not abandon me."

"I understand better than you might suspect. Nobody is perfect, and perhaps it is a flaw in ourselves to expect so."

"Thank you for your understanding." His sentence sounds unfinished as if there is a thought on the tip of his tongue waiting to be spoken. It remains unsaid. "Good night."

"Good night, Daniel." He turns to leave, and I close my door.

I shake my head and walk over to the washbasin. Taking the ceramic ewer, I fill it with lukewarm water and wash. After slipping into a nightgown I crawl into bed, hoping for a dreamless sleep as I do every night.

CHAPTER 10

Nine hours later, I again find myself sitting at a table with Briony and Daniel. Jeffrey is taking an early call in the library. It must be from the museum, for there are few private homes with telephones on the island. This time we sit in the conservatory, and a wan Niobe has brought in a tray of freshly baked rolls, the aroma they emanate making my mouth water, and small bowls of jewel-colored jams. They are the most colorful things in sight, for the sky outside is gray, and sad raindrops spatter against the glass panes around us.

Jeffrey walks through the doorway as I am liberally slathering orange marmalade onto the steaming bun on my plate. "That was Laria," he announces with no preamble.

"What did she say?" Briony looks alarmed, and I set down my knife.

"Dymas was there yesterday evening before Nikolas got home. Good thing, too, because Laria swears he knew nothing of her and Caspar. Then again, wives have been known to stand by their husbands—"

"Not if she thought Nikolas harmed Caspar" Briony shakes her head, "I know Laria, and when she confided in me I was certain she had stronger feelings for him than she was willing to admit."

"Well, Dymas was clearly not convinced either, he stayed to talk to Nikolas."

"Oh dear!" I press my lips together.

"It's all right. Dymas is competent enough. He didn't simply come out and ask, 'did you kill your wife's lover?'" We all notice Daniel flinch, and Jeffrey quickly adds, "I apologize, I should not have been so blunt."

"No, go on. It's fine."

"In any case, he left evidently satisfied, and Nikolas is none the wiser."

"Oh good," Briony sighs, her shoulders dropping.

"Good? Don't you think he has a right to know the truth? Don't we promise each other honesty in our marriage vows."

"And obedience," Daniel adds with a sly grin.

"And servitude," I chime in. Put like that, marriage is losing much of its appeal in my eyes.

"Very amusing. Truly, if it were me, I would want to be told." Jeffrey sounds serious and we desist in our taunting.

"But it was over!" Briony says strongly. "What good would it do any of them to dig up past mistakes? Nikolas would feel betrayed and hurt, Laria repentant and guilty and the child . .." She drifts off and Jeffrey sighs, taking her hand.

"Perhaps. But is it not wrong somehow that we should know, and Nikolas remains kept in the dark?"

"Morality aside, I would very much like to speak with the police inspector. He did say he would keep us abreast of progress in the investigation," says Daniel.

"You could call him. Ask for him to come over, or for you to meet him at the station. You can use the car. I am afraid I need to go into town today. Paul is dropping by to fetch me, so the car is yours."

"Must you go today, Jeffrey? Look at the weather. Besides, you work too much as it is." Briony frowns and pushes away her plate with a half-eaten triangle of toast.

"They need me to help them review a few new pieces from the excavation. I won't be very long. Why don't you go into the village with Daniel and visit Laria? Oh, and Evie," a smile is stretching across his mouth, "you may drive."

And so it is. An hour later, the three of us sit in the lovely Delage, rolling down the lane. While the rain has ceased, the uneven road is now dotted with puddles and dips, and I drive more slowly than I would like to.

The lane curves often as it wraps itself around the mountain, and we climb slowly down to the village of Miklos. The moisture in the air, mingling with the heat rising from the earth, creates valleys of eerie white fog, like milky puddles below us. More than once, I strain to see properly what is almost in front of me, for fear of driving right into such a deceptively solid mass. This is not quite how I imagined my first drive in this deluxe contraption, but if I return it unharmed I may get a second chance soon.

Finally, though really it has only been a few minutes, we see the shadowy gates of the village ahead. The drive seems to have taken longer than my walk with Daniel yesterday, conditions being what they are. But we have arrived, and I hope by the time we leave, it will have cleared up enough for me to test out a higher gear.

Daniel called the Miklos Police Station after breakfast and was told by a constable, Inspector Dymas will be in and able to meet him around eleven. Briony called Laria (what a marvel the telephone is!) and annouced her intention to visit.

She is in better spirits now that we are out of the house. The fear and anxiety we all feel there is weighing her down especially. My mind keeps swinging back to the argument and the accusations made last night at dinner. Was Caspar truly such a disagreeable fellow? I cannot judge him from our sadly short acquaintace. If he truly was using Daniel, and if Daniel was aware of this, perhaps their friendship was not as solid as he pretends. Of course he has an alibi, so I shall not permit suspicious ideas to create ugly pictures of him. In any case, I cannot truly see him as the villain of this story.

Briony gives me directions to Laria's house, and I manage rather expertly, if I say so myself, to maneuver this unwieldy driving machine down alleys meant for donkey carts and bicycles and come to a stop in front of the modest villa. Briony does not want to hear what Dymas has to say. It is probably best for her to have a private word with Laria without Daniel and myself intruding.

This settled she steps out of the car, clutching her hat and managing to push down the gauzy fabric of her skirt before the sudden rush of wind can render her indecent.

"Come back here when you finish at the station," she shouts before dashing for the door, without awaiting an answer. Just as I am steering the car perilously around the tight bend, I see Laria's door open in the rearview mirror and Briony's pink-clad figure disappearing inside.

Onward the car rolls, and I try, with intense focus, not to scrape the expensive paintwork along the uneven walls on either side of us.

"You can breathe, you know" Daniel says, and I hear humor in his voice, though I dare not turn to glance at his face.

"I find depriving myself of oxygen helps my concentration."

"Ah, well, as long as you stay conscious . . ."

"Very amusing." I try to sound vexed, though my tense smile tells another story.

Somehow, without fainting, or marring the car, we arrive at the eggshell colored block of stone and stucco, Miklos Police Station. After I manage to park the car without a scratch, we disembark, and Daniel gives a little bow.

"Most impressive."

"Why, thank you." I drop into a little courtsey, this small attempt at levity a faint mask for our anxieties, before we enter through the arched wooden door into the cool interior of the building. Once inside, we are confronted by a young, mustachioed and uniformed policeman. "How can I help you?" He asks politely.

"We have an appointment with Inspector Dymas. He is expecting us. My name is Daniel Harper," he gestures at me, "this is Lady Evelyn Carlisle." I didn't think the title would mean much here, but the young man's expression softens instantly and a blush creeps into his cheeks.

"Oh, yes. Please, follow me." As he turns around, Daniel raises his eyebrows, and I shrug. I wonder why it should matter on Crete that my name carries the title of "lady"? What vengance do they believe I will wreak if they are not agreeable?

The young man leads us down the main hall, past a row of three desks, behind which policemen are sitting, writing, reading, or staring curiously as we pass. At the end of the hall, he stops at a closed door and knocks twice.

"Come in!" The muffled voice of the inspector calls out in Greek.

Our guide opends the door and presents us to Dymas, who is sitting behind a broad desk, his jacket slung over the chair behind him, shirtsleeves casually rolled up to his elbows, exposing muscled and tanned forearms.

"Mr. Harper and Lady Carlisle, Sir," the younger man announces, standing with a very straight back.

"Ah, yes, please come in." The inspector stays seated and beckons us forward. There are two stiff-backed chairs standing before his desk, and we take our seats. "Georgiopolis, you may go." He dismisses the young policeman, who obediently turns and closes the door soundlessly behind him.

"We wanted to know, if you had found anything new you can tell us?"

"I have not arrested Nikolas Zarek, if that is what you are asking, Mr. Harper." Dymas is speaking English now, accented, but clear and confident.

"I know. May I ask, why not?" Daniel sounds vaguely annoyed.

The Inspector exhales loudly as he leans forward in his seat, resting his elbows on the tabletop before replying. "The answer to that, Mr. Harper, is that I do not believe him guilty."

"How can you be so confident? He had a strong motive, while I must admit I was recluctant to accept it at first."

I remain silent, waiting for Dymas to reavaal anything of use.

"Mr. Harper, I understand your desire to find the responsible party and have him or her punished. However, Nikolas Zarek, even if he knew of the affair, could not be the killer." The ugly word is softened somewhat by his gentle tone and pleasant accent, but I cannot help wincing.

"You don't want him to be guilty, if that is what you are implying."

"He has an alibi. One I have already confirmed."

This quiets Daniel, so I take my chance to ask, "What sort of alibi?"

Dymas hesitates, probably wondering how much he is obligated to tell. He sighs after a moment and relents, likely deeming us harmless enough for this small enlightenment.

"He was assisting a birth. Seven hours, in fact."

"Oh."

"Indeed. I will not elaborate, needless to say there is a witness, three, in fact, not counting the healthy baby boy."

Daniel nods more to himself than to us.

"Yes," Dymas draws out the word, rubs the stubble on his chin and folds his hands together.

"Do you have any other suspects?" I venture, copying his gesture.

"You will understand, I am under no obligation to share such information with you. It would be against protocol."

"Oh, come now man! Protocol? Since when has that—" Daniel leans forward, agitated, and I interrupt before he manages to alienate the inspector.

"Daniel! Please, he is only doing his job." I place a calming hand on his shoulder. He breathes deeply and nods. Dymas' gaze follows our exchange, lingering on my hand. He narrows his eyes for a second, creasing his brow. I withdraw my hand, resting it once again in my lap.

"I understand your concern, Mr. Harper, and I will therefore tell you this much: We do have other leads we are investigating. I cannot tell you more that this stage. You will understand such precaution."

"We do, Inspector," I answer before Daniel can add anything else. "Nonetheless, I am worried. My cousin feels quite unsafe at the villa as, I confess, do I. Could you at least reassure us nobody there is under suspicion? Whether everyone's alibis have been confirmed? It would be a great relief to know even so small a fact." I smile, trying to look sweet and helpless, the kind of creature one can confide in, one will seek to reassure. I must do so with some success, because after a pause, the inspector nods.

"I can confirm, they were all where they claimed to have been."

"And Yannick, the chauffeur? I've been ever so worried," I clutch my little purse and look at the older man with big eyes. "I have been thinking and thinking. Might he not have had the time to go back to the villa between dropping us off and picking us up in Heraklion?"

"Lady Carlisle, you don't have to try so hard," Dymas grins, and I straighten in my seat.

"Whatever do you mean?"

"I think he means, he isn't quite buying into your act." Daniel, too, is grinning and the men are, at least in this, of one opinion. I roll my eyes and cross my legs in a blythe show of nonchalance.

"Oh, fine."

"As I was saying. Your staff, all three of them, have confirmed alibis." Dymas sighs. "I shouldn't tell you this, but if you swear you will keep it to yourselves . . ." Daniel and I nod in unison. "Very well, Yannick was meeting Niobe at her parents home. They are courting."

"Niobe and Yannick?" My jaw drops as I picture the unlikely couple.

"Her family lives just outside Miklos, and both were there the whole time in question. Now," Dymas expression grows stern, "I must ask you not to tell their employers of this. Both wish their attachment to remain private for the moment. Suffice it to say, they are accounted for."

I draw breath, opening my mouth to keep on questioning when, without a warning knock, a frazzled policeman with wild black curls bursts through the door. His face is flushed with excitement, his forehead wrinkled in concern. He throws a quick glace at us, then shouts out a word even I can understand instantly, fire. The inspector jumps up and crosses the room in three long strides. They begin to speak in hurried voices in the local dialect, making it impossible for me to follow the exchange. Daniel and I get to our feet, our conversation is officially over. The policeman darts from the room, and Dymas turns back to us.

"A fire in a house three doors down. I must go and help." The police station doubles as the fire station, and putting a fire out is a communal effort.

Dymas rushes out, Daniel and I exchange an uncertain glance when the inspector's head peaks around the door again.

"Come, man! We have a fire to put out!" Daniel follows without hesitation, and I, not wanting to be left behind run after them.

The fire is not yet an inferno. The great danger is of it spreading, thus setting the neighboring buildings aflame, spelling disaster. The heavy smell of smoke is already thick in the air, and I feel a hum of familar dread. Looking around for the pump, I find only two lines of men and women, leading to the well. Buckets are passed on, and before I know it, I am standing behind Daniel and the inspector in one of the lines. Everything is happening quickly. When Daniel turns to reach for the first bucket, I catch an expression of surprise and perhaps a hint of admiration flicker across his features.

The buckets are heavy, and even though I hold each only for a second, my arms and back begin to ache within moments. The fire doesn't easily give up its fight. Where is the rain when we need it? The dampness of the morning has evaporated and does nothing to aid in our efforts. As I move along in this strange dance of turning, holding, passing and repeating, my eyes take in the orange, red, yellow flames as they devour the narrow house. They flare out in angry tendrils from the windows where blackened shreds of curtains flail like frantic limbs. Fire. My breathing grows faster, the hairs on the back of my neck stand on end. My arms, now wet from spilled water prickle with goosebumps. Fire. My knees are weak, still I keep moving, passing bucket after sopping bucket. Steam rises from the ground as the flames blacken the yellow stone, spitting bursts of sooty ash, crackling and hissing like a thousand snakes. Despite shouts of the people around me, I am deafened by them alone. And the smell. The chocking clawing monster trying to savage my insides, filling my lungs, trying—

"Evelyn? Evelyn!" I have stopped moving. A man pushes me aside and continues passing buckets to Daniel, whose voice is ringing through the fog. I cannot move. I can ony stare. I want to run away. I can't bear it, can't bear the acrid smell, the stinging in my eyes, the violent, ugly, terrible color of the blaze. I am not seeing the little yellow house anymore. It has been replaced by a large Tudor manor. Flames are shooting violent hissing sparks from the roof, glass bursting in the windows . . . tears are running down my face, wet and uncontrolled. Suddenly I feel a hand on my shoulder, shaking me.

"Evelyn!" Tears blur my vision. I blink and see Daniel's hazy face, behind him Dymas, wearing a bemused expression. I look over their shoulders. The fire is gone. The house a blackened, sooty mess. Swallowing, I wipe at my face with the back of my hand.

"Here," Dymas passes me a handkerchief.

"Are you all right?" Daniel asks, confusion evident in his voice. He has rolled up his sleeves, still the front of his shirt is soaked. Dymas hasn't fared any better. I turn my gaze to the charred skeleton of the house, making certain no flames stick out their taunting tongues at me.

"Yes," I run a trembling hand over my clammy forehead, "I . . . it was just a bit much." My breathing is ragged, the smoke suffocating, the long-dormant monster awake and hungry. A spasm of fear runs through me. I let out a cough, my whole body trembling with its force. I want the smoky blackness out, all of it. I want no trace of it to touch me.

"Let's get her back to my office." Dymas' voice allows no objection. Daniel nods. Both men lead me back to the police station. I am numb as they place me in the seat I occupied earlier.

Dymas reaches under his desk into a drawer and pulls out a nearly full bottle containing a clear liquid and three tiny glasses. He sets them on his desk, filling them nearly to the brim.

"Here," he slides two glaces over to Daniel and me, "drink, you'll feel better."

Without thinking, I take a generous sip. I splutter, coughing more violently than before as the liquid burns away at the inside of my mouth, a river of fire down my throat.

"Easy!" Dymas shakes his head and takes a sip from his own glass.

"You shouldn't have come out! It was dangerous. Briony would have my head if anything happened to you." Though his words are spoken with a force ill disguising his distress, Daniel doesn't look angry.

"It's all right. I'm fine now, truly."

"She was brave to come," the inspector startles me with his comment his black-eyed gaze focused on me. "I must thank both of you." He graces us with a rough smile and holds up his glass.

Daniel begins to say something, opens his mouth, then decides otherwise and raises his glass. My hands now calm again I join them and as we clink together, take a tiny sip. It's not so bad the second time, maybe because I can't seem to taste anything anymore. At least the bitter tang of smoke clinging to my throat has been washed away.

"Was anybody hurt?" I find my voice again to ask the question weighing heavily on my mind.

"No, there was nobody in the house. They work in town. It will be a bad shock, and I have no way of reaching them to give them a warning. The husband works as a fisherman, and his wife does cleaning jobs, so they will not have access to a telephone."

"How awful! At least no one came to any harm."

"That is a relief." Daniel puts down his half-empty glass. He glances at the large clock, ticking away behind the inspector on the wall beside the window. Turning his head to look at me he says, "We should go. Briony will be waiting." He looks uneasy, his jaw tight and lines crinkling his furrowed brow. I glance from Daniel to the inspector, who gives an almost imperceptible nod.

"Are you up to it, Miss Carlisle?" I notice he has dropped the "lady" again and smile.

"I think so."

"Then let me show you the way out." Dymas rises from his chair, his trousers stained and crumpled, he moves around the desk and opens the door. "If you will follow me."

Daniel and I get to our feet. To my relief, my legs have regained a sense of gravity, and they neither sway nor buckle below me. Nevertheless, I do not hesitate when Daniel offers me his arm.

As we cross the hallway and walk towards the entrance, I notice the curious stares we seem to attract. Daniel and Dymas certainly look less than pristine and, as it happens, so do the other policeman we pass. The fire has united us, and as we behold each other sooty and dissheveled, standing at the door, I cannot help but laugh, whether out of relief or anxiety I cannot say. For a moment, I am the only one, then Dymas joins in, loud and open mouthed, then Daniel and the four or five men around us. If an outsider walked in and saw us now, they would think it was a madhouse rather than the police station!

After a few moments, we wipe the tears from our eyes and bid farewell. Dymas executes a tiny bow, and I wave at the men standing behind him.

"Goodbye, and thank you for your help. I will contact you if there are developments." There it is again, the reminder of why we came here at all. Daniel and I turn away to find the car.

"Perhaps I ought to drive. I only had a sip, and you do seem a bit shaky, if you don't mind my saying." Daniel suggests as we approach the peacefully waiting car.

"Yes, I think that would be wise. If not the fire, then the fire-water would most certainly have incapacitated me. What was it?"

Daniel grins and opens the passenger side door. I climb in and watch him walk around to the other side. Once he is seated beside me, and the motor is rumbling eagerly, he replies, "Ouzo. Very popular here. Laria and Nikolas brought some the other night. I assume you did not partake?"

"I think I would have remembered, or certainly my tastebuds would."

"Or not." Daniel chuckles.

"Very amusing." I lean back in the seat. The leather is cool and pleasant, and I am trying not to think about wearing my soiled clothing on it.

"Evelyn?"

I look up. Daniel is staring at the narrow road, though the car is not yet moving. "Yes?"

"During the fire, what happened?" He turns to face me, and I feel cornered, but also warmed by his gaze.

Breathing out slowly, I clasp my hands together. When I was a child, I used to close my eyes and pretend that my mother or my father was holding my hand. I tried to remember what it felt like. They had smooth skin, soft, yet not as childishly soft as mine. My father's hand was large and dwarfed my own, my mother's smaller, with long delicate fingers. I would let myself dream they were walking with me. That we were running away together. That they had come out of the flaming inferno, held my hands and swung me into the air, like they used to. That I screamed with glee.

"It brought back a painful memory." I want to leave it, want to go back in time to a moment ago when we all stood together laughing in relief and understanding. It is not like me to play games, to give hints and to taunt and deny the truth. "My parents died in a fire." The words sound hollow as I utter them as though they are some line written by somebody for me to reapeat when the situation arises.

"I am so sorry." Daniel frowns, not looking away. His green eyes rest on my face with neither pity nor lack of feeling, but something akin to understanding.

"It happend long ago." Another line. Is it me saying these words?

"Time doesn't heal all wounds, contrary to popular saying." The veracity of this statement startles me with its simplicity.

"Indeed, it does not."

"Do you like to think about them?" I meet his gaze as he speaks, and for a moment I fear he will turn away, discomfited by the intimacy of the situation, but he does not waver.

"Sometimes. Not like today."

"No, that must have been a terrible reminder."

I press my lips together and nod. "Yes, it was. I saw it all again. The house, the flames, the smell of it burning . . ." My voice trails away as I ward off the new onslought of memory.

"How old were you when it happened?"

"Four, a small child. It was so long ago, and I was a distance away. Still, it is never easy."

"Of course. I understand." The words, though I have heard them countless times before, carry a different weight spoken by him. I wait a few seconds before answering.

"I know." I let the words resonate, giving him the chance to realize I comprehend the scope of his pain. In a way it unites us, a very sad thing to have in common. He seems to read my thoughts, for he echos the sentiment with a wry smile.

"A dismal bond we share."

"Truly awful. There must be something better. . . Let me think," I straighten in my seat, sensing the moment for melancholy has passed, and we need to bring light back into our hearts and minds. "Do you enjoy chocolate?"

"I adore it!"

"Me too!"

"Splendid," Daniel grins, turns the key to start the motor, "then we shall base our friendship on a shared love of chocolate."

"Perfect. I am also fond of summer."

"As am I, another commonality. My my, Lady Carlisle," he maneuvers the car away from the sidewalk and onto the main road, "I believe we're not such a sad lot after all."

CHAPTER 11

The short drive to Laria's house is not unpleasant. We discover neither of us favors ouzo, while we both like a nice brandy. The only conflicting point is the question about Hector or Achilles being the true hero of The Iliad. I am firmly on the Trojan's side, while Daniel misguidedly argues for the arrogant Greek. We are at in impasse. I believe I will win him over yet.

At Laria's house, Daniel squeezes onto a bare patch of scorched earth. Miklos really is built for nothing larger than a very moderately sized donkey cart, and this metallic monster, marvelous as it is, simply does not fit. Still, I must commend Daniel's efforts, even though I privately believe I could have parked it at a better angle. I follow Aunt Agnes advice in this situation and compliment him. Men require more attention and adoration than a puppy. I cannot comment on the validity of her statement in terms of it applying to the entirety of the gender. With Daniel, however, it does the trick.

"Well done, what a tight spot," I said admiringly, and he gives me the old shrug, all the while looking pleased with himself.

We climb out of the car, and I nearly bang the door against a lamppost, seemingly having materialized out of thin air. Fortunately, I notice it at the last moment and catch the edge of the door. Wedging myself out, I join Daniel on the other side, and we walk up three steps to the front door. It is painted a lively orange, and two large, overflowing terracotta flowerpots stand on either side. The door is opened upon my knocking.

"Come in, come in." Laria steps back into the shadows. She leads us into the well-lit where Briony is perching on a low sofa, the child, Kaia, showing her a doll. Briony's face is aglow, and her eyes transfixed. She barely notices as we enter, muttering only a quick, "hello," before helping Kaia braid the doll's unruly yellow hair.

"She looks like you!" Kaia says excitedly, pointing at my cousin, who blushes with delight where offense may be in order, judging from the tattered appearance of the toy. Still, I am pleased to see her happy, though this will make it all the more difficult for her to go back to her childless home.

"Please sit, sit." Laria gently pushes us to another sofa. "Can I get you something to drink?"

"No, thank you." Daniel and I reply, and she sits down in one of the armchairs.

"We didn't want to intrude, we just wanted to hear how you were today?" I smile at her, hoping she isn't angry at us for informing the police of her relationship with Caspar. Sitting here, in her lovely home, with her lovely child, I feel a stab of guilt. But Dymas found Nikolas' alibi without telling him a thing, so no harm done, I hope.

"No trouble. I am better now, thank you."

"Laria," Daniel begins, rubs his chin, a gesture I have noticed he favors when nervous, "I am terribly sorry about sending Dymas here."

"It's all right," she turns her pretty head to the side, dark curls flowing across her shoulder.

"I didn't want to cause any trouble for you or Nikolas, I hope you know."

"I know," she sighs, tugging at a strand of her thick hair. "I understand what you were thinking. I won't deny the thought crossed my mind."

"Everything was cleared up? Dymas, we just saw him, said Nikolas has an alibi."

"Yes, 'an alibi'. What a strange word? He was at a birth. I know the woman. She had a baby boy."

"I'm so relieved," I give her a cautious smile.

Kaia turns around, noticing us only now.

"I know you," she trundles over to me, her big eyes curious. She pets the fabric of my skirt.

"Why are you so dirty? My mama says I have to take a bath when I get dirty. Also sometimes when I'm not dirty. I like baths, so I don't mind," she shakes the doll, "she likes baths, too." Ah, that would explain the knotted hair and worn off facial paint.

"Well, I like baths as well. Daniel," I wave at him, "and I, we were helping put out a fire, and we got dirty. We wanted to come visit you and your pretty doll before we take a bath."

"Do you want to hold her?" Kaia asks, now a little shy. I smile and hold out both hands as if receiving an infant.

"Of course, what is her name?"

"Helen, like the most beautiful woman in the world. My mama told me the story. Once there was a woman called Helen, and she was very pretty. She married a man, but then she was put under a spell, so she fell in love with another man, and they lived happily ever after." Kaia bends her head, her face dreamy and glowing. A little romantic in the making.

Briony, Daniel, and I cast curious glances at Laria, who shrugs. Has she simply told her daughter a harmless version of The Iliad, or is she mirroring her own situation in the tale? The same thoughts are on my companions' faces, I observe, though none of us dares to ask, especially not in the presence of the child. Whatever Laria has said, I do not believe her relationship with Caspar was a simple one. She is clearly well situated here. She has a nice home, a healthy, happy child, a husband who seems devoted. Why would she endanger all of this security to embark on a meaningless affair? It does not add up. Perhaps Daniel, Jeffrey and even Dymas can be convinced of it, but they do not understand a woman's mind. I cannot imagine a woman with so much at stake would take such a risk if her heart was not compromised. Briony said she thought Laria loved Caspar, and I am inclined to believe it is the only possible explanation. Does one fall out of love in so short a time? Something must have happened to change Laria's mind. If only I could be blunt and ask. Carried away with my thoughts, I barely register the conversation around me and find myself startled when Briony is suddenly standing beside me, tapping my shoulder.

"Evie?"

"Yes, oh . . ."

"We had best be going. Kaia looks exhausted and, if you'll forgive me, so do you Laria. Get some rest now, you've had a rough two days."

Nodding, I get to my feet. "Thank you for having us. I was very happy to meet you again." I bend down to pet Kaia's curly head.

"And Helen." It is a statement. This girl knows her mind. I smile.

"Of course, and Helen."

"Do say hello to your husband and give him our best," Daniel adds as we walk to the door. With her back to me, leading the way, I notice Laria's spine stiffen slightly at his mention.

"I will. Thank you." At the door, she gives us all a weary smile and clasps her daughter's hand, holding on for stability.

"Bye then."

"Goodbye!"

We bundle through the door, waving as we go. Kaia makes Helen's hand wave as well. This visit has done Briony good. There is a bounce in her step, for which I mentally thank Laria's charming daughter. I only hope it won't dwindle once we get home.

We climb into the car, and Briony asks what on earth happened to make me relinquish my proud grip on the steering wheel to Daniel.

"It's a long story. I will say that fire and fire-water were involved, and I no longer felt up to the task."

"You mentioned fire. Oh, Evie, I wasn't thinking. Are you all right? How awful!" Her face is full of understanding and sympathy. Briony, better than anyone, knows my fears, just as I know hers.

"I'm fine now." I reply, not wanting to go down that dark and uninviting alley again. I glance over at Daniel, who is concentrating very hard on getting us back onto the passably wider main road. Briony takes this as my attempt to silence her, lest she betray me before him.

"Sorry." She pulls a guilty grimace and presses her lips together.

"No, please don't worry. Daniel knows. It's no secret. Still, let us speak of something else."

"Right," Briony assents. "Do you have any news?"

"Dymas didn't have much to say, except that Nikolas has an alibi, which you know." I hesitate, not wanting to go back on my word. "Niobe and Yannick do, too. It has all been confirmed." I don't know why the two of them would want to keep their liaison a secret, but at least with Daniel as a witness, I shouldn't divulge this to Briony. I am certain she and Jeffrey are very tolerant employers and would be happy for them. They will have their reasons for discretion, perhaps more to do with the problems of a Greek girl marrying a Polish man, than anything else. I do not know how traditional her family is, or what is expected of her.

"I must say, it's a relief to know our closest friends and staff are not involved. Of course I never thought they were," Briony says.

"Did Laria have anything important to tell?"

"Well," Briony pauses, undoubtedly for effect, and Daniel tenses slightly. "I don't know how important this is, she did tell me how they met. I could not recall, and you won't believe where it was?"

"At her daughter's birthday celebration." Daniel's voice is flat, and he is trying hard to keep any judgement out of it.

"Really?"

"Yes, really." Briony sounds almost elated at this scandal. "Nothing happened for a while." She glimpses over at Daniel and blushes. "Sorry, Daniel."

"Go on, I can cope. I am more or less an adult."

"Right, apparently they met coincidentally a week later at the market. I don't recall Caspar ever having taken an interest in the market," she shakes her head, and I fear her drifting off in a completely different direction.

"Briony, what else did she mention?"

"Oh, they simply talked a lot, sat down in a café and chatted for hours. She said he understood her, and that they were connected somehow. She couldn't ignore that."

"Poor Laria."

"She does seem quite stricken. I honestly do not know how she hides it from Nikolas. I think Kaia keeps her busy and reasonably distracted, but she isn't happy."

"Did she explain why she ended the affair?"

"No, she only vaguely hinted that she felt too guilty about it all and didn't want to ruin her marriage."

"Sensible enough, I suppose." I comment, not at all satisfied with this answer. "There is something she isn't telling, don't you agree?"

"Perhaps she is embarassed. I know I would be," Briony hastily adds, "not that I would ever—"

"Of course not," I reassure her. "Now that you, Daniel, and I know, and there is a murder investigation, she must realize that candor is important. Whatever she is keeping secret may be a vital clue to the murderer's identity."

"I have told you all she said. Still, I got the strongest impression all was not right between her and Nikolas."

"Did you note her tensing when Daniel mentioned her husband?" Daniel asks, now sliding the car through the town gate. I didn't even notice passing down the main road. Daniel must be a better driver than I was willing to credit.

"I didn't pay attention. I was chatting with Kaia. Isn't she darling?" Briony beams.

"Very. What about the story of Helen? Do you thing Laria was simply shielding her child from the truth of its rather unhappy ending, or was she telling her own tale?" I shake my head, wondering aloud.

"If she was, it's not very subtle." Daniel doesn't take his eyes off the narrow, dusty road as he answers.

"No, I don't suppose it is. Even if she loved Caspar and wanted to run away with him, she broke it off, and her husband has an alibi. I would say that chapter can be closed." Briony leans back in her seat, quite satisfied at having made her point.

"Nikolas and Laria can be ruled out, I think, as can your staff, and the four of us. Who else did Caspar know here? Did he have many acquaintances, or did he perhaps do business with anyone?" I shake my head as one question after another floods into my mind. Daniel sighs. In the distance I already see the gleaming ivory of the villa, a striking contrast to the gray clouds crowding the sky.

"We can't assume each and every person he had contact with wanted him dead. How can we possibly know where to begin?" He sounds distressed, though there is spirit in his tone. He is sad, upset, grieving, but spirited nonetheless. He is waking up again and hunting for the truth.

"There must be a few people who had arguments with him or some he did not like. Can you think of anyone?"

"No, not really." Daniel slows as he turns into the driveway. The wet gravel has turned a dark gray, mirroring the clouds above, and I hear as much as feel the heavy tires crunching over it.

"Well . . ." Briony's voice sounds uncertain. Both Daniel and I turn our heads. Thankfully Daniel has halted the car by now.

"What is it?" I ask.

"I don't know, perhaps it is nothing. Probably."

"Out with it!" I plead at the edge of my seat.

"Darius had an argument with him a while ago. You remember, Daniel."

"That was weeks ago, surely things had been smoothed over sufficiently by now?"

"What happened?" My eyes dart from Briony to Daniel.

"Caspar and I joined Jeffrey to have a look at the dig a few weeks ago. Darius was there and very proud, too. They had only just discovered a new set of rooms, and everyone was excited. Caspar was a little careless, picking up priceless bits of terra-cotta and Darius got angry. He said, or rather implied, Caspar was incapable of understanding their value, he had no business there, that he was basically an ignorant snob. Well, Caspar thought Darius was arrogant, and he was insulted, so he took a copper vase from the dig home to the villa."

"Was it found out?"

"Of course," Daniel lets his hands fall into his lap in a gesture of resignation. "Darius immediately discovered the object's absence and deduced it must have been Caspar who took it to spite him."

"Did he return it?"

"Yes, it was a very silly situation. Darius in one corner stamping his foot, and Caspar in another tossing about a priceless antique. In the end, it was resolved once the vase was returned. Darius and Caspar hardly had any contact afterward, for all I know. I kept a close eye on him. I didn't want him going around offending people. Didn't want us to be run off the island, or cause Jeffrey or Briony any trouble."

"You're a good man, Daniel, but we would have been all right."

Briony smiles sweetly.

"I don't think Darius is a likely candidate— "

"No, Evie, leave it to the police, please. Don't go digging about upsetting yourself or anyone else, and I don't want you to put yourself in any danger." Briony's smile from a moment ago has faded, and she is looking at me with a stern, pleading expression.

Oh, all right. "I will let the police do their job."

She gives me a scrutinizing look, knowing full well what a vague promise I have made, but seems in no mood to argue. "Good. Now, let us get inside, it looks as though we haven't seen the last of the storm, and you two need a wash and some clean clothes."

We climb out of the car as the first splatters of rain begin drumming against the windshield and run for the house. Once inside, we slip off our sodden shoes and hurry to our rooms to make ourselves a little more presentable again.

"I'll send Niobe to draw you a bath!" Briony calls up after me. A nice hot soak will be just what I need to cleanse me of the remaining traces of the fire. True to her word, Briony sends up the maid within moments. Niobe, dark circles below her eyes, disappears into the bathroom.

Glancing into the mirror I am not entirely thrilled with what I see. Beyond the dirty, crumpled clothes and dissheveled hair, I look gray. Perhaps it is a nasty trick of the light, filtering through the thick cover of clouds and barely illuminating the inside of the room. I turn away. There are bigger things to worry about. What Dymas told us of the alibis provides only minimal reassurance. Whoever committed this crime had easy access to the grounds and must have been familiar with Caspar and therefore probably with Daniel, Briony, and Jeffrey as well. I contemplate this, tensely feeling the muscles in my forehead pull together. Whoever it was must have known Caspar was alone, mustn't he, or for that matter, she? Yes. This thought rouses me, and I begin pacing about the room. Who could have known he was alone?

Then again . . .

The murderer, if he was known to Caspar, would not necessarily have needed him to be alone. Rat poison or strychnine is easily transported. If he had found several of us in residence, he might have simply changed his plans to wait for a better opportunity. Poisoning is not a spur-of-the-moment vim. Not that I can speak from experience.

"Miss Carlisle?" I spin around, my hands on my hips in frustration.

"Niobe, yes?" I drop them, opting for a friendlier stance. The poor girl looks done-in, and I am tempted to send her off to enjoy the bath herself. She certainly gives the impression she might profit from a good long soak.

"Your bath is ready, Miss. I added some lavender oil. I hope it is to your satisfaction."

"Thank you, lovely." I begin removing my bracelet and the pins from my hair. Niobe turns to leave, but half-way to the door she stiffens and slumps forward, clutching the top of the dresser, toppling over a small vase of pink flowers.

"Oh!"

"Niobe, what is it?" I stride across the room to her. "What is the matter? Are you in pain?" A silly question, her face, as I now see, is contorted in misery.

"I am fine . . ."

I shake my head.

"You're not. Come and sit down." Carefully supporting her by the elbows, I lead her over to the chair. Her face has relaxed again, the pain subsiding, unless she is simply putting on a brave face.

"I am better, thank you."

"We must stop meeting like this," I smile in an attempt to put her at ease, while remembering her fainting spell a few days ago. "Perhaps you should see a doctor? Shall I call for one?"

"No!" Anxiety tugs at her features. "It is fine."

"Niobe," I crouch down beside her on a footstool. "Honestly, is everything all right? You can tell me. I might be able to help. Briony and Jeffrey wouldn't want you to suffer. They won't dismiss you if you aren't feeling well."

Niobe swallows, bites her lower lip and shakes her head.

"I am not ill."

"But surely this isn't normal. You should at least see a doctor. Is it money? I can lend you money to see him, if you need it."

"No, it is not that."

"I can't force you to tell me what is wrong, but I promise you can trust me. I want to help." She hesitates, eyeing me with her dark scrutinous gaze.

"I am with child. I am not ill." This takes me by surprise, though I could kick myself for my naïveté. I mustn't say anything to make her regret this confidence.

"I see," I say slowly, "are you certain?" This seems like a safe thing to say, while my mind races.

"Yes. I went to the doctor two weeks ago."

"To doctor Zarek?"

She seems puzzled for a moment at this enquiry and shakes her head. "No, a doctor in Heraklion. I didn't want anybody I knew."

"How do you feel?" The question surprises her as though nobody has asked it yet. On second thought, considering how secret she has kept this news, it is likely nobody has. I feel a stab of pity for her, all alone with her frightening, exciting news.

"I do not know." In a gesture that appears unconscious, she lays a hand on her flat stomach.

"I may be overstepping, but Niobe, does the father know? Does Yannick know?"

"Yannick?" The surprise on her face is genuine and leaves me puzzled.

"Yes, Yannick. You two are a couple, are you not?"

"How do you know this, we were so careful?"

"I'm afraid Yannick is your alibi and you his, that is how I know. "You do not understand." As if only now noticing her hand, she lowers it onto her thigh.

"What do you mean?" I am not getting very far in my understanding of this woman. Again, I notice her wavering before giving an answer.

"Many people here do not like me marrying a Pole. They think I should marry a good Greek boy, but . . . but he is very kind, and he will be a good husband." If only she didn't look so worried, this arguement would be far more convincing.

"Forgive me for being blunt, however, if there is something upsetting you, you can tell me. I am not scandalized so easily."

"Scandalized?"

"Shocked." Niobe nods and takes a slow breath, shifting her gaze to the open window where the sky is dimming ever so slightly, and a pair of birds are singing a cheerful song.

"Yannick is not my child's father. He knows and still wants to marry me. I cannot tell this to the people in my village, so they cannot understand that he is a much better man than any of them. It is very difficult, yet I must keep it secret, and you must, too." She returns her focus to me, locking her eyes on mine, extracting a promise that goes beyond spoken words.

"I will not breathe a word." As I make this promise, I worry about facing Briony while protecting Niobe's secret. We normally confide in each other on most matters. I ease my conscience by telling myself it is in her best interest to be spared the news that even those out of wedlock have greater luck in conceiving children than she herself has had thus far. Oh, it is all such a balancing act, pleasing one without offending another.

"Thank you. I do not want to cause any trouble." Niobe looks down at her hands, folded in her lap, and I wonder whether she knows what her news may do to her mistress.

"It will be all right." I hope. "When will you marry? It should be sooner rather than later, for the sake of propriety." I am sadly aware of the harsh societal judgement an unmarried mother faces, even in these modern times.

"My family is not happy about it. I cannot explain the truth to them. They would be disgraced and my father . . . No, I can never tell him." She hugs her arms around herself miserably.

"Niobe," I lower my voice ever so slightly, "tell me to mind my own business, but are you in love with Yannick?"

The bluntness of the question clearly catches her unawares, and her eyes widen in surprise, not disguising a flicker of fear. "Of course. Yannick is a very good man. I care for him very much." Not exactly a resounding declaration of her affection, though one I am able to believe.

"I hope you will be happy together." I smile, suddenly very tired and eager to sink into the bath, by now lukewarm at best. Not wanting to be rude, I stand, unable to feel entirely at ease with this young woman and her plans. "Are you better now?"

Niobe nods and gets to her feet, looking less fraught. I hope unburdening herself, even to a stranger, has helped her. I have great sympathy for her situation, but there is something in her manner that unnerves me. Suddenly, as I walk her to the door, a memory of her wearing an anxious expression and speaking in hushed tones with Caspar the eve of the dinner party returns to me.

"Niobe, may I ask you one more question?" I say before I can stop myself.

"Of course, what is it?"

"How well did you know Caspar Ballantine?" I watch her carefully, trying to for innocence in my voice, to disguise my roused curiosity.

"What do you mean? I saw him here. I knew him only a little." Her tone is even, and I chide myself for attempting to detect signs of distress or dishonesty in her delivery.

"I was simply curious as I saw him speaking to you at the dinner party. Do you recall? I was worried he might be bothering you and thought about stepping in, but I did not want to interfere. I hope I did not make a mistake in staying back?" I emphasize this last comment as a question, careful not to alarm her by sounding harsh or suspicious.

"I can't remember, perhaps he wanted more wine. He did not bother me."

Liar. I would stake my grandmother's diamond bracelet on it. She has something to hide, this lady of mysteries. I will not get it out of her tonight. She will already be questioning her wisdom in confiding in me at all. I can tell from the set of her jaw, she will reveal no more.

"Good," I reply with pretend relief. "I had best get myself cleaned up now. I hope you are better, and if there is anything I can do to help, please let me know."

With that we part. I leave the door a fingerswidth ajar to hear her footsteps descend the stairs, then close it firmly. Somehow I do not trust her. I know she has an alibi, and I am being absurd, but I believe, with some conviction, that she is lying about Caspar. There was an intensity to their conversation that had nothing to do with wine. Perhaps he is the child's father? He certainly enjoyed the attentions of more than one lady, whether appropriate or not. Or am I simply allowing my riotous imagination too loose a reign to run where it pleases?

Shedding my dress, I toss it over the chairback and enter the bathroom. The air is warm and scented with lavender and the bathwater is still pleasantly warm. As I ease into it, the tension in my weary body begins to ease. It has been a long day, and I am sorry for everyone I have encountered.

Sinking further into the large tub, leaving only my face floating above the surface, my normally auburn hair turns a deep coffee brown as it dances around my face in the water. I enjoy the sensation of my ears being submerged, unable to register the reality of sound. Do fish hear? I wonder. Or do they swim about in an endless fog of non-sound. The silence is pleasing. Soon enough, the voices in my mind will beckon again, and I will be forced to listen.

Raising my head, I experience a slight pop as my ears adjust to the change in pressure. My body is more relaxed now, but I cannot find a place of calm inside myself. It is strange how at odds body and mind can be, and still they work together by some peculiar almost unfathomable mechanism.

I rest my head on the small towel folded against the rim of the bathtub and stare up at the swirls in the plaster ceiling, wondering, not for the first time, whether it was a mistake to come here. At least being here, I can help Briony cope with this difficult situation. She will inevitably soon discover that Niobe is pregnant. How will it affect her? I exhale a heavy lungful and close my eyes.

When I was younger, alone or afraid, I often tried closing my eyes, telling myself I must think of something entirely frivolous. I would focus my mind on the pretty dress I had seen on a mannequin in Selfridges or what I would like to have for pudding; only such matters would be allowed. Building a wall in my mind, I barred all serious concerns, protecting myself. It was a high wall, thick and sturdy, but still it failed too often to count. Through some gap the ugly thoughts slipped inside, memories, fears and gnawing anxieties, and I would wrench open my eyes as though escaping a waking nightmare.

Today I do not even try this evasion. I am not a child anymore, even though, at this moment, I feel remarkably small and vulnerable. I allow my mind the freedom to wander down the dark alleys and the shadowed recesses that cause my skin to crawl. I have been here less than a week, yet so much has happened. I have trouble believing it.

Images flash before my eyes of the ferry, of Yannick and the Delage, the dinner party, the Agora, the dead, dead body of Caspar. Normality and horror. Isn't that the way of the world? Goodness is so often overshadowed by the dark. Light always the more fragile entitity.

We all have a shadow following us wherever we go. Is this duality of light and dark in human nature simply something we must learn to accept? We all harbor some unattractive qualitites within ourselves, should we simply expect them on some occasions, to manifest themselves as something truly horrendous? If this were the case, life would be hardly worth living. What would life be if it was not treasured, loved, protected, mourned by somebody? Lazily accepting evil in the world as status quo cannot be an option. No, the day I stop being shocked and saddened by tragedy and evil, is the day I lose faith in humanity, and that day is not today.

With renewed energy, I open my eyes. My hands and fingers have wrinkled like the prunes I had at breakfast. With a sigh, I rise and carefully climb out of the bathtub, cold water dripping from me and running in little lavernder-scented rivulets down my limbs.

Swathed in a large, soft towel so white it competes with the delicate whisps of clouds now drifting across the sky, I wander back into my bedroom. It must be nearly time for dinner, and I find myself unenthused at the prospect of company. We are all miserable, and sitting at the table, exchanging niceties and garbling on about the weather and the food, seems a trial. Every time I look at Briony I worry, thinking about her outburst in the café. Regarding Jeffrey, I wonder about his lack of interest or awareness of my cousin's unhappiness, and I find myself blaming him, knowing it is not my place to interfere. Daniel is at once the most difficult and the most intriguing company. Agony emanates from him in almost palpable waves, and still we have laughed together, despite everything that has happened in this short span of time.

How I wish I was a child, ignorant of future pain and wholly satisfied with the world. To go back to a time when I could play in the garden for hours on end, have an extra bun at teatime and declare all well with life. If only wishes weren't just wishes. If only, if only . . . I banish this notion, but cannot help wondering, isn't it true? I have so much others only dream of and still am not satisfied. There I am again at the crux of human fallability. We want what we can't have and react either mournfully or despicably.

With a sigh, I pull on fresh clothes, a floral dress, longer than the present fashion, touching almost mid-calf, and a soft cardigan of the palest mauve. I am not aiming to impress tonight, simply to be comfortable in my skin. All the better if said skin is in contact with silk underthings and a cashmere cardi. Glancing at the wall-mounted clock, I observe it is only ten past five. Dinner won't be before seven, and though I have little appetite, I do not quite know what to do with myself until then.

Uncertainly I stand at the door. Silence. Suddenly an idea invades my mind. Caspar's room. The police searched it, but what if they missed something? They haven't been back to the house since they've known about Laria and him. Maybe he left behind some clue to who might hold a grudge against him, or with whom he may have quarrelled.

I open the door an inch or so, feeling like an inturder, creeping about. What am I hoping to achieve? I slip out of my room and pad across the hall to stand haltingly before Caspar's door. If I discover something, I will have to admit where it was found. Unless I put it back and discreetly hint that there may be something to be found. Altogether a rather troubling dilemma.

Before my mind knows what my body is doing, I find my hand resting on the brassy doorknob. Do I dare? Is it not in some way sacrilegious to enter a recently murdered man's domain? Certainly the police have already done so . . . Oh, hell.

CHAPTER 12

Turning the knob, the door slowly opens, and I am grateful to whoever in this household diligently sees to oiling hinges as there is not a squeak to be heard. For a moment, I hesitate, standing on the threshold. Once I step across, I will be a trespassing into a dead man's private quarters. There is something quite disturbing about this thought. Then again, I am only trying to find out who wanted him prematurely gone from this earth, trying to get justice for him. Yes, I nod to myself, probably looking faintly mad to anyone who might be observing this little tableau. An immediate chill runs down my spine as I enter the room. Is it colder in here?

Looking around, I take in that the window at the other end of the bedchamber is open, allowing a gust of cool afternoon air to waft in. No ghostly spirit lurking about then, only my morbid imagination combining with the elements.

Carefully, I lean the door against its frame, not closing it entirely, just enough not to look suspicious to anyone passing by. Right. I rest my hands on my hips and scan the room. It is smaller than mine, with a view in the opposite direction. The bed is neatly made as though never slept in at all. For some reason, this feels particularly sad to me, and I stand at the edge of it, thinking that not long ago a man, very much alive, rested here, not knowing he would soon be forced into a permanent slumber. Pulling myself away, I walk across the room to the only object of real interest: a large steamer trunk below the window.

The trunk is not securely closed, limp straps hanging down the front begging to be opened. This is it, I tell myself. Once you open it, you can't go back. You will be well and truly snooping in a murdered man's possessions.

My hands are clammy. The air from outside is blowing right into my face as I stand wringing my hands before the leather case.

"What are you waiting for?"

I nearly jump out of the open window at the sound of that voice. Instead of lurching forward to my doom, I stumble back a step or two into a decorative screen. I must look as guilty as they come.

"You are searching for something?" Daniel is standing in the doorframe, arms folded over his chest, his expression unreadable.

"No, I. Oh, Daniel, I am sorry. I had this idea." I shake my head, as if marveling at my own stupidity.

"Go on." He hasn't moved, not a muscle.

"I thought," I begin, feeling the burn of shame on my cheeks, "I might find something that would provide a clue. I shouldn't have. I am sorry." Taking a few halting steps towards him, I intend to indicate my contrite intention to leave. I meant to harm, but his tall form is blocking the doorway.

"The police searched already. They say they found nothing of importance."

"Yes, of course. I was foolish, fancying myself a sleuth of some sort."

"The police is Cretan," Daniel's tone is even, not harsh, which reassures me, "they might not know exactly what an Englishman values or where he keeps it." This statement surprises me and I stand still, waiting for him to go on.

When the silence begins to drag, I inquire, "You mean, you know?"

He considers this for a moment, then takes a small step into the room. I can see it is causing a similar strain in him as it did in me. Nobody wants to invade this space. There is something eerie about it, despite the lightness of the furnishings and decor; a heavyness that permeates the air we are breathing.

"Caspar kept a diary his whole life."

"A diary?" I am unable to keep surprise from my voice. Caspar Ballantine was not, by my estimation, the type to keep a diary, to reflect much about anything, let alone in writing. I immediately chide myself for these uncharitable thoughts and remind myself I barely knew him and now never will.

"A journal of sorts. When we were children, he would write down how many fish he caught in the stream or about winning a game of cricket. Later, I don't know what he wrote, but he carried it with him, even in the trenches."

"Do you think the police found it?"

"They left a receipt, which is in my room. Let me see whether they included it." He turns and without looking at me, disappears for a minute. When he reappears, he strides through the door with less hesitation, brandishing a piece of paper.

"And?"

"No, nothing. They didn't take much at all, only his passport and travel documents." There is an undercurrent of anticipation in his tone, and the tense muscles in my shoulders ease a bit.

We look at one another, neither daring to say what possiblity we may explore. Finally, Daniel moves toward the trunk in a few decisive steps. He kneels down on the carpet, then looks up at me standing nervously at a distance.

"Come now, you wanted to explore, now let us open it together. For what it's worth, I don't think Caspar would be offended to have a beautiful woman go through his things." As he hears himself say it, I can tell he hadn't meant to. To ease his nerves, I brush it off and step over, crouching down beside him.

"Ready?" We look at each other. I nod, and we both hold our breaths as he swings open the lid. What we find is vaguely disappointing at first sight. A pile of tangled and carelessly tossed in clothes, which fill the trunk nearly to the brim.

"Well, this looks very ordinary," I say, not sure whether I could suggest rummaging through them. Fortunately, Daniel echoes my thoughts and begins the unpleasant task of unpacking. I decide to let Daniel complete this task on his own. It would not seem right for me to touch these clothes. Daniel was his friend, if anybody has a right to interfere with Caspar's belongings, it is him.

He empties the trunk, piece by piece, making a neat pile on the side. There is tension in his jaw as though the task requires deep concentration and self-control, which perhaps it does. Within a few minutes, the pile of wrinkled shirts and trousers beside us has grown, and the trunk is nearly empty. So far, Daniel has unearthed nothing even remotely resembling a diary. Finally he is done, and we lean forward to peer into the carvernous case.

"Nothing," I shake my head. For good measure, Daniel reaches down and runs his hand around the flat base. No hidden compartment or secret space pops up to reveal anything. I must confess, I am disappointed.

"To be honest, I hadn't thought he would hide anything particlarly precious here. He had very little trust in people." Daniel says this almost by-the-by.

"Why not?"

"What?" Daniel is distracted, sorting the clothes back into their former place.

"Why didn't he trust people?"

"Oh, that." He slows his movements long enough to catch my eye for a second. "I sometimes thought his mistrust of people reflected his own character."

"You mean," I venture carefully, "that he himself wasn't quite..."

"Honorable? No, I suppose he wasn't." Daniel sounds almost cheerful, which puzzles me. Still, it is better than melancholy.

"Well, the situation with Laria probably shows it rather well."

Daniel makes a small noise, which I take as a sign of agreement. "If only that had been all." He stops what he is doing and turns, leaning against the wall, looking directly at me for a moment, gauging how I might react to whatever is on his mind. A strand of his dark brown hair has tumbled onto his forehead, and his cheeks are slightly flushed from his efforts. I dare not move or break the gaze, not wanting him to snap out of this phase of openness and trust, reverting to his state of quiet melancholy.

"Tell me," I encourage in a quiet voice. His chest rises and falls evenly a few times, before he finds his voice.

"Laria was not the first married woman he took up with. Nor would she have been the last."

"It happened before."

"A few times, yes. He did care for them. Once or twice, I even believed he loved them. Of course, it could never lead to anything."

"The women might have left their husbands."

"Perhaps," he shrugs, pushing the strand of hair from his forehead. "They never did though. To make things worse, they were often wives of his friends. This affair with Laria was not a great surprise to me."

I take a moment to absorb this, then ask, "Was Nikolas his friend?"

Daniel emits a sharp chuckle, sounding both amused and saddened as his mouth twists into a smile that does not reach his eyes. "No, not at all. In fact they didn't like each other."

"It must have felt even more of a conquest when he charmed Laria into this . . . whatever it was."

"Exactly. I think that is why she ended things. She must have realized how badly it would hurt Nikolas and how little it would hurt Caspar. She is not a fool and likely came to the conclusion eventually."

"Briony thinks Laria loved Caspar."

"Perhaps she did. Perhaps she does."

"You do not believe she had anything to do with his," I swallow awkwardly, "his death?"

"No, I don't. People kill in bouts of passion and jealously and rage. I have only ever known her as a calm and reasonable person. And further,

I don't think Caspar mistreated her. His women never hated him, he was always a gentleman in their eyes."

This notion seems odd to me. How could a woman with any degree of sense be so duped? Caspar was, even in the short time I knew him, transparent in his designs. I cannot imagine he never broke a heart, never inflamed one to the point of fury. We do strange things when we love or, come to think of it, when we hate.

"You don't believe it?" The small, bemused smile is still playing on his lips as he speaks, and its presence makes me bolder.

"I do not. No half-way self-respecting woman would let herself be toyed with in this way and then harbor no resentment when she discovers the true nature of things."

"I was under the impression, they knew exactly what they were getting into most of the time."

"What do you mean? You cannot imagine he told them their great love was only temporary, until he decided he had enough! He must have duped them into loving him. Using them and tossing them aside."

"So many questions." Daniel dips his head back for a moment, and the light from the setting sun, pouring its last deep golden rays through the open window, highlights the structure of his face; the straightness of his nose, high cheekbones, and angular chin. I might have mentioned it before: Daniel is not at all bad to look at. He turns his face to me, and the light is replaced by shadow.

"Do you have any answers?"

"Some perhaps. Caspar was not cruel. He did not want to hurt people. Not in the war and not afterwards either. He wanted to be happy, and he wanted to make people happy. That was by far his best quality, one which unfortunately turned into egotism at times."

"Go on."

"He was discreet, careful to keep the wives in good stead with their husbands. He made no promises, at least that is what he told me. You understand, I did not find this aspect of his life particularly pleasing."

"I didn't think you would." Turning to the side, I lean against the base of the trunk, my legs folded decorously to the side. I am glad to be wearing my cardigan as the air in the room has grown even colder, and sitting on the floor amid Caspar's possessions could give anyone a chill. Still, there is an odd comfort in the situation, which sets my mind at ease. I sense no hostility or anger in Daniel's company. He might have resented my intrusion, instead he has accepted it quite easily.

"What are you thinking, Miss Carlisle?" Daniel is looking at me intently, his emerald eyes sparkling in the low light. A shiver runs through me, whether of anxiety or anticipation I cannot tell.

"Nothing." I lie. If he notices, he doesn't seem to mind.

"Shall we abandon our search?" His voice is low, his gaze even. I shake my head, to pull myself into the present. He takes this gesture as an answer.

"No, I didn't think so. Well," he pushes himself off the floor, towering over me and reaches out a hand, "better keep going. Briony will want to feed us soon, and I don't think I can come here again today."

I reach up, liking the way our hands fit together, the contrast of my white and his tanned skin. He pulls me up, and for a moment we are only inches apart, his face close above my own. Then the spell is broken. I let go of his hand and take a tiny, clumsy, step backward. He is grieving and in need of comfort, I ought not fancy myself with ideas of anything else.

"I'll start with the closet, shall I? You could search the little dresser by the bed, if you don't mind." Daniel suggests. Turning away I bite my bottom lip, the sting waking me, bringing me back to the present. Concentrate, Evie.

Kneeling down again, I think how wise it had been to forgo stockings, for they would have been riddled with runs and holes from all of the kneeling on the bare wooden planks. Carefully, I open the first of the three narrow drawers in the bedside table. The top drawer contains a small, leatherbound Bible. On first glance, I think it is "the diary" and am about to alert Daniel when my eye falls on the etched in title. It would appear unlikely of Caspar to keep a Bible beside his bed.

"Was Caspar a religious man?" I ask, more to say something to interrupt the silence of our search, than out of genuine interest.

"Not particularly, why do you ask?"

"There is a Bible in his dresser."

Daniel grins. "Caspar opened it about as often as it snows on the Acropolis. It belonged to his mother. She was a devout woman, and he never met her. She died in childbirth, and he had little that belonged to her."

A cad, a philanderer, and a man who yearned for his mother. I turn back to gently place the small book into it's previous home.

The second drawer is empty, and even my ardent search around the inside produces nothing but a splinter in my finger. Opening the third, it looks as empty as the others, and wary of another painful sliver of rough oak wood ending up embedded in my hand, I cautiously feel around inside. I expect nothing and am stunned to touch something smooth with the tips of my fingers. Eager now, I reach further . . . Can it be? The spine of a book. The diary? Grasping the object, I pull it out. It had been standing propped vertically against the very back of the drawer. Niobe, dusting and cleaning would not have opened it far enough to even catch a glimpse of the precious item.

"Daniel!" I cannot hide my excitement, though I remain careful not to alert anybody else. "Look." He takes a sharp breath as he sees what I am holding. "Is this it? Do you recognize it?" I scramble up, holding the rectangular book bound in smooth, chocolate brown leather.

"I think it is." His eyes are wide as they meet mine. In unspoken union, we crouch on the edge of the bed, having, for the moment, forgotten its prior sanctity.

"Here." I hand the journal to him, the thought of opening it myself completely out of the question. He takes it and holds it for a moment as one might an object one has never encountered before.

"Yes, this is it. His latest journal." He presses his lips together, and his knuckles whiten as he clasps the book.

"What do you want to do?" I can barely disguise my eagerness to delve in. He swallows, blinks a few times, and for a terrible few seconds I fear he will begin to cry. What will I do then? I cannot think of anything to say. It would be worse for him. A man has his pride. Thank goodness, we avoid that awkward situation as he takes control of himself again. He glances at his wristwatch. I reach over to turn on the small lamp on the bedside table, which casts a surprisingly wide glow around the room.

"Thanks. It's only twenty past."

He isn't willing to say that this will give us a moment to have a look at the contents of the journal, before we have to go down for dinner and drinks. Keen as I am to know what Caspar has written, I feel uneasy about the idea of reading his private thoughts and trying to pry into a life I never had any part of.

"Daniel, I'll give you some privacy. It would not be right for me to read this." Getting to my feet before I can change my mind, I take a few determined steps to the door. "I will see how Briony is. Take your time." Daniel, despite his solid frame and broad shoulders, looks lost and forlorn sitting on the corner of his dead friend's bed in the meager yellow light, holding the journal like a hostile object.

"Thank you."

I linger for a moment on the precipice of walking back, putting an arm around his shoulders and a comforting hand on his, then restrain myself. He needs to do this on his own. He will tell me if he discovers anything important, of that I am certain.

Without another word, I turn on my heel and silently as a cat retrace my steps and descend the stairs.

CHAPTER 13

Once downstairs, I drift towards the sitting room where the quiet scratch and hum of a gramophone record is coming from. Entering, I recognize the melancholy voice of Bessie Smith singing the blues. I am surprised to hear it here, of all places. I would not have known the soulful jazz musician myself, had it not been for a dear friend in London who introduced me to her and taught me the Charleston when we should have attended the "Ladies Lecture on Etiquette."

Briony is sitting on one of the low settees, eyes closed, her foot tapping to an imaginary rhythm. As my heels click against the marble floor, she opens them, but doesn't smile.

"Is everything all right? You look—" I break off, noticing the line of her mouth is one of anger, not sorrow.

"If I look upset, it's probably because I am." She states this in a tone so reminiscent of the one she used as a child, I cannot help but smile.

"Why? What has happened?" I wander over and crouch on the seat across from her, resting against the cushions in my back.

"It's not a lauging matter, Evie." She crosses her bare arms over her chest.

"Well, enlighten me. I have no mind for guessing tonight." My patience for childishness is not abundant after the serious scene I have come from. "Out with it!"

"It's Jeffrey."

I groan inwardly. I have been here less than a week and find misery and discord in all the married couples I encounter. With the exception of Paul and Rosie, who may have other concerns.

"What has the man done now?" I should be more patient, yet I cannot deny I have the strong urge to take Jeffrey and Briony by the hands, like children who need to be guided, and lock tem into a room to sort themselves out, or at least to talk things through, like the adult couple they are. Such judgement is easy for me, I confess, as I have no experience with marriage or, for that matter, with any proper romantic attachments to draw from. Instantly repentant of my impatience, I smile and settle back to listen.

"He's not here."

"Jeffrey?"

"Of course, Jeffrey, who else?" She shakes her head in exasperation.

"Sorry, go on."

"He promised he would be here by five. I told him I needed to talk to him. I said it was important, and he isn't here!"

"It's not yet half-past," I glance at the beautiful cherrywood grandfather clock in the corner. "He may well be here in a moment or two."

"He might have called, if he was going to be late."

"Perhaps he couldn't. Didn't have time or—"

"Stop defending him, Evie!" Oh, dear, now she is angry with me.

"I am sorry, I don't like seeing you upset."

"Well, I am. This is not the first time. He does this all the time. Leaving me here, pleading with the cook to keep the food warm, trying entertain the guests, his guests, while he is busy with some pile of rubble, or bits of useless glass. I have a lower priority in his life than that rubbish!"

"Briony, I am certain it isn't so." A weak answer, I know, but what am I to say? Jeffrey is not a bad man. Nevertheless, my loyalty is always with Briony.

"Evie, he isn't interested in me. I am just his little wife who sits at home or goes off to make social calls. I left my home for him to have this opportunity. I at least expect him to show some understanding."

Now we are heading into dangerous territory. I can hear the resentment in her voice and it worries me. "Briony, you know this isn't fair. He adores you, you know he does."

"He may have, not anymore."

"You've not been married three years!"

"Exactly. How could he lose interest so quickly? I did everything he wanted, getting married so quickly, moving here, and what do I have to show for it? A distant husband and an empty nursery." We have arrived at the source. All that ails Briony inevitably leads back down this much-trodden path.

"Don't blame Jeffrey. You have not been married long. Countless couples take longer to have children than you."

"Evie—" she twists the dainty fabric of her skirt in her clenched hands and whispers, "he has given up on even trying."

"Oh." I may be unmarried, but I have for sometime been quite clear on what is required for a preganancy to result.

"What do I do about that? He is busy. He has to go to work. We have to host a dinner. We have to go to a dinner, a function and so on. It is always about him and his work and fawning over his colleagues, who make digging around long-gone people's property appear crucial to the development of humanity! I am alive now, I want to be happy now!" Her voice has grown shrill, her cheeks pink to the point of feverishness.

"Please, Briony, calm yourself. You are right to be upset. Still, getting agitated will do nothing to improve the situation."

"Then help me." Briony looks at me, her eyes swimming with tears. I drape an arm around her shoulder, wishing that I could.

"What shall I do? I do not believe Jeffrey would take kindly to me ordering him to impregnate you." This produces a sliver of a smile on my cousin's face.

"I suppose not."

"Well, you suppose correctly. I can talk to him, but I honestly doubt it would do much good, except make him believe that we are discussing him behind his back."

"Which we are."

"Indeed. Still, I doubt your relationship would benefit from him discovering this."

"Probably not."

"He would feel under attack in his own home, and, if anything, he ought to feel less so."

"You are right as usual," she concedes; a sentence I never tire of hearing, though in truth it is a rare occurrance.

"Give it time, Briony. I know you are struggling. Jeffrey loves you, I know it, and I am certain you do, too."

Her shoulders rise as she inhales deeply. I remove my arm and find a clean handkerchief in my cardigan pocket and press into her hand.

"Thank you." She dabs at her eyes.

"Better?"

"A little." She turns her head, giving me a sheepish look. "I am embarassed, Evie. I shouldn't have said all of this. I am simply not feeling myself. Haven't been for some time. I know people change when they get married, and I haven't changed in a way I like. Maybe Jeffrey has become aware of that." Her quiet confession pains me.

"I don't like you being sad." A banal thing to say, still it is out before I have heard it in my mind. Besides, if there is one person I do not have to impress with the elegance of my speech and thought, it is Briony.

"I am a terrible host. Luring you here under the pretense of a holiday, and now you get is misery all around; Caspar being killed and me moaning all waking hours. It isn't right, and I am sorry."

"Don't be. You know I am always on your side, though I will say, I am immensely relieved you have an alibi for the murder, so my loyalty must not be tested."

"You shouldn't joke like that." She smiles, if faintly. The force of the storm has passed for now.

"You're smiling again!"

"Yes. Thank you." She sniffles once or twice and tucks the handkerchief into her pocket. Just then, we can hear the sound of the heavy entry door fall shut, followed by footsteps. A moment later, Jeffrey appears in the doorway. He looks disheveled and sun-burnt, the eggshell color of his shirt a strong contrast to the tomato-esque tone of his skin.

"Hello, sorry I am a bit late. Paul and I were drawn into a discussion with Darius, and he does go on."

"Oh, has Paul come with you?"

"No, no. Only dropped me off. Said he had to get home to see how Rosie was. I'll wash up, and then we can eat. I am ravenous."

Without another word, he disappears and we can hear him plodding up the stairs. Everything in this open house creates an echo. This can be both impressive and at times startling.

"You see? He apologized for being late!" I try to make this out to be a great and wonderful thing. Briony, not easily deluded by my ploys, only shrugs.

"It's the least he can do. Let us leave it. Tell me something interesting."

When we were younger, and Briony entertained her suitors while I was at University, she would always ask me, upon our twice-monthly meeting, to tell her something interesting. As it happened her stories of debutantes and jilted lovers were much better than my bland tales of dull professors and the tedium of translating Latin.

"You ask too much. It has been a long day." I lean back into the sofa, feigning a yawn.

"Fine, I will excuse you this time, though I must point out the very curious fact that you spent much of this long day with our dear Daniel." There is a distinctive twinkle in her eye and an unmistakable insinuation in her tone, making me toss a cushion her way. She easily evades the gentle missile and grins in an all-too wicked manner.

"Whatever your immoral thoughts, I recommend you banish them immediately. Daniel is a good man, and I a decorous," I alter my voice to mimic Aunt Agnes, "and respectably lady."

"Indeed." Briony cocks her head and raises an eyebrow, and while her line of questioning is decidely uninvited, I am relieved to find her spirits so quickly restored.

"Yes, indeed. I will hear no more on the matter. Rather, you may tell me something." At Jeffrey's mention of Paul, I remembered Rosie, his wife, and her oddly unnatural demeanor, which left me unnerved and confused when we met.

"What may that be?"

"Rosie, Paul's wife, what happened to her?" At this, the playful grin on Briony's face disappears and thin lines crease her forehead.

"Oh, Rosie. So you noticed." Shrugging, she adds, "Of course you did. It is difficult not to. Yes, poor Rosie."

"What happened?" I repeat, sitting up in my seat.

"She drove an ambulance in France. Very brave, came as a volunteer."

"Was she hurt?"

"Oddly, she wasn't. Came through it completely unscathed." Briony shakes her head.

"Did she meet Paul during the war?"

"No, they were engaged even before she left. He was at University when she decided to leave, to go off to the front. I doubt very much he was happy about it. There wasn't much he could do. By the time he found out what she had done, it was too late."

"But what happened then? You are telling me the story of a woman full of courage and will-power, and I am sad to note this, but Rose is nothing like that anymore." Briony loves telling a story, and I am keen to find my answers before we are interrupted for dinner.

"It is so tragic." Briony shakes her head, blond curls bouncing, "She arrives at home, is paraded around for her efforts, and finally marries Paul.

Two months after the wedding, a car collides with her bicycle on her way home one evening. The driver never stopped and was never found. She was unconscious for days, and when she woke up, she was not the same."

"Oh, Briony, how terrible. Poor Rosie, poor Paul."

"Yes, they are both very sweet. Rosy does speak occasionally. Not much, still I think it gives Paul hope."

"How long has she been this way?"

"More than five years."

"Such a long time. Do you think she is aware of it at all?" I ask, trying to imagine being trapped inside a body that will not function as I would like it to.

"I do not know. Paul seems certain his old Rosie is in there still. I can tell when he looks at her, at least a part of him believes she will recover."

"What a tragedy, for them to be robbed of a proper future together. I should like to have met Rosie the way she used to be. "

"As would I. Looking at her, one would never think there is anything at all amiss. She gives the impression of being the picture of strength and good health."

"Yes, I thought the same when she was here." We are silent for a moment. I reflect back on the tall, strong-looking woman, and I remember likening her to the fierce warrior, Brunhild, who was robbed of her powers. An eerie parallel! I won't share it with Briony, she will only think me morbid.

"Shall we go to the dining room? The men ought to be ready soon." Briony's eyes dart over to the clock quietly ticking in the corner, and she adds, "It is nearly time anyway."

We leave the room and find ourselves running into her freshly-laundered husband and Daniel, descending the last few steps. Together we make our way into the well-lit dining room where the four of us naturally drop into our regular seats at one end of the long table.

Jeffrey asks what we have been up to and is in better spirits than the rest of us. We oblige by giving him the news of the alibis, at which he exclaims relief, "I never doubted them for a minute", and of the fire, "terrible, just terrible."

The evening is pleasant, and I ease into conversation as it turns from the events of the day to literature, and then to the difficulty of obtaining good English beans here. I comment that I have not suffered from their absence, whereupon Jeffrey, and surprisingly Briony (apparently united in their strong feelings on canned beans) argue, "Give it week!"

Thinking of food, we are served a delicate salad of tomatoes and spinach with warm walnuts, cubes of meat and vegetables on a little spit called "kebab", and a rare treat, or so I am told, Bird's custard with rum-soaked figs. Altogether this is a pleasant conclusion to an otherwise draining day.

CHAPTER 14

We retire to the conservatory, none of us able to enjoy the terrace yet, as the view is inevitably of the oak tree, shielding a dead body only too recently. While we make ourselves comfortable around the table, Niobe brings out a tray of heavy brandy glasses along with a full decanter and a plate of cheese and grapes. Without saying a word. she disappears again like a spirit. My oblivious good humor is shaken by seeing her so soon after her confession, and the mysterious unease concerning her character returns.

"Are you all right, Evie, you have suddenly gone a bit pale?" Briony asks, leaning forward in her seat.

"Yes, fine." I must be unconvincing in my reply, for Briony looks at me with narrowed eyes before turning to the tray and its contents.

"Here, have a sip." She tipples a finger or so of liquor into my glass. I take it, but do not drink, preferring to swirl its contents around, creating a small eddy as it whirls slowly up the sides.

"Cheers!" says Jeffrey, and we all obligingly raise our glasses. "To us. To good company and good friends!"

We lean across the large table and chink our glasses together. Only Jeffrey takes a sip. Daniel, who has been making a good attempt at lighthearted conversation throughout the meal, has grown quiet. I catch his eye across the table. He seems to be trying to say something, but being unfortunately obtuse when it comes to the deciphering of subtleties, I cannot quite comprehend what this may be. Finally, he breaks eye contact and looks at both Briony and Jeffrey, before opening his mouth to speak.

"I think there is something you all should know. Something I have only today discovered." His voice is calm in spite of the tension in the tight set of his jaw.

"What is it?" Jeffrey responds to the change in tone. I put my untouched glass on the table.

"Before dinner, Evelyn and I discovered Caspar's diary."

"His diary? Where?" Jeffrey sounds puzzled. Briony remains silent, cradling her glass in both hands and flashing me a questioning look. I raise my eyebrows and shrug, not knowing what Daniel might be about to share.

"In his room."

"You searched his room?" Jeffrey leans forward, craning his head in Daniel's direction.

"Yes, I know it seems an intrusive thing to do—"

"No, that isn't what I meant," Jeffrey shakes his head, though it is exactly what he meant.

I can only commend him for attempting to make the situation less awkward. Silently, I hope Daniel doesn't mention that this search only began after he discovered me already practicing my sleuthing skills in his friend's room.

"It's all right," he says, rubbing his forhead, his brows tensely knitted together. "It was not something I planned. The police have already been through his things, so my doing so did not seem harmful. Besides, Caspar would have done the same and sooner, too. He would have wanted me to understand what happened, to resolve this."

"Likely as not," Jeffrey concedes and takes a small sip.

"As I was saying," Daniel continues, "we found his diary. He kept journals all his life. Until today, I never knew what he wrote in them."

"Didn't seem the type to write about meeting Mr Jones at the club for tea, did he?" Jeffrey shakes his head. "So, what did he write about?"

"That is the strange thing. Every page is written in a sort of code."

"Code?" I cannot help but ask, wishing I had stayed upstairs to read it with him.

"Was he some kind of spy?" Briony looks hopeful.

"No, no I am sure it has a different meaning. In fact, I have a vague idea what the code may be."

"And?" Jeffrey gives off an air of exasperation.

"It reminds me of a code we used as boys. Not just Caspar and me, quite a few boys in our school knew of it. We thought we were very clever, leaving these coded notes which our teachers could not read, though in reality, it was not terribly clever."

"Were you able to decipher any of it yet?" I ask.

"Not yet. But if I am correct in my assumptions, it is not going to take very long. Caspar only wrote about ten pages ,and those all seem to be made up of short sentences, almost as though he was making brief notes rather than writing about any one event."

"And how do you know it isn't all meaningless?"

"I don't, but what if he wrote down something leading us to his . . ." Daniel falters for a second, "his murderer."

"Why don't you explain the code to us? My mind is still clear enough, tonight, to take on some new information. If we all know it, we could work through the book together."

Daniel considers Jeffrey's suggestion, and I can tell he is uncertain about entrusting his friend's diary, and thereby his private thoughts, to us. After a moment though, his face clears, and he nods.

"Fine. Let me go and fetch it and some paper."

He gets to his feet, scraping the chair on the tiled floor, and leaves the room. We remain silent while we wait for him to return, which he does in due time, carrying the ominous journal and a small writing pad and pencils. Like eager students, we crowd around him.

"Here, see this," he says and opens it to the first page. What meets our eyes is a set of neat letters and numbers written in a slanted, angular hand. Each line consists of no more than three words, and ends in a number.

"You recognize this?" Jeffrey raises his eyebrows.

"At least I think I do. Look," he tears a piece of paper from the writing pad and draws a small chart.

	1	2	3	4	5
A	A	B	C	D	E
B	F	G	H	IJ	K
C	L	M	N	O	P
D	Q	R	S	T	U
E	V	W	X	Y	Z

"Oh, I see!" I cry, excitedly.

"Yes. It's really very simple, we were only boys so it seemed remarkably clever to us then, but it is far from mind-boggling. You combine a letter and a number to represent the new letter. So, B3-A5-C1-C1-C4 is . . ."

"Hello!"

"Exactly, as I said, not very complex, just a nuisance for whoever finds himself confronted with it."

"Well, whatever Caspar wrote this journal, he considered the precaution of writing in code a necessity."

"It wasn't exactly lying about the room either," I interject with a small grimace. "It was in the drawer of his bedside table, pushed spine-side-up against the back. You could only find it if you felt around for it."

"How mysterious. Do you think we ought to call the police, surely they will want to see it?" Briony asks wide-eyed. We give each other questioning looks.

"If we find anything, we will tell them. Thus far, all we have is our late friend's journal." Jeffrey answers diplomatically. He is keen to start the process of decoding.

"Why don't we each take four rows per page," suggests Daniel, his eyes alert. "There are sixteen on each page, and nearly ten pages are filled. It should not take terribly long."

Daniel passes around pencils and paper, and we sit crowded around the unassuming diary. As we begin, silence descends on the room, and all we hear is the scratching of lead on paper. It takes a few lines to get into the rhythm. Daniel is much quicker than the rest of us and has his lines translated first, waiting us to finish, so he can turn the page.

After ten pages of tedious work, Jeffrey lays down his pencil and stretches his fingers, making them crack. "This is futile, if you ask me." He leans back in his chair and rubs his eyes.

"I must say, it isn't Shakepeare." I also put down my pencil, my finger stiff, though my mind is whirring and alert.

"I can't say I am surprised, but all of this must have some meaning. He wouldn't have bothered with the secrecy, if it did not."

"Perhaps he wanted to annoy anyone who tried to read it?" Jeffrey yawns.

"It was hidden, I don't think he expected it to be read. Besides, he couldn't know he would be dead soon." Nobody argues with this, and Daniel goes on, "Let us put together what we have translated thus far."

With less excitement than we had shown minutes ago, we puzzle together each page of translated work.

JACK	ADLTR	PAYM	10
JACK	PAYM	MON	7.20
RACE	WIN	4	
INV	WITH	COLEM	20
SUIT	AT	JONES	6
MARLAND	THF	PAYM	12

Several dates are written chronologically at the top of each page, and we see that the journal is less than a year old.

"It looks like a catalogue of money, does it not? Bookkeeping?" Briony is the first to offer her suggestion, twisting a curl around her finger.

"Yes, exactly." Jeffrey nods and absently pats Briony's hand, a gesture both sweet and condescending. I hope she views it as the former.

"He has kept a record of his spending and income. Quite an ordinary habit, is it not?" I ask, trying to hide my genuine uncertainty, not having ever been much in the practice of doing so myself.

"I agree, it looks like simple bookkeeping. My question is, why use code? And what is 'JACK ADLTR'? A name, do you think? I can't remember any Jack with a last name beginning 'Ad—'. We have known a lot of the same people, having been friends since childhood." Daniel furrows his brow, running a finger over the words as though this might help him to decipher their hidden meaning.

"What if 'ADLTR' means something else," I point to the translated pages. "'PAYM' undoubtedly means 'payment' and 'MON' is probably 'Monday'. 'ADLTR' could be an abbreviation for the service he is paying this Jack person."

We all sit still for a few moments, running possible options through our minds.

"Alterations, maybe?" Briony sounds unconvinced.

"No 'd' in that, though." Jeffrey shakes his head.

I cannot help but notice that this strange course of events has created a situation in which we are all—including Jeffrey and Briony—firmly united. It is good to see my cousin and her husband closer again if only for the moment, however much I wish the circumstances were different.

"Add letter? Would that make sense?" I suggest, certain it does not, but nevertheless eager to make a contribution.

"Not sure what it could mean . . ." Daniel looks unconvinced.

"Nor am I." We smile across at one another. It has grown pitch-black outside and it feels cozy sitting here, in this room of glass, with people I like all hunched together around a little table lit by the gentle golden glow of two lamps.

"Does 'ADLTR' recur in any other line?" I take up the sheaves of translated words and glance over them.

"Anything?" Jeffrey asks.

"No, not that I—" I reach the end of the fifth page. "Wait, here is another mention of it." I point to the short line toward the bottom.

CHARL ADLTR PAYM 12

"Well, let us assume 'CHARL' stands for 'Charles'. Charles requires a payment of 12 Pounds for whatever 'ADLTR' is."

"If we leave the deciphering of that particular abbreviation, the remaining ones are reasonably plausible." Jeffrey's eyes run down the list once more.

"What about 'THF?'" asks Briony.

I can tell she is eager to draw Jeffrey's interest, for as she says it she looks directly at him, flattering him with her attention.

"'THF' could be anything starting with 'the.'" Jeffrey scratches his head, leaving a tuft of blond hair standing at an odd angle.

"Yes," Briony agrees slowly, "but he has kept all other notations as separate words. It would be strange if he broke the pattern by combining two. Also," she sounds more confident, her voice gaining strength, "he never uses articles or sentence form, so why would he here."

"You could be right." Jeffrey sounds surprised. I feel almost insulted on Briony's part for his apparent lack of confidence in her intelligence.

"Certainly she is." I try not to be too defiant in my support. "I would not have thought of that."

Briony smiles gratefully, and I return it, wishing I knew which leg, in that jumble under the table, is Jeffrey's, so I could give it a nice kick.

Suddenly, an idea crosses my mind, and before I have time to think of it's insinuations, my mouth has taken over.

"Thief!" Everyone stares at me. "Thief. 'THF' could stand for thief. What if Caspar knew this Charles to be a thief." As I am speaking, the implications of this possibility occur to me. Oh dear.

"'Charles thief payment 12.'" Daniel's voice is even. He looks across at me, and I know his mind and mine have reached the same conclusion.

"Blackmail?" I word this as a question, though from the tight expression on Daniel's face, I need not take this precautionary step.

"Oh." Briony bites her bottom lip, and Jeffrey swallows, his Adam's apple bobbing nervously.

"Yes."

Daniel has grown pale, and I wish I had never made the connection. What use is all this detective work? Caspar is still dead. And Daniel is the one getting hurt. I stay silent, not trusting myself to speak.

"Daniel, can this be?" Jeffrey leans forward, his hands interlocked in his lap.

"You knew him, Jeffrey." Daniel closes his eyes, rubbing his temples in a circular motion. When he opens them, they look tired. These few moments have added pounds to the weight of his eyelids.

"But why?"

"Why?" Daniel sounds incredulous and gets up, beginning to pace in the rather limited space. "He was not a saint, now, was he?" He shakes his head, angry for the first time.

"But blackmail. He had his own money?"

At this Daniel startles, regaining his composure before I can be certain it was not simply a trick of the light. "I always thought he did. We didn't discuss it much."

"Naturally."

Jeffrey nods in understanding. We have all been taught from a young age, it doesn't do to talk of money. Such an attitude is easy when money has never been a concern at all. I feel a tinge of shame. I am here with trunks full of beautiful things, in a grand villa, with a chauffeur and a cook and a maid, and none of it is remotely a result of my own merit.

"He said he had invested well. His mother came from wealth, and he inherited a fair bit when he came of age. He never really worked, but I never thought he supported himself with something like this." Daniel gestures at the journal. "Blackmail. My God, he could have had enemies everywhere he went!" He shakes his head in a hopeless, exasperated manner, dropping his hands at his sides.

"Look at the dates, this may not have been going on for long." Briony offers.

"Ha!" Daniel's voice is sharp and tinged with bitterness. "I doubt very much this was a new proclivity of his. He kept a journal all the time I knew him. I am not saying he was blackmailing everyone from childhood on, but it appears he had quite an elaborate system in place. The irony is, he probably did use that money to invest and was able to live off those profits."

"So," I swallow, feeling a palpable density in the air, before managing to continue. "'ADLTR', could mean adulterer." I allow my gaze to touch upon Daniel's face and hear Briony emit a small gasp beside me.

"'Adulterer.'" He frowns and turns to face the window, his back to us. I watch his unhappy face reflected in the glass.

"Well . . ." Jeffrey says as though there is something to follow, but even he is out of words.

"Do you recognize the irony in it?" Daniel asks, still turned away from us, his hands in the pockets of his trousers, "Caspar was the one having affairs. He was as much a part of adultery and theft as anyone else." His voice rises, whether in anger or sadness I cannot tell.

I sift through the pages again, searching for some particular detail. Not finding it, I glance up to see Daniel staring at us, an expression of weary resignation marring his handsome features.

"There are no women's names." I cannot be certain whether this is good or bad.

"So, he wasn't blackmailing his lovers." Jeffrey vocalizes what we are all thinking.

"A gentleman and a fraud." Daniel rolls his eyes.

"Perhaps we ought to go bed." Briony looks around the table.

I cannot help but gratefully agree with her. Jeffrey is not hiding his exhaustion either, suddenly ten years older. Daniel has just discovered his closest friend was a criminal, and Briony is probably as overwhelmed by this drama as I am.

"Yes," I catch her giving me a grateful smile. "Let us stop for now. We should sleep on it and discuss what to do tomorrow."

"You're right. I am so sorry about bringing all of this into your lives." Daniel gives Briony a contrite look.

"Don't be a fool, man." Jeffrey gets up and claps Daniel heartily on the back. "None of this is your fault. We could not have known, none of us."

"I should have. I suppose I always knew he wasn't the best of sorts, but he was a good friend to me and he never asked me for anything."

"Whatever else he was, remember him as your friend, Daniel. Don't let all of this," I wave vaguely at the heap of papers on the table, "cloud your memories, the happy memories."

"Well said." Jeffrey sighs, and Briony and I get to our feet, carefully scooping together the diary and translated pages, which I hand to Daniel.

"Here, you keep these. We can decide what to do with them tomorrow. It is too late to call Dymas or the police now, and nothing more can be done today."

Daniel takes the bundle, holding it carefully as though the edges are searing hot and sharp as blades.

"Yes, tomorrow."

We all turn to the door, Jeffrey the last in the line, is left to extinguish the lamps.

CHAPTER 15

The morning begins by the summoning of the police, called by mutual agreement after a quick breakfast. Inspector Dymas promises to arrive before noon and stays true to his word, rapping the brass knocker at eleven twenty-eight. Briony leads him into the conservatory where he sits, unwittingly, in Caspar's chair. We pass around the usual greetings; offers of tea or coffee are made and politely refused.

"You said you have found something I should be aware of?" Dymas leans back, crossing his arms over his broad chest, a gesture that in him expresses curiosity rather than rudeness.

"We found something you missed when you searched Caspar's room." Daniel places the diary along with the papers of translated notes on the table and pushes them toward the inspector.

Dymas looks at them for a moment, then picks up the small, leather-bound book. Flipping through the first few pages, he frowns, creasing his forehead. Every movement of his face leads to another, an intricate network.

"What is this?" Dymas looks at us in turn.

"It's a code." Daniel is the first to reply, pointing to the sheets of paper. "We were able to translate it last night. The code was not very difficult. Caspar and I used it as children."

"I see." Dymas takes one of the translated pages, his eyes dart across it, narrowing as he nears the bottom. "Are they all like this? So short?"

"Yes. Initially we thought it was bookkeeping."

"Bookkeeping?" Dymas sounds confused, and I chime in.

"Keeping a record of your money. Expenses, savings, earnings, and so on."

He nods and picks up another sheet of paper. "What is the importance of this? It is a good record, but why did he write it in code? Why did he hide the journal?"

Daniel flinches at the inspector's questions.

"Caspar's records weren't purely of a legitimate nature."

"Illegal gains, you mean?"

"Ill gotten gains, certainly," Jeffrey adds.

"I understand," Dymas says slowly and allows himself another moment to take in the strange words and numbers on the page, then places it carefully on the table. His face is difficult to read. "Mr. Ballantine was stealing?"

"Blackmailing," Jeffrey supplies.

Dymas raises a thick eyebrow. "The names of his victims are recorded here? Do you recognize them?"

"No, not really. Some are abbreviated, and all of them are first names only. I might know them, Jack for example, but then, it's such a common name, I could easily be mistaken." Daniel shrugs.

"The journal is less than a year old. Did you not say you traveled together these past months?"

"Yes, but again, we met many people, and he could have had other acquaintances I was never introduced to. He liked to gamble, go to parties. I am writing, and prefer quiet time to work. Some of our days were inevitably spent apart."

"What is your book about?" Dymas rests his large hands on the table.

"It's a travel book." Daniel is uncomfortable answering, one can see in the tightening of his features. In fact, this is the first time he has mentioned his writing. Maybe doubts his abilities?

"Interesting. Well, I am glad you kept me informed. It may help us to discover someone on the island with whom Mr. Ballantine had illegal dealings, and who may have had a motive."

"How will you do that, with only first names? Even those are shortened in some cases. Here," Daniel points to a line on the paper in front of him, "this name, 'CHRSTS' or this one, 'DARS', or, 'PHLIP', or 'ARSTO'?" Daniel turns to the inspector, frustration drawn across his face. "The most recent entries must have been made here on the island, there are only nine since we have been on Crete. Of those three have dubious connotations."

"Well, 'CHRSTS' is surely 'Christos' and 'PHLIP' must be 'Philip'. I will make a list of the recent entries and ask my colleagues to help. Which are the names of his blackmail victims?"

I wince at the word, still thinking of Caspar as the ultimate victim.

"Let me see." Daniel furrows his brow and runs his eyes down the last page.

Jeffrey and Briony, who have remained almost silent in the exchange, sit closely beside one another, tired and edgy, with lines drawn across Jeffrey's forehead and visible tension in my cousin's expression.

"Here we are." Daniel takes a pen to circle three lines on the piece of paper. "Look." He turns the page around to show it to us.

TYMN	THF	2000DR
DARS	THF	3500DR
PHLIP	ADLTR	2000DR
DARS	OWES	9000DR
TYMN	WED	1000DR

"So 'DARS' and 'TYMN' appear twice and he has added what they owed him in Drachmae not Pounds. The adulterous Philip seems to have been spared a larger part in this affair." Dymas seems bemused, the corners of his wide mouth slanting ever so slightly upwards. Odd man. I almost shake my head.

"Have you any other ideas, inspector?" I want to remind him that this is a serious matter, nothing to be grinning about.

"No. None. Your friend has been very discreet and thereby difficult to understand. So far we have no new leads, I am sorry to say. I have spoken to the list of people you supplied, people with whom he was in contact or who he had befriended. In the short time he was on Crete, he made quite a few acquaintances. Still, as far as we have been able to investigate, none had a motive to do him any harm. Even if they did," he lets his words hang in the air for a moment, "they have alibis. They are not easy to confirm in some cases. Many people here work by a daily routine, most do not even own watches. We have to track their movements by asking who saw them and when. This is a time costly task, and Miklos does not have the resources or manpower you may be used to in London. We are already borrowing three men from the next district."

"We understand." Jeffrey's tone is clear and not lacking authority. "And we appreciate being kept informed. It is a very difficult time and a disturbing situation we would like resolved as quickly as possible."

"Of course, Mr. Farnham. I should be on my way. May I take these translations?" Dymas gets to his feet and at Daniel's agreeing nod, gathers together the pages of translated notes.

We all get to our feet. After a muddle of scraping chairs against tiles and shuffling of bodies around the table, we escort Dymas through the door and to the main part of the house.

"Thank you for coming, inspector." Briony smiles, and the policeman returns her demonstration of courtesy, generously flashing a glimpse of his even white teeth.

"Thank you for being so cooperative." He gives a tiny bow, which sends a flush of color up Briony's neck. Then focuses his dark gaze on me. "Miss Carlisle, may I have a quick word?"

The others look at me, and for a tiny moment I fear he will arrest me, as one does, naturally. Yet he keeps smiling, and I follow him to the door while the others retreat to the conservatory, probably speculating on what I might have done. Much as I am myself at the moment, I must admit. We reach the door, which he opens, and without a word we step outside.

"I am sorry, Miss Carlisle, you are not in any trouble," Dymas says as we stand beneath the portico, the sun already glowing brightly, making the police car gleam.

"I am relieved." I reply, my heartbeat lowering its nervous pace again.

"Yes," he falters, glances at his hands gripping the notes. "How are you today, Miss Carlisle?" The question catches me by surprise, and I take a moment to comprehend what he is saying.

"Well enough, I suppose. Good of you to ask."

"I meant after the fire. You were quite shaken." His expression is kind, his face showing sincerity and care.

"I was. It was a shock." I stammer and force a brave smile, though I can see his hooded gaze is not easily fooled.

"Yes. Well . . ." he pauses, waiting for me to finish his sentence. When I do not speak, he continues. "I must get back to the station. If you think of anything else, you know where I can be found." He hesitates for a moment longer, and I cannot shake the impression there is something remaining unsaid.

"Inspector?"

"Yes?"

"Is there anything else?" I ask boldly.

"No, nothing. Nothing. Good day to you, Miss Carlisle."

"And to you." I watch as he turns and wanders over to his car, his tall, broad frame casting only a sliver of a shadow as the sun is nearly exactly above us. As he waves a hand and rotates the wheel to direct the car onto the road, I turn and go back inside.

Closing the door, I exhale slowly, not yet able to relieve the tension in my chest. Smoothing down the front of my cotton shift, I make for the conservatory, which has become our unspoken gathering place.

My instinct was correct. Daniel, Briony, and Jeffrey are clustered together around the table, which has been laid with small plates and bowls of "light lunch," or so Eleni, the cook believes. Sitting down beside Briony and Daniel, I answer their unspoken questions by telling them of my mysterious conversation with the inspector. None of them appears satisfied. I have offered all I am able to disclose, and we are soon distracted by the delicious scent of the food before us.

As we spoon some of everything onto our plates, no reference is made to the diary or its implications. We are all tired and a little wary of a subject that, while on our minds, does nothing to improve the general opinion of Caspar or our personal state of mind.

"Your cook is a treasure," I remark as Niobe brings in a tray of coffee and small rectangular cakes. I take one, declining coffee.

"Yes, she is wonderful. Thank you, Niobe, you're a great help as well, of course. We couldn't manage without you." Briony smiles at the young woman, and I suffer a pang of anxiety for keeping the news of Niobe's pregnancy from my cousin.

"Thank you, Mrs. Farnham. Can I get you anything else?"

We all decline, fully sated. The sun is streaming through the windows, and the late April air coming in is cool enough to keep us from roasting. Outside the window lies the pretty tiled veranda, illuminated and inviting. Beyond that oasis of lovliness looms the dark oak. I shiver slightly and focus my gaze back on my companions.

"What now?" I wonder aloud, tracing along the rim of my saucer.

Jeffrey sighs and Briony nibbles on one of the little cakes.

"Caspar's father called before Dymas got here." Daniel focuses on his hands, clutching his cup, perhaps seeking comfort from its warmth.

"Did you tell him?" Jeffrey asks.

"Of course. I had to." Daniel sets the cup aside gently and runs a hand through his hair.

"How did he take the news?"

He drops his hand onto his lap."Better than I had expected. He stayed calm. They weren't terribly close, so I wasn't expecting an outburst."

"His only son has been murdered." I am unable to hide my incredulity and cannot imagine feeling anything less than destroyed in his situation.

"He has always been a stoic man." Daniel shrugs.

"But—"

"Evie," Briony places a hand on my arm and shakes her head. Fine.

"No, Briony, it's all right," Daniel gives a weak smile. "I understand your surprise. I know him, and I knew his reaction would not be one of uncontained grief. He is what he is. He lost his wife and went on living. Now he has lost his son."

"Poor man." Briony says.

"He will cope in his own way."

"What about the funeral? It has been days now, shouldn't they release the body?" Saying this may sound crass, but Daniel's acceptance of Mr. Ballantine reaction to the death of his son has rankled me, and I am irritated enough to voice my thoughts.

"No. Not yet. As it's a murder, they won't allow the transport to Britain in time. Caspar's father has asked me to deal with the arrangements. I would like to have him laid to rest here."

"But Daniel he's English. Surely—"

"Leave it, Briony." Jeffrey shakes his head, silencing her protestations.

"I know what you are thinking. Still, it is for the best. He didn't want to go back home. He didn't have anyone there who particularly cared for him, not even his father." He turns to me as he says this. I remain silent.

"Whatever we can do to help with the arrangements, you will let us know. You are not alone." Jeffrey answers, draining the last of his coffee in one final gulp.

"Yes, to be sure, Daniel." Briony adds her assurance.

"If there is anything I can do . . ." I offer out of politeness, though the prospect of funeral planning, even, or especially for a man I barely knew, whose dead body I had the misfortune of discovering, fills me with dread.

"Thank you for your offers. We will see how to proceed when the time is right."

CHAPTER 16

Shortly after Niobe returns to clear away the remains of our meal, Jeffrey excuses himself, saying he has work to do. Daniel also drifts off, explaining he has neglected his writing for too long.

Briony and I sit for a few minutes longer, gazing out of the windows where the wispy branches of young trees rock lazily back and forth against the bright, cloudless sky.

"Briony?"

"Yes?" I continue to watch the tranquil scene outside, thinking of how to word my question to arouse the least degree of suspicion. Seeing Niobe just moments ago and watching her interaction with my cousin, has reminded me of the great dilemma of her situation and of the air of mystery she wears like a shroud. I won't betray her secret, but I must find out what I can to better understand her.

"How well do you know Niobe?"

"Niobe? What has brought this on? I know her about as well as one knows an employee of nine months. She was recommended by the wife of Jeffrey's colleague. We had a different girl before. Why do you ask?"

"Only curiosity, you know me." I smile as convincingly as I can. "And Yannick? What brings him here? He is Polish, is he not?

"Polish, yes, though he lived in England when he was hired to deliver the car, drive it and accompany it on the ship. Jeffrey asked him to stay on."

"Just like that?"

"Jeffrey did telegraph the company that employed him to ask for references, and they thought highly of him. We haven't had a problem, and I believe he is quite content."

"Doesn't he have family in Poland? He has stayed here for almost a year without any prior planning?" I wonder aloud.

"I asked him, of course. He said his family is happy he has found good work. He sends them money, so it is all for the best."

"I see." I cannot help but wonder whether I— had I a family—could simply do what is necessay and leave them behind?

Briony smiles knowingly. "People do it all the time. Immigrants come and take the jobs we are too lazy or arrogant to take ourselves. It's complicated at times, but I like to think we treat Yannick well."

"Of course you do. And I understand. I just wonder . . . he must miss his family." Perhaps lonliness makes him even keener to start his own with Niobe, accepting a child that is not his.

"I am certain he does. He telegraphs and sends money, and one day, they will be reunited."

"Yes." Maybe.

"Don't look so doubtful. He is a grown man. Let us talk of something else. There is so much sadness and misery. I want to laugh again, Evie. After everything we have been through these past few days and my own state of mind, I long for light-heartedness. We need to cheer ourselves up or at least find some distraction." Briony sits up in her chair, the wicker creaking ever so slightly.

"What do you have in mind?" I ask, thinking that distraction is exactly what we need.

"Let us go for a picnic tomorrow! It will be Saturday. Even Jeffrey can tear himself away from the museum for a few hours. Actually, we could make a day of it." Her eyes are gleaming suddenly, and I can see her mind running ahead, planning the fillings of the sandwiches and which hat is best worn at a picnic.

"A lovely idea."

"We shall take you to see Knossos!" Briony announces, her cheeks turning pink with excitement.

"Knossos. Oh, excellent! I have always wanted to see it."

"Yes, and Jeffrey won't complain because he adores old things, even if they are crumbling ruins," Briony rests her chin on her fist and angles her head in contemplation. The rays of lights streaming in from above turn her hair into a helm of glowing gold.

"Perhaps we should ask Darius to come along?" I add, thinking of the insight the small, neat man could provide on such an outing.

"Yes. Very good idea. We might ask the Zareks and Paul and Rosie to join us, too. Or would you mind?"

"Not at all. The more the merrier. In fact, why not ask the inspector as well!"

"Oh, I don't know—" Briony looks at me with a slight downturn of her mouth before realizing my less than serious intent and grinning, wiggling her head. "Very amusing. Nine are plenty. I will ask cook and Niobe to prepare something for the picnic, and then we will give them the rest of the day off. There, you see what a good employer I am?"

"Indeed. I had no doubt as to that. You know," I venture, leaning my elbows on the table in a manner that would have drawn Aunt Agnes' ire, "you might give Yannick the day off as well."

"Yannick? But who will—" Again a look of understanding dawns upon her face. "You want to drive? You do not even know the way?"

"Someone can sit beside me with a map. I happen to take very good directions. I am like a dog in that respect."

"Ha! A dog, more like a bull or a mule, stubborn as they come. Oh, don't look at me like that." She sighs melodramatically. "Fine, I will try to convince Jeffrey, and then you shall have free reign, or wheel."

I am confident in Briony's skills of persuasion regarding her husband. We sit together a while longer, planning and giggling like the schoolgirls we sometimes still wish we were.

Jeffrey easily agrees. Daniel also appears somewhat lifted by the idea of a day-trip, though Knossos is no farther away than Heraklion. Briony spends the afternoon being driven around and on the telephone, busy with last minute invitations to friends. To her unconcealable delight, Laria and Nikolas are bringing little Kaia along. Paul, Rosie and Darius, too, have accepted the invitation. Thus we are to be a party of ten on our little picnic tomorrow. After some assurances of my capability at the wheel, Jeffrey concedes, not without a hint of wariness, to let me be chauffeur for the day. Much excitement abounds.

CHAPTER 17

My day begins with the pleasant shower of sunshine I have already grown used to and must never take for granted. Today it is all the more welcome, for our outing is dependent on the benevolence of the elements. I hope Zeus, whom in my mind I declare responsible for such matters, is having a generous day.

Upon getting dressed, a process requiring several trips to Briony's room for approval, I venture downstairs. I have finally settled on a pair of wide seafoam linen trousers, and a simple white blouse with short sleeves and a rounded neckline, which Briony argues I will dirty in no time, crawling about the ruins "all mannish-like", she said, but I would not be swayed. Her comment last evening regarding my apparently occasionally stubborn nature may not, in fact, have been entirely fictitious.

As I step onto the landing, Briony, in blue and white seersucker, darts out of the sitting room, notices me, and gives an almost imperceptible shake of the head, probably in view of my choice of wardrobe. She disappears in the kitchen from where I hear the raised voice of Eleni the cook. Oh dear! I have not in all my years of privileged living met a cook who tolerates anybody interfering in her domain.

Turning towards the conservatory, I hear the low voices of Daniel and Jeffrey, and smell the rich bitter aroma of dark coffee, mingling with buttery fried eggs.

"Good morning, gentlemen." I smile at them as I enter. Today should be a good day for all of us, I hope.

"Morning, Evie." Jeffrey is in the process of mopping up the contents of his plate with a slice of toast.

"Hello." Daniel smiles back and removes the sheet of newspaper from my setting. "Looking forward to today?"

"Oh yes," I begin to pour myself a cup of the black brew, adding a generous spoonful of sugar. "The weather seems to be playing along. Will we pick up Laria, Nikolas, and Kaia? How will we all fit into the car?"

"No, no. They will drive themselves. Nik has an old motor, a bit rusty, but reliable enough. Paul, Rosie and Darius live close by. They will meet us at the site."

"Good." I begin buttering my toast, debating whether to top it with honey or some jewel-colored apricot marmalade? I take another slice of toast. Dilemma solved. "Jeffrey?" He looks up.

"Yes?"

"Is Sir Arthur Evans in residence these days?" The Sir Arthur Evans in question, being the chief excavator of the site and quite a celebrity in these post-Schliemann days. Schliemann being the fortunate fellow who stumbled upon no other site but that believed to be ancient Troy!

Jeffrey shakes his head, dashing my hope to come upon the man himself digging around in the dirt.

"I am afraid not, Evie. He's in Oxford. He is in his seventies. Travel for him is not as easy as it once was."

"So, you've not met?"

"Never, sadly."

"I visited the Ashmolean," the museum in Oxford, of which Sir Arthur was Keeper, "and saw quite a number of the Minonan artifacts he brought back."

"Very impressive and a great help to me when I was preparing to come here. Have you been to see it, Daniel?"

"I have, though I confess, I was rather negligent when it came to the artifacts collections. I went to see the paintings." Daniel takes another sip.

"If you ever go back, you must have a look. The collection is truly impressive, not as good as the one in our museum in Heraklion, but undoubtedly invaluable nonetheless." For a few minutes we ponder this, and I try to recollect whatever I saw and read about the site at Knossos. I do not want to appear ignorant in the company of archaeologists and native Cretans.

"Have you seen Briony?" Jeffrey wonders with raised eyebrows, the change in topic of conversation startling me for a moment.

"Yes, as I came down. She was a little agitated."

"She is convinced there isn't enough food. You have been dining with us for a while now, has our cook ever let you go hungry? No, I thought so. Briony needs to have something to worry about. It's her way."

I rather dislike the way he says this, and am formulating a sharp retort when the lady herself joins us. Her face is flushed as though she has been laboring in a bathhouse, and she is fanning herself.

"Briony, here, sit yourself down." Daniel has jumped up to pull out a chair for her, and she rewards him with a grateful smile. Jeffrey remains completely unaware, try as I might to stare daggers at him.

"Is everything all right?" I ask, taking a bite of toast number two, and deciding that the tangy flavor of the apricot marmalade may even warrant a third piece.

"Oh, yes. Fine." She nods, patting down unruly strands of hair.

"Won't you have something to eat?"

"No, no. I ate already, thanks."

"Been up for ages," Jeffrey comments, from behind his newpaper, "busy, busy, busy." His tone implies the opposite.

I lay down my knife. "Yes, Briony does a remarkable job managing such a large house."

"I always say, 'hire more help'. She doesn't want any." Jeffrey adds. The newspaper rustles as he turns the page.

One ought to snatch it away from him and thump him over the head, I think, barely managing to leash my temper. Instead of acknowledging her labors, he simply implies any hired help could do her job.

"Some people—" I begin when Briony cuts me off with a sharp shake of her head. I roll my eyes, aware that Daniel is watching the display. Jeffrey doesn't mean anything by it, I tell myself. He doesn't see that his wife is struggling and not with the housework. But that is not my tale to tell.

"You said you have seen Knossos before, Daniel. Am I remembering correctly?" I try for a friendly tone to steer the conversation back onto a sunnier path.

"Only on a passing visit. Caspar had no patience for archaeology, and I spent most of my time exploring the living cities and towns."

"Have you seen much of the island? I must go back to explore Heraklion more extensively, to see the harbor when my legs aren't made of jelly."

"Yes, the journey can be a trial. Perhaps I can take you some time next week? I have to pick up a few books."

"That would be wonderful!"

"Good, it's settled then."

It takes us another forty minutes or so to wash up, heave the gargantuan picnic basket into the car, make certain we have our hats, and turning the car back because, as it happens, Jeffrey has forgotten his glasses and recruits us to search, my good self eventually finding them dangling precariously from his jacket buttonhole. Needless to say, we all breathe a sigh of relief upon finally hearing the rumble of the tires on the road beneath us.

"You must give me directions," I remind Daniel, sitting beside me. Jeffrey wisely elected to sit with his wife.

"We should keep to this road for while. We'll see signs, I think." He rustles the map. I have to fight the temptation to peak at it myself. Jeffrey would have apoplexy. He is not fond of my driving.

"Fine, fine." I say breezily. I want this day to be fun and distracting. We have had so much anxiety these past few days, a little outing with some friends will be just what we all need. Briony, though she does not mention it, is thrilled to have little Kaia along, and I hope seeing her with the child will give Jeffrey the kick he needs.

I concentrate on the road as it leads steeply up and down, wrapping itself like a coiled snake around the mountains. Slowing down and speeding up, I cannot quite manage to emulate the smooth rhythm Yannick achieves when maneuvering these hairpin bends. Hearing a sharp intake of breath more than once from the seat behind, I know instinctively that it has escaped from Jeffrey's quivering lips. My cousin is made of sterner stuff. I should teach Jeffrey to drive, to set him more at ease. Then again, poor Yannick might be out of a job, and we can't have that.

The car rolls along, strong and solid; my grip on the wheel firm and confident. All around us the landscape is uneven, with craggy yellow stone rising on our right and green dotted valleys dipping dangerously to our left. The roads on Crete are not built for motorcars as there aren't many around. They are most often used for carts, donkeys, horses, or bicycles.

We encounter very little traffic of any sort, and the journey becomes more relaxing, at least for me. I cannot speak for Jeffrey, even though I am trying to stay as far from the cliffs edge as possible to spare the poor man's nerves. Not to mention preserve our lives.

At some stage, the road widens slightly, and we begin to encounter a few more travelers throwing clouds of dry dusty earth into the air as they make their progress.

"There was a sign. Don't turn into the city, follow that road—" Daniel points. "There, it should come up soon."

"Yes, I see. Cheers. Everything all right back there? Not long now. Did you hear, Jeffrey?"

"Yes, yes. Pay attention to the road." Comes his tense reply. I do hope he isn't too badly out of sorts. I really don't see how my driving differs so greatly from Yannick's. Really, I may be a bit choppier with the turns and drive at a slightly higher speed, other than that . . .

Taking the road to the right, it is only at the last minute that I see an oncoming cart, the size of a lorry, lumbering toward us, and swerve to avoid a collision. Fortunately, the road is just wide enough to allow an inch or two between our vehicles. The driver of the other car doesn't seem bothered and motors on. I hear a distinct gasp from the backseat.

"Sorry."

"Just get us there in one piece, Evelyn." Though I cannot see (to think of the drama should I turn my head for the tiniest moment!), I can easily imagine Jeffrey is saying this through gritted teeth.

"Will do." I reply cheerily and notice it rubbing of at least on Daniel, who, as I observe from the corner of my eye, is grinning. Briony is soothing her husband's nerves, murmering something in a low, calming tone.

"And here we are," Daniel's announces. There is a dusty sign and beyond the crumbling ruins of pale yellow stone.

I maneuver the car into an empty spot near two other motors and turn off the engine. Jeffrey sighs with relief as do I. I suspect we probably have different reasons.

The excavated site is now before us, and I am keen to set my feet on the ancient ground and to delve into whatever remains to be discovered.

"There come the others." Briony points over the seat to the little group of Darius, Paul, Rosie and the Zarek family heading in our direction.

We scramble out of the car to meet them. The air is warm and dry, smelling of dust and wild thyme. I adjust my straw hat with a wide brim to shield my face from the blinding light.

"Hello!" Kaia is the first to reach us. Today she is wearing a sweet floral dress with matching ribbons in her wild mass of curls. In a jolly mood, she bounces and skips around like an excited pup. I elect not to share this comparison with Briony, who looks delighted and aglow.

"Not so wild, Kaia, and put on your hat, child!" Laria reaches us, shaking her head.

The men nod at one another, clapping each other on the back as though they had battled through a game of rugby. Rosie remains standing stiffly beside her husband, basking in the sun.

"How are you? Have you adjusted to island life?" Laria asks with a smile. I cannot see her face, shaded by the rim of her hat, so I am hard pressed to judge her emotional state.

"Yes, I have. I come from an island, so water all-round is not all too novel."

"I always forget!" She smiles. I am glad to observe her cheerier manner. The last time we met, her mouth was turned decidedly in the opposite direction.

"Shall we go in, have a look around?" Jeffrey asks. I imagine he considers himself the leader of the group, in spite of Darius and Paul being equally knowledgeable. Again, I shall not share these critical thoughts with my cousin. Perhaps Jeffrey is simply terribly relieved to be out of the Delage where he was subject to my whims and wheels.

We stroll along, and I watch other visitors already inspecting the pale yellow remains of once glorious buildings. As we reach the entryway, a shiver passes down my spine. How many people from all walks of life have wandered these narrow streets before me? Men and women, husbands and wives, children, elders, all with their own lives, worries, fears, and joys. What would they think if they could see it now? Probably not very happy thoughts. Oh, to have seen it in all its original glory, what a site it must have been!

"Evelyn? Shall we keep moving?" Laria is regarding me with a bemused expression. I am barring the way, staring dreamily at a crumbly set of buildings she must have passed countless times before.

"Oh, yes, quite."

We begin to make our way up the gentle slope. Some of the buildings are still partially supported by stout columns; others have collapsed into unrecognizeable heaps. The central part of the palace is an elevated structure, with a set of columns holding up one side, while its back walls have all but disintegrated. In my state of rapture I nearly trip over a rock on the uneven path and am steadied by the surprisingly strong grip of Rosie, who has soundlessly materialized at my side.

"Thank you!" She stares at me, nods and releases my arm.

Laria points to a rectangular building on our left. "This is where they discovered frescos. Minoan frescos. They have been repaired and are still remarkable."

"Can we see them?" I ask as the men approach.

"The frescos?" Darius looks at the structure, blinking behind his specs.

"I'm afraid not, they are going through a process of restoration." He shrugs apologetically.

"Oh well, perhaps another time."

"Do you plan on staying longer?" he questions as we make our way along the path, sloping upwards to emphasize the ascent to the main palace and throne room.

"I believe, I shall. I like it here." I cast a quick glance around at the others, who are milling about only steps away. "As long as my cousin and Jeffrey will have me."

Darius' expression turns grave. "I worried what happened to poor Caspar might have frightened you off."

Right, there we are again. I take a deep breath, searching for a response. I had wanted this to be a day of distraction, and now Caspar is here again, in the midst of this ghosttown. Rather appropriate, now that I think of it.

"It is terrible, but evil can be found in any place. I am afraid running away will not help me outrun my memories."

"Of course, of course. I should not have—"

"Please," I interject with a placatory smile, "do not apologize. It is only natural to wonder. I have great faith in the abilities of Inspector Dymas and hope he will bring resolution to the horrible affair." The word elicits an expression of extreme discomfort in Laria, who has been walking silently alongside us. I catch her eyes veering in the direction of her husband, standing within earshot. Nikolas, however, seems completely at ease and is chatting amiably with Daniel.

"Of course. I will speak of it no more." We slow down as we approach one of the more intact structures.

"This was the throne room." Darius points to the building. It may have once been terribly grand, with solid pillars supporting its sides and ramps leading up an inpenetrably thick wall.

"How do you know?" I stare up, shielding my eyes from the sun.

"There is a throne, and benches made of alabaster."

"Really? Incredible."

Darius appears happy in light of my enthusiasm and continues with his narration. "This is not all part of the original complex. It was destroyed over eight-thousand years ago. What we have here today originates from a time around 1350 BC."

"To think people quarried and transported all of this stone and knew how to create such solid structures so very long ago. A proficient people, the Minoans!"

"Indeed."

"Is Darius feeding you information, Evie? He is the expert, of course." Jeffrey joins us as do the others, and we stare ahead for a few silent moments, absorbing the reality that we are standing amid a priceless relic of human history.

"Mama, I am hungry!" Kaia interrupts this moment of awe, a collective chuckle ensues, drawn back, as we are, into the inescapable present.

"Yes, darling, soon we will have a nice picnic."

Little Kaia's patience is tested in exploring the rest of the site. Darius, Paul, and Jeffrey, our guides, toss out facts and anecdotes as we move along. Daniel, not contributing to this tour, has fallen into step beside me. Occasionally, I glance over at him, and occasionally he glances back. We hardly speak, listening instead, feeling momentarily released from the burdens we carry, enjoying good company and fine diversion.

After a while, we reach the end of the tour near the place where we started and come upon a small patio and green area where other people are already resting their weary feet. There is a scattering of trees providing some shade in one corner. Driven by mutual instinct, we head in that direction. Jeffrey and Paul have gone to fetch the picnic basket, and Briony is setting up two large blankets in a green check pattern on the ground.

The food arrives, and all exclaim in awe at the generous quantities. Kaia, in a case of eyes-bigger-than-stomach, fills her plate to accomodate a very large person long deprived of any nutrition and begins gorging herself unabashedly, seated beside Briony. Briony looks on in delight as a palette of various condiments is smeared around the child's mouth.

We settle down to enjoy the picnic. There are sandwiches with egg and cheese, triangular pastries filled with Feta and spinach, small chunks of meat on skewers, tins of olives, anchovies, fruit and freshly baked lemon biscuits. No one will go hungry, not even the ants that keep trying to creep onto the blanket and are forced into a hasty retreat when Kaia begins stomping on them. A darling child!

"What do you think? Did you enjoy it?" Daniel asks between bites of spanakopita.

"Oh, quite marvelous. Unlike anything I've ever seen."

"Evans took some liberties with the renovation process, but not being an archaeologist myself, I think it all looks utterly believeable."

"Indeed. I should have liked to have viewed the frescos, but perhaps another time."

"Has that inspector Delos or Domas or whatever his name was, found anything new?" Paul asks.

I am so startled by the sudden question, natural as it is under the circumstances, I nearly choke on my food and need to gulp down a large mouthful of cold tea to stop my racking cough.

"Dymas is the name. Well, not really." Jeffrey shakes his head.

I hope he doesn't say anything about the diary. Of course, these people are their friends and have their alibis as far as I am aware. Still, it would not feel right in light of the ongoing investigation to go around giving away clues, betraying Dymas' confidence.

Paul chews and swallows elaborately. "I cannot imagine what is taking so long. Surely, there must be leads. This is a small community."

"Exactly. That is why people are sticking together. No one wants their friend or neighbor to be accused of being in any way involved in this." Nikolas is reaching for another sandwich. "These are excellent, Briony, by the way."

"I shall tell our cook." Briony replies, still smiling dotingly at the child, who, as far as I can see, is getting dirtier by the minute!

"Are you saying people know? That people are keeping quiet?" Daniel's half-eaten spanakopita sits suddenly forgotten on his napkin.

"No, no of course not." Nikolas shakes his head. "I am sorry. I only meant people will be wary of cooperating. No one, and forgive me for saying this, will be keen to expose one of their own in a case that they don't think concerns them, because the victim was English."

We are silent for a moment. I do not know whether to be insulted or grateful for his candid bluntness.

"Nikolas, please, you are upsetting everyone." Laria intervenes, two lines appearing on her forehead.

Nikolas takes another hearty bite. "I only want my friends to understand what is happening. Dymas will know this, too. What happened was tragic—is tragic—however, I somehow doubt it will ever be resolved. The murderer used rat poison, no?" At our nods he continues. "Everyone has rat poison. No one saw anyone coming to the villa? No one except Caspar was there? Or were any servants around?"

"None," Daniel answers, clenching his jaw.

"Right, no evidence, no witnesses. What can Dymas do? He even contacted us," Nikolas shakes his head in wonder, "looking for alibis. I mean, really."

"I must say, that was a bit disturbing," Paul adds. "Understandable, though." He turns his attention to Rosie to offer a sandwich, which she takes without change in her expression. I wonder how much is getting through to her. How sad for Paul, having known her the way she once was. He obviously still dotes on her, coaxing her along in her current state as though she is a helpless child. Compassion is a good thing, and Paul is a good man, standing by her so resolutely.

"Dymas seems competent enough," Jeffrey's tone is bordering on defensive, and I hope he won't say something foolish or damaging.

"Yes, I am sure he is." Darius adjusts his specs, frowning uncomfortably. Either the conversation is troubling him, or these pesky ants have crawled up his pantleg.

"Competence is all very good," Nikolas raises an eyebrow and pops a black olive into his mouth in a practiced motion. "I still have my doubts. What if it was a foreigner?" He looks at Daniel. "You two were traveling around before you came here, what if he was followed? What if the murderer is long gone, back home, task completed?"

"Nik! Stop! You are upsetting everyone with your remarks. I don't want Kaia to hear this." Laria cries out, her voice as sharp and strained as the tendons in her neck. She is right. Everyone looks tense, with the notable exceptions of Rosie, who is staring dreamily into nowhere, and Kaia who, without our noticing, has befriended a stray dog and is feeding the poor creature anchovies straight from the tin, howling with glee when it licks her hand. I predict a long, soapy bath in her future.

"Fine, fine. I am sorry, if I offended anyone." Nikolas concedes half-heartedly.

"It's all right. We are all speculating." Jeffrey admits.

"Well, I certainly hope it will soon be resolved." Darius sets down his empty plate and brushes his lips with a napkin. "Dymas, when we spoke, appeared a shrewd man. Further, he is a local, so he will know how to speak to people."

"We can only hope."

"Yes, and Evie and Daniel have been playing detectives." Briony comments absentmindedly, trying to wipe Kaia's face. I stiffen, noticing that Daniel mirrors my motion, though no one else seems to notice.

"Oh, not really," Daniel lends voice to my thoughts. "We only spoke with Dymas, to find out whether he has discovered anything new he might tell us. Beyond having found who did not do it, there wasn't much news."

"It was a horrible thing to happen, such a waste." Paul's face pales as he speaks the words. I can visualize images of Rosie as she was, dancing tauntingly through his mind. So much in the history of this world may be called a terrible waste. A waste of life, of resources, of joy, of tears. We live in a world full of trap doors and jagged edges and are still ill equipped for dealing with such unpredictable obstacles.

"Humans have always had an ambitious attraction to depravity." Daniel mutters almost to himself. Nonetheless, I am certain we all heard the bitter words and felt their truth resonate in some shadowy place within ourselves.

Finally, Jeffrey clears his throat. "Perhaps we ought to pack up. I am being assailed by ants, and I could not eat another bite."

"Yes, let's."

Everyone agrees. There is a palpable sense of relief as we begin to fill the basket with empty containers and scraped-clean plates. I get to my feet, stumbling slightly and not for the first time relieved I chose trousers over a skirt. Brushing crumbs from my lap, I glance at the others. Paul is pulling Rosie to her feet. Her face is pink and she looks so alive, were it not for an emptiness behind her eyes that must burn Paul everytime he looks at her, searching for the woman he once knew.

Darius and Nikolas are on their feet now. Darius is disshevelled, his linen trousers lined with creases, and his hair, without the cover of his hat, sticking up at odd ends. Nikolas watches Laria and his expression, not seen by his wife who has her back to him and is speaking with Briony, is one of unconcealed anger. I am startled to see his normally benevolent face in such a grimace of ire, and force myself to look away. In that moment one thing, however, seems utterly transparent: He knows her secret.

CHAPTER 18

Upon reaching our respective motorcars, we begin our goodbyes and promise to do this again. Kaia is tired and sucking on a finger that I hope someone thought to wipe clean at some point after her feeding the dog or baking mud cakes. Laria looks exhausted, and I feel for her. Being in Nikolas' company must be very difficult right now, unless she isn't aware of his ambiguous emotions. I could be mistaken, I tell myself, climbing into the drivers seat, yet knowing with some certainty that I am not.

It takes a few minutes to position the picnic basket, which may have diminished in weight, but has maintained its unwieldy girth. At last, we are all seated and settled and I can begin to breathe again.

"Evie, what is it? Something is obviously bothering you." Briony comments from behind me. I bite my bottom lip and swallow. The other car is pulling out of the spot beside us, and we all wave until they are out of sight.

"Nikolas knows."

"What? What do you mean?"

"How do you know?" Jeffrey says, his tone indicative of doubt.

"He was rather brusque with her." My cousin is less skeptical. Daniel has turned to me, his expression unreadable.

"When I saw the way he looked at her just now when we were packing up, you should have seen his face. He is suspicious, I can't explain it, but he knows. I am certain." I shake my head, wishing I could conjure up the image for them to see.

"I believe you are right." Daniel says gravely. "He was short with her more than once, and didn't even speak to her much of the time."

"She was busy with Kaia. It's understandable he wanted to speak to the men instead."

"They were different with each other today, Briony. At the dinner party he doted on her, they seemed so well suited. Today they were like a completely different couple."

"Caspar was there that night. If Nik knew, he was putting on a show to make it clear that Laria was his and not Caspar's. To illistrate to Caspar that he had lost." Daniel says.

"If Nikolas knew then, Laria did not. She claims she never told him. What if Caspar was the one who enlightened him? What if he boasted to Nikolas about having bedded his wife? When Laria ended the affair, Nik thought he could retaliate by putting on a united front at the party to warn Caspar off."

"Could be," Jeffrey mumbles.

"The other possibility is that Nik found out during or after the party and killed Caspar for it." Daniel's words have been coursing through my mind these past few minutes, so I do not gasp as Briony does when he utters them.

"Goodness!" Jeffrey's voice is hoarse and in the mirror I watch him running a hand through his hair and shaking his head.

"It is only a thought, of course." Daniel adds weakly.

"What if he did it? What if we just sat around having a picnic with a murderer?" Briony's voice betrays her distress.

"He has an alibi. We must not forget that."

"Yes, he has an alibi," she echoes with relief.

"An alibi for a poisoning may be a little vague. The bottle might have been given to Caspar at the party."

Oh heavens, this is getting worse. I start the motor, more for something to do than a desire to return to the scene of the crime in any great hurry. As the engine roars to life I say, "Surely inspector Dymas thought of something like this? It is quite obvious, now you've suggested it."

"I certainly hope so. Do you think we ought to call the Inspector?" Briony replies.

"On a Saturday evening? No, we couldn't. Got to give the man a day of peace."

"I doubt he will be in today in any case." Daniel rubs his temple.

I steer the car onto the main road. The heat of the sun has caused the mud to turn to dust, and as I barrel down the lane, clouds sweep up behind us. At least our conversation is providing enough distraction for Jeffrey; he hasn't gasped or cursed once yet.

"It wasn't Nik," he says, making it sound as if the very notion is absurd, which, in away, it is as is this entire situation.

"What makes you so certain?" Daniel asks.

"For one, Nikolas Zarek is a respected doctor. A doctor! He saves lives. Giving Caspar a poisoned bottle of wine is too uncharacteristic and risky. Anyone might drink from it. He wouldn't be so careless." His head turns from left to right in the rearview mirror.

Daniel interjects, "If he was in a passionate rage, he may not have been in his right mind."

"But he was not in a rage, was he? If he did give the bottle to Caspar at the dinner, he was very calm and at ease as you all observed. That is the only time he could have done it, and I am telling you, he did not." Jeffrey's judgement sounds final. I am still unconvinced.

"Perhaps you do not know him as well as you think?"

"What is that supposed to mean, Evie? The man is angry because his wife was unfaithful. It is understandable. That hardly makes him a killer."

"It certainly gives him motive, and let us not forget, his wife's lover is now dead!" Immediately I regret my outburst. My tone, especially on "dead" was rather shrill. I can hear Daniel's slow intake of breath and hope he is not too upset by my words.

"We have to accept Nikolas as a possibile suspect. Poisoning is done by a calculating mind. He is a physician, intelligent and level-headed."

"But—"

"Please, Jeffrey, let me finish. I don't believe it was Nikolas, but as Evie said, we have to consider it. You are the only one of us who did not see Laria's reaction to Caspar's death. She was distraught. She loved him. If we, being relative strangers could see this, her husband would have noticed, too."

"You overestimate the perceptive powers of a spouse, Daniel." Briony says, a statement quite shocking had she not lightened it with a chuckle.

In a piqued tone Jeffrey asks, "Is there something you wish to tell me, dear?"

I can only hope she delivers something very placating now as we have at least ten minutes left in our journey. Ten minutes of awkward silence can be as miserable as an all out row, which I am not keen on either, I must add.

"No, dear. Nothing at all," Briony says. Jeffrey shows himself suprisingly content with her answer and asks no more.

"So," I venture, "did we all have a nice day?"

CHAPTER 19

We reach the villa as the sun begins to turn the sky golden. Pink and purple streaked clouds float featherlight above us. The day was a long one, and I am weary from the soles of my feet to the crown of my head.

Jeffrey hauls the empty picnic basket out of the car, and we all make our way up the short gravel path to the door. Niobe, efficient as ever, is holding it open and taking our hats.

Knossos was fascinating, and I am determined not to let worrisome suspicions spoil the memory of the day. We agree to meet for a quick bite in an hour, and I drag myself up the stairs, eager now to shed my "comfortable" shoes, which seem have grown teeth and are devouring my feet. Upon reaching door to my room, Daniel's voice stops me in my tracks.

"Evelyn!" I turn around.

"Yes, Daniel?" He climbs the final stair and stands in the soft light filtering in from the window above.

"What do you really think?" There is a note of pleading in his voice I cannot interpret.

"I honestly do not know. It is all such a muddle in my mind. I don't want to start imagining horns sprouting from everyone's head, but it is hard to ward off suspicion."

He takes a step forward, out of the light. "Are you afraid?"

I swallow and with a dry throat answer, "I would be mad not to be. I am afraid of this killer, of what still might happen." Helplessly, I shake my head. "There is so much to be afraid of, and I am so tired of it all." Before I know it, I feel the familiar sting of tears in my eyes. "Oh, look at me. I am sorry. It's been . . . difficult." Wiping at my eyes, I attempt a smile. "Much more for you, of course. I am normally not a weepy girl, you must believe me." I am babbling now, overcome with the embarrassment of the moment. At least the light is dim enough to hide my blush.

"It's all right." Hesitantly he reaches forward and, with a gentle motion, wipes a tear from my cheek. "There, that's better," he retrieves his hand, letting it hang at his side.

I nod, unsure whether I am disappointed or relieved. Looking down at my hands, I search for something to say.

"Evie, Daniel, have you grown roots?" Jeffrey's voice interrupts my confusion. He appears at the head of the stairs, clutching a cup of tea and holding a folded newspaper squeezed under his arm.

Instinctively, almost guiltily, Daniel and I back a step away from one another.

"Jeffrey . . . We were just—"

"Look at this," Jeffrey ignores us and hands Daniel his tea, unfolding the paper. He steps into the light. "Utter rot, but I had to show you."

I join them as my curiosity is awakened in an instant. The moment between Mr. Harper and me is well and truly over.

"Englishman Murdered on Cretan Holiday!—War-veteran Caspar Ballantine poisoned on holiday. Authorities are investigating the atrocious crime against a citizen of the crown."

"Typical Daily Mail, I get it on Saturdays, because of the late post, but I thought you ought to read it." Jeffrey frowns. We turn to Daniel, who is looking surprisingly calm.

"Daniel?" I ask, nervously twisting the ring on my finger.

He rubs his chin. "There we have it. It was hardly going be kept secret, and why should it be. It won't be news in a day or so. Life goes on. Something terrible will happen someplace else, and no one will think of 'war-veteran Caspar Ballantine.'"

"You're not upset?"

"Death and murder are always fuel for media attention. I had hoped Caspar's father would be spared reading about it, but I am not shocked. If anything, I am more determined to discover the truth. If it was Nikolas, I will have him punished, and, if not, may he live a long and happy life. Now," he neatly folds the paper and hands it back to Jeffrey, "if you will excuse me, I must get changed. Today left me positively filthy." With that, he turns and steps into his room, closing the door firmly behind him.

Jeffrey and I look at one another, our faces mirroring expressions of incomprehension and bewilderment. "Well . . ." he begins.

"Indeed." With that we part company. Once in my room, I tear open the windows to catch a glimpse of the glowing orange sun as it dips below the horizon. The air blowing into the room is cool and refreshing, making the curtains twirl about me like writhing spirits.

There was a brief moment with Daniel when I thought . . . Perhaps not. Perhaps I am simply tired and dreaming of something sweet and good and detatched from the sadness and pain that has brought us together in this place.

Running a hand through the tangles in my hair and detatching several pins, which clatter like needles to the ground, I lean forward, my hands braced against the wooden sill. Poking my head out of the window, I want the cold breath of wind to ruffle my hair, to brush over my skin. As I cast my eye over the small grove of olive trees below, I notice Niobe dressed in her pale orange shift, dark hair whipping about her face. Craning my neck a little further, I see another figure, taller, but not by much. A man, his back to the house. From his stance and the paleness of his hair, I am certain it is Yannick.

Fighting a twinge of guilt for spying, I try to hear what they are saying. I know, I know, I should close the window and contend myself with brushing my hair, but sadly I am neither so good nor so moral.

To my disappointment and Niobe's fortune, the wind, shaking the branches of olive trees, noisily rustling their leaves, makes eavesdropping a challenge. Straining, all the while making a dedicated effort not to fall out of the window, I listen.

"...asking questions..." Niobe is pacing now, clearly in a state of agitation. Yannick places a hand on her shoulder, but she shakes him off.

"...nothing... don't worry..." Yannick says something in a placating tone. Niobe stops pacing and stands before him, her hands placed on her hips in irritated defiance.

Whatever is said remains a mystery. I cannot hear it in my secret perch. A moment later, they part. The maid strides off in the direction of the villa, leaving Yannick standing in the shadows of the trees, a forlorn figure, until he finally retreats in the opposite direction.

A lover's tiff? Perhaps. Niobe is a strange fish, and I wouldn't be surprised if there is more to her engagement with the Polish chauffeur than I can understand. We shall see. Or not, I suppose. My curiosity has been roused. Now I must get myself ready to behave in a civilized manner for what is certain to be a decadent, but morose sort of dinner.

I shake my head and close the window, skewering my big toe with one of the fallen pins as I turn toward my wardrobe. Serves me right for snooping.

CHAPTER 20

Dinner consists of light vegetable broth, baked fish, stuffed with dill and capers and drizzled with lemon juice, and a selection of imported chocolates from Fortnum's. I am only moderately hungry after our midday orgy and hope I don't offend the cook by sending back my plates less than polished.

Conversation centers around our excusion, though we are evidently rather wary of mentioning Nikolas, Caspar, or Dymas, as though invoking them would conjure up a stormcloud looming dark and forboding above us.

"Do you have any plans for tomorrow?" Briony asks, eyeing the last caramel. I push the tray towards her, and with a vaguely guilty expression, she pops the sweet delight into her mouth.

"I am not sure. I truly ought to write some letters or read. Day of rest and all that." I lean back in my chair.

"Must get some work done," Jeffrey rests his elbows on the table, and with a hint of amusement, I watch Briony fight the urge to tell him off.

"Work, work, work." She sighs, refraining from adding any more to fuel the flame. No one wants another evening of tension.

"And you, Daniel?" I turn to him, my right hand fiddling with the beading of my dress.

"I must get some writing done. My book is looking more like a generously sized letter at this stage. I confess, it is too easy to be driven to distraction these days. I find myself thinking of countless errands more pressing than writing another page."

"We will lock you in your room and not let you out until some work has been done." Briony smiles and Daniel returns it, the corners of his eyes crinkling like fine crepe de chine in the soft light of the candles.

"I will probably fall asleep or make it my mission to escape. It is no good. I am always searching for inspiration and find instead only diversions."

"Our very own Dickens!" Jeffrey chuckles and takes a small sip of his cognac.

"As he said, 'Procrastination is the thief of time.'"

"David Copperfield," I exclaim.

"Quite right, I am impressed." Daniel inclines his head in a little bow.

"I prefer Miss Austen. Dickens is far too gloomy for my taste." Briony swirls the rest of her wine in the thin-stemmed glass.

"Or Joyce, brilliant man, Joyce." Jeffrey adds. The rest of us begin to chuckle.

"Joyce! His writing is as dry as the sands of Egypt." Daniel shakes his head. "Give me Dickens or dear Miss Austen, but please, oh please, spare me Joyce." He grins, and Jeffrey looks affronted.

"But Ulysses, what a masterpiece! Come now, you must admit that!"

"A tome is what it is. A cursed tedious tome, and I shall never forget battling through it. Although I will admit, it is memorable." Daniel concedes with an expression of cheer, which has been absent from his face all the time I have known him. Had I been aware a mention of James Joyce would brighten his spirits, I would have brought up his name in every conversation. Maybe, he is merely relieved that, for once, the topic of conversation is normal and easy, and we are all laughing together, or at Jeffrey, for that matter. All in good humor.

We talk a while longer of books we have read, pictures we have seen, topics that engage rather than enrage. After we have retreated to the sitting room with coffee and cognac and the elegant grandfather clock chimes eleven, we decide in a chorus of ill-disguised yawns, that sleep may be in order.

In my own company once more, the door of my room, closed, the house silent, I recognize my pleasure in being here. For days I have been battling my sense of sanity—dubious at the best of times—as to whether I ought not go home again. However, sitting together with a group of kind people, people I care for and who care for me, has restored my faith in my decision.

I wash quickly, slip into a soft cotton nightgown and open the window again to allow fresh air and the soft light of the moon to filter into the gloom. The large bed seems to welcome me with open arms, cool smooth sheets enveloping my tired body in a gentle embrace. My head nestles into the pillow, and my thoughts drift away.

CHAPTER 21

I wake with a start. DARS THF. Darius. Thief. The code, the journal. The jumble of letters dances through my mind. We have been blind! Darius. He was blackmailing Darius. Him a thief? Can it be? How would he have known? A moment of doubt plagues me, but I bat it aside. Instict tells me I am right. What should I do?

Sitting up in bed, back straight, jaw tight, I decide to tell the others. I can't let this remain unsaid. Swinging my legs over the side of the bed, I search for my slippers, still lost to the dark of the room. As I make for the door, I pull on my robe.

The hallway is dark and utterly silent, and I suddenly feel foolish about rousing everyone to bring up a miserable new development, especially after we had such a lovely evening together. With some hesitation, I stand in front of the door to Daniel's room, which is closer than Briony and Jeffrey's. Should I really wake him? Yes. The idea has firmly taken root in my mind, and I cannot shake it off until I have passed it on.

Two gentle knocks against the door. Stepping close, I hold my ear to the wood. Nothing. I knock again. What if he doesn't answer? I listen. There is movement. I hear the approach of shuffling steps.

The door opens and a puzzled Daniel appears, patting down his hair. "Evelyn?" he whispers. In the gloom I cannot read the expression on his face. "Is everything all right? Has something happened?" His questions are hurried, and he leans slightly towards me as he speaks.

"Yes, no. I don't know . . . Daniel—"

"Wait, let me get a candle." He disappears for a moment, then reappears, spectre-like, holding a flickering candle that sets his face aglow.

"Daniel, do you remember the 'DARS THF' entry in Caspar's journal?"

He wrinkles his brow. "Yes, what of it?"

"I think, it means 'Darius,'" I explain, conviction suddenly absent in my voice. "Darius Thief."

Though the hall is still dark, I can see Daniel pale, his expression changing immediately. He opens his mouth, shakes his head and rubs his chin before finding his tongue.

"My god! You are right. How could we have missed it? All of us." He runs a hand through his hair and I see the other, still holding the candle, trembling slightly, causing rivulets of molten wax to run like tears down the sides. Carefully, I take it from him, thinking of Briony's dismay at wax stains on the carpet.

"I can't be certain, of course, but it is too coincidental, do you not think so? Or did Caspar know any other Darius?"

"No," He shakes his head. "It's not an uncommon name, but we've been here only a little over two months. How many people named Darius would he have been likely to meet?"

"If he had known more than one, he might have added the first letter of the last name to his code. Although he would have known which Darius of his acquaintance he was blackmailing," he winces.

I add a meek, "sorry."

"Sadly, I believe you are right. How could he do this? Darius is a friend, how could he blackmail him?" Daniel leans against the frame of the door. "I don't think I knew him very well at all."

"Don't let all this spoil your memories of him." Without thinking, I place a hand on Daniel's arm.

"He was a blackmailer, a womanizer, a philanderer . . . I have been blind." Knowing nothing to say in defense of his former friend, I opt for silence. He goes on, "And Darius a thief? I cannot believe it? He is so proper. Civilized in every way. Quite a bore, if you pardon my judgement."

"Maybe it was a misunderstanding. Caspar might have read too much into something he knew little about."

"It must be true, if he kept it written in that nasty book of his." Daniel sighs. "I suppose, we ought to tell Jeffrey and Briony."

"They will forgive us if we wait until the morning. I am sorry to have disturbed your sleep. I wanted you to be the first to know. The news will keep. We can let them get a few more hours rest."

"Yes. You're probably right."

"Daniel . . . do you think this means Darius might—"

"Be the killer?" Daniel shrugs, "I do not know. I know too little of what I want to know and too much of what I don't."

"We will have to tell Dymas."

He gives me a resigned nod. "We will. It must be resolved soon, somehow."

"I hope so." We stand together another moment, silent, the quivering light of the candle enveloping us in its soft glow, casting dancing shadows onto the walls.

"We should try to get some more sleep." Daniel says, making no move to back away. We always seem to find ourselves in moments such as these where some intangible force holds us together, but something more powerful pulls us apart.

"Yes," I say quietly, knowing more sleep will be hard to come by this night. I turn around still holding his candle, its warm light guiding me safely to my room.

CHAPTER 22

Jeffrey and Briony take the news with surprising calm. Jeffrey shakes his head and mutters something like, "what is this world coming to," and his wife, shadows beneath her bright blue eyes, shakes her head and stirs half-heartedly in her porridge.

Daniel and I decide to go into town and learn whether the Inspector can be found on a Sunday. Jeffrey is keen to withdraw to the library to work, and Briony begs off as well, claiming the urgent need to catch up on her letters, reminding me that I really ought to do the same when time permits.

Dymas, as is discovered by a quick telephone call, is at the station, closing a different case and will see us before he goes home at midday. Once dressed, we borrow two bicycles and make our way down the gravel drive to the main road. It is a warm day, the sun climbing ever higher into the cloudless blue, the fragrance of wildflowers and herbs along the lane filling our nostrils. We reach the road and swing ourselves onto the saddles. I am wearing soft brogues, which make the act of pedaling up and down the uneven landscape slightly more manageable. My hat, a straw cloche with a smattering of tiny flowers on the side, shades my face. The air sweeping at us as we roll down to the village is glorious and fresh and makes me grateful, once again, to be alive in this place.

Once in Miklos, we climb off our bicycles, pushing them along, until we reach the police station. Leaning them against the wall, trusting in the goodwill of the villagers not to steal or vandalize, we enter.

I straighten my hat and smooth the front of my blouse. Daniel watches with a curious expression. After a short conversation with the desk sergeant, we find we are in luck. Inspector Adriano Dymas has returned from another inquiry and can be found in his office. We follow the sergeant down the hallway to the familiar door. His short knock is answered, and we are admitted.

Dymas is seated behind his desk, much as we last left him. Sleeves folded up to his elbows, which are resting on the tabletop, littered with papers. He looks up as he sees us enter and gets to his feet.

"Inspector, these are—"

"Yes, yes. Thank you Stavros. Hello, Miss Carlisle, Mr. Harper, you wanted to speak to me?" He motions to the empty chairs in front of his desk.

"Inspector, have you had a chance to think any more about the entries in the journal?" Daniel asks as we agreed he should.

Dymas frowns thoughtfully. "I am afraid I can add nothing new to what we already know. You have wasted your journey."

"We think we may have come across an enlightening idea," I start, my eyes focusing on the inspector.

"Oh?" He forms a steeple with his hands, elbows again resting on the table.

"We think the 'DARS THF' entry stands for 'Darius Thief.'"

Daniel continues, "The only Darius of our acquaintance is Darius Calandra, a curator at the museum in Heraklion. Of course, it is possible Caspar knew another man of this name, but I think it unlikely."

"Darius Calandra?" Dymas' eyes widen. "Darius a thief? I cannot believe it. He is the picture of a model citizen."

"That may well be." Daniel concedes. "But he is human, and humans make mistakes. Theft is one thing, murder another."

"Good God, man! Now he's a murderer? This is maddness. I know Darius, he is not a violent man."

"Think of the way Caspar was killed," I am trying for a calm tone, "poison is not a violent weapon. It creates distance between the murderer and the victim. It is clean and difficult to trace. An intelligent man like Darius might have considered this."

Daniel raises his hands in a placatory gesture. "We do not want Darius to be guilty, but if Caspar was blackmailing him, there is a motive. Further, if Darius didn't go to the police about the blackmail, he was likely guilty of the theft he is accused of."

Dymas shakes his head and leans back in his chair, eyeing us with wary eyes. "I hope you are wrong. He is a good man, and he would have ruined his life, if this is true."

"Someone ruined Caspar's life," Daniel coldly retorts. "True, it seems he was not a very good man. Nevertheless, he was alive, and now he is dead. He deserves justice, if nothing else."

"Of course. I apologize." Dymas nods. "I will think about how to act on this new information."

"Surely you will question him?"

"Yes, that is certain. Still, how to do it without causing alarm? I need to have a strategy. Darius is an intelligent man. He will wonder why I am asking, and he may panic. I interviewed him shortly after the murder to establish his alibi, since he was on the list of your dinner guests and therefore one of the last people who saw the victim alive. His alibi sounded solid enough. He was at the museum. A number of people confirmed this."

"He would only have needed an hour to go to the villa and come back. He has a car. Daniel, do you remember, we saw him driving to the villa days after the murder when we were walking to Miklos?"

Daniel nods. "His car would not have been as fast as the Delage. It may have taken him longer to get there and back to Heraklion without anyone noticing his absence. Perhaps you are right, inspector. I hope so."

"I will call the museum to see whether he is in today. We may have resolution by this evening. I will inform you of any news or," he adds frowning, "if an arrest is made." Understanding this to be our dismissal, we rise. Dymas, too, gets to his feet.

"Goodbye." Dymas looks weary as we take our leave. I share his hope that our suspicion is proven wrong. Darius appears like such a mild-mannered and kind man. While this does not prove his innocence, it makes me wish for it.

"What are you thinking?" Daniel's voice pulls me back to the present. We are walking down the narrow, sunlit alley running along the side of the police station. Few people are about. Those who are send us friendly smiles and go about their business.

"I don't know. I just don't know what to think."

"Isn't it somehow surprising that such crimes still shock us?" Daniel asks, without turning to me. "We have experienced so much violence, so much human evil in our lifetime, and still we are disturbed by a single man's murder." His tone is matter-of-fact.

"Wouldn't it be terrible if we didn't care, if we weren't disturbed by such tragedy? Isn't it a sign of our humanity that we react to new horrors with sadness, anger and fear?" I watch his profile as he gives a gentle nod.

"Let us have something to drink." Daniel gestures at Hector's Café, which has appeared right when we need it. Upon settling into the same chairs we occupied days ago, Daion, the owner, approaches with a cheerful smile.

"A coffee and—" Daniel casts me a questioning glance.

"A lemonade, please." Daion disappears inside, returning within moments with our drinks and a small plate of rectangular biscuits.

"On the house," he says, and turns to a group seated at another table opposite us.

Daniel hestitates a moment, eyeing me curiously. "I am sorry if I spoke too harshly. I am not truly so cynical." He takes a small sip of coffee and winces as it scalds his tongue.

"It's all right. I understand, and in many ways it is true."

"Hm . . ." is all he adds.

I let my gaze wander to the people strolling by, allowing Daniel a moment to collect himself and steer the topic of conversation onto a different path.

"Oh, damn," he exclaims, surprising me. I nearly knock my glass off the table.

"What is the matter?"

"Sorry, sorry." His right hand has flown to his forehead. "I forgot to ask Dymas about funeral arrangements. I wanted ask how soon we can bury him."

"I suppose he will tell you once they release the body."

"You are probably right. Still, I would like to get it over with. There need to be some measures taken toward resolution, not only for me . . ." He breaks off, gazing at his hands.

"For Caspar as well?" I finish the sentence. He looks up and nods.

"I am not a religious man, but somehow I feel his spirit, does that sound mad?"

"Not at all," I reply.

"I want him and this horrible business laid to rest."

"We could go back to the station, if you like?"

"No, no. You are right. Dymas will tell us."

I nibble at one of the biscuits for something to do, to give myself a moment to think, rather than much of an appetite. Daniel mentioning Caspar's spirit touched a raw nerve near the surface of my too-thin skin. The idea of spirits, ghosts of those loved and lost hovering around, has always been a comforting idea for me. While some memories can be sheer misery, the thought of some part of my parents accompanying me, warming me, is one I secretly cling to with all my heart. When the distractions of everyday are not enough and lonliness looms, I draw strength from these spirits, be they real or in my mind.

"Evelyn, are you all right?"

"What? Oh, sorry. Yes, I'm quite all right." I smile and take a sip of the lemonade.

"Did I upset you?" His forehead creases, and he presses his lips together.

"No, don't worry. I was only thinking."

"What about? Your family?" Catching himself in this intimate enquiry, he blushes and quickly adds, "Sorry—"

"You must stop apologizing!" I cannot help but smile at his tense face. "It's all right. I won't collapse at your feet at a sign of distress."

"I know you won't." His expression softens. "You have proven yourself quite courageous."

"Have I? I haven't done anything."

"Oh, you may not notice it, not every woman would be able to cope with what has happened—"

"Not every woman!" I shake a finger in playful reproach. He grimaces.

"Again, I apologize. Every person. Better?"

"Go on."

"I am only saying, you have coped very well, considering that you came here for a relaxing holiday in the sun. I am grateful to be able to discuss everything with you. Jeffrey is a good friend, but he is busy with his own life and didn't much care for Caspar. Briony and I don't truly have very much in common. Besides, she is clearly troubled by something herself." He lowers his eyes for a moment and swirls the remaining coffee in his cup.

"I am happy you trust me." My tone is light, though I feel the weight of what he has said, acknowledging the strange bond, which has formed between us as a result of this tragic event.

"Cheers to that." Daniel lifts his cup and I clink mine against it.

"To good friends!"

"Indeed, good friends." Some emotion I cannot identify crosses his suntanned face, and then it is gone.

CHAPTER 23

After our refreshments have been removed and our bicycles retrieved from the police station, we are on our way again. The ride is more difficult this time, mostly uphill and soon the muscles in my calves burn from the effort. The air is pleasant, neither too hot nor too cool, and I enjoy the awareness of my body's strength as we labor up the winding road.

My mind drifts to the conversation we had at the café. Daniel is afraid of being happy, of laughing, of enjoying life again. He feels the heavy weight of guilt, much more than I do. It is a guilt that comes from surviving, from being the one that remains to live a life of which only a shell remains all else having been shattered and broken. I am certain he is lonely, too. Drifting from one place to another, not finding an anchor, not wanting. Is he escaping to outrun memories or ghosts? Mentioning Caspar's spirit revealed a glimpse of his turmoil.

We reach a bend in the road, and Daniel glances back at me, making sure I am following. Nothing is said. We let the wind tug at our hair, and I fear for my hat. As we ride along the side of the mountain, gulls circle above us, white and gray shrieking figures in the peerless blue sky. Despite anxiety weighing heavy on my mind, my muscles relax. This island has crept under my skin. The ever-present sun, the vibrancy of colors, smells of salt, and herbs and dry earth fill my senses with something akin to ambrosia. It is a balm for my scarred psyche, and I apply it with devotion. My skin has taken on a healthy, golden tone, and my cheeks feel hot and flushed as I pedal harder. The sun is in our backs now, and its warm rays caress the exposed skin at the nape of my neck.

When we turn again, a group of Kri-Kri—Cretan mountain goats—come into view, cocking their heads at us as we roll past. To our left a small orange grove appears, a lush speck in this barren scene. I wish I could paint, or had a camera that could capture these striking contrasts. In truth though, a picture could never evoke the majesty of this place. What makes it come alive—what makes me almost sense the very heart of the earth I tread on—is being here in this very moment and creating a living memory inside of me. What is an image of the sea, if I cannot smell the salt? What a photograph of the donkey, if I cannot hear its friendly bray? Whatever happened, I am here and I am alive.

Supplied with renwed energy by this elation, I push past Daniel, lifting my hat in salute, and roll down the last stretch of dirt road to the villa, glowing pale and beautiful ahead.

When we enter the house breathless from our effort, which turned into a race I am proud to say I won, we are greeted by Niobe, bearing a tray.

"Mr. and Mrs. Farnham are in the conservatory. If you care for lunch, it has only just been served." She lowers her gaze, and we follow her through the main part of the house to the back where the conservatory is located.

"Evie, Daniel you're back! And in good time too." Briony gestures to the empty chairs. "You've not eaten, have you? Cook made roast lamb with mint sauce and potatoes. Almost like a proper English Sunday lunch."

"Smells wonderful." Daniel pulls out my chair before taking his usual seat beside me.

"Yes, lovely." I add, hungry now, after the strenuous ride.

"So," Jeffrey begins as he fills his plate with slices of fragrant lamb and rosemary potatoes, "did you speak to Dymas?"

"We did, thanks," Daniel takes the plate Briony has filled for him. "It was rather strained, to be honest. He hates the idea of Darius being a suspect."

"As do we all," Jeffrey comments, dowsing his lamb in green speckled sauce. "Darius is a respected member of the staff and a good friend."

Briony nods her agreement. "I can't believe he could hurt anybody. He's such a lamb. Oh—" she looks down at her plate, "well, a dear, I meant."

"Indeed. However, if Caspar was really blackmailing him, and if the theft Darius is accused of in the diary was real, he has motive." Daniel dips a bite of the pink meat into his sauce.

"Since, he never went to the police about being blackmailed, it would seem at least that part was true."

"Why did all this have to happen?" Briony lowers her fork to her plate, the potato speared on its prongs left uneaten.

"It is partly my fault." Daniel says, and we all turn our eyes on him. He sets down his cutlery. "Had I not brought him here, none of this would ever have happened."

"Daniel," I reply solemnly, "you cannot blame yourself. You did nothing wrong. You took your friend along to visit a beautiful place, to meet kind people. You must forget this absurd idea that you carry any blame for what has happened."

"Exactly," Briony nods.

Jeffrey swallows his last bite and pronounces, "With Caspar's penchant for blackmail as is evident from that little book of his, he made enemies wherever he went. If he had a habit of such behavior, he would have created a hostile environment anywhere." I open my mouth to admonish him, when he holds up a hand. "No, let me finish. I am not saying he deserved any of this, heavens, who does? All the same, he made his life unsafe, doing what he did. You are not responsible for his actions, Daniel, nor for the tragedy which befell him."

Daniel takes a thoughtful sip of his wine before saying, "I want to believe you are right."

"'Of course I am," Jeffrey insists, helping himself to another spoonful of potatoes.

"Right, now that's settled," Briony sits up in her seat. "I have received a leaflet about a nameday festival for Saint George on Tuesday evening. Should be good fun and some distraction for us. What do you think?"

"Wonderful," I answer, dragging a chunk of potato through the sauce on my plate. "Is it in Heraklion?"

"Well, there, too, but I thought we'd go to the one in Miklos, show the locals our faces after everything that has happened."

"Good idea," Daniel nods. "I must say, Briony, this lamb is absolutely delicious. Best Sunday roast in memory."

Briony beams as though she herself had anything to do with the preparation. "Thank you! Tuck in, but leave a bit of room, there's apricot tart for afters."

CHAPTER 24

"Afters" as Briony called dessert, has done us in. Sated to the point of bursting, we break apart. Daniel to call Caspar's father again, and Jeffrey to work. Judging by the sound of snoring echoing through the walls, this means, "to nap."

Briony and I settle in the sitting room. She begins to do some quick-fingered stitching on a white pillowcase, and I flick open a copy of Evelina.

After a few moments where the only sound is that of dry pages being turned, Briony says, "Evie, what will you do when this is over?"

I lower the book onto my lap. "What do you mean?"

Briony hesitates, the fabric of her pillowcase creasing in her clenched fists. "Will you go back home? To London?" Her voice is calm, trying for a neutral tone. I know her too well though, noticing the twinge of ill-concealed anxiety.

"I wasn't planning to. Not yet, at least. I don't want to intrude though—"

"No, no!" She shakes her head with force, blonde waves bouncing above her narrow shoulders. "That isn't what I meant at all. I just didn't know whether you would want to stay after what has happened." Her eyes meet mine. "You left London to escape sad memories, and now you have been dragged into this miserable affair. It's not the holiday I had in mind for you when I sent the invitation."

"Oh, Briony, of course not. No one was to know any of this would happen. However, it's not the same as at home. Those memories claw at my heart. Caspar . . . well, I didn't know him, did I? Don't misunderstand, I am horrified at what happened to him, certainly I am, but his ghost does not haunt me. Do you understand?"

She nods, her face briefly brightened by a smile. "I hoped you would say so."

"I told you I would stay as long as you needed me, and meant it wholeheartedly." I squeeze her hand.

"With you and Daniel here, the house doesn't feel so empty. It sounds like a terribly selfish reason to keep you here, but you know what I mean, don't you, Evie?" I nod. The situation hasn't brought Briony and Jeffrey closer together yet after all.

"Evie?" Briony bites her bottom lip, signifying something serious on her mind.

"What is it?"

She swallows, dragging out the moment before answering, "Will you come to Zaros with me tomorrow?"

"Zaros? I've never heard of it. Where is it?"

"A town nearby. The truth is . . ." her words trail off, and she looks at her lap where she is still holding onto the little pillowcase with white knuckled vigor.

"Yes?"

"I want to visit an orphanage."

This was not the response I had anticipated. In truth, I do not know what I had expected her to say. Briony is ordinarily not one for scandals or great surprises.

"Don't be shocked." Her lips are a pale thin line.

"I am not shocked, only a little surprised. Of course, I will go with you. Happily," I add.

"Really?" Relief floods her face, and traces of pink appear in her cheeks.

"Yes! Did you think I would not? Really, you ought to know me better. Tell me, how many children will we be returning with?"

Shaking her head she emits a mirthless laugh. "Oh Evie, I wish it were so simple." She leans back into the cushions, releasing the creased pillowcase with a sigh.

"Can't it be?"

"Nothing is ever simple, Evelyn Carlisle, you should know by now."

"You must do what you think is right, Briony. What can be wrong with being happy?"

"It may come at the cost of my marriage?" She doesn't look at me, speaking almost in a whisper.

"Would it?"

Another sigh, her eyes still somewhere near the ceiling.

"It is much harder than when we were children. We could easily convince ourselves that we would get everything we wanted when we were all grown up. We would be married to the most handsome men, our children would be best friends. Being happy was a basic assumption."

"We read too many fairy-tales."

"Little girls always read fairy-tales. Why do you think we were so mislead, sitting at home, while the boys went out shooting with their fathers?"

"They made us happy, Briony."

"Deluded and naive."

"We saw what we wanted to see. A princess, a prince, a happy ending. We ignored the fact that the witch and the wolf kept reappearing, or that the princess was the one to make the greatest sacrifices. We were not deluded, we were children." I pause, and when she does not respond I add, "And when, not if, when you have a daughter of your own, you will tell her the same stories we were told, because you will want her to believe in happy endings."

"I will." Briony says in a dreamy voice.

"It isn't so bad here, is it?" I try to coax out a sense of contentedness. "The weather alone ought to give you reason to smile. You have had a lot to worry about lately. Life will calm down again, and I will still be here and so will Jeffrey."

"I know." She turns her head in my direction. "I should not complain, I have it so good in so many ways, it's just . . ." She gives a little shrug, "everytime I have a moment of quiet, my mind turns back to the child I might have had. It is as though I have a chronic ache, a chronic emptiness, which nothing, no matter how wonderful, can fill."

"We will go to the orphanage tomorrow, only you must promise to do nothing rash. Jeffrey must be a part of the decision, whatever may come. He loves you, Briony, I know he does."

"Yes, but it isn't enough. I am greedy, Evie, God help me, but it isn't enough."

CHAPTER 25

The day drifts by with surprising speed. I read my book, take a long bath, join the others for dinner, and drop contentedly into my soft bed. All the while, Briony's words echo in my mind. In truth, there is nothing to be done. Jeffrey is too traditional to accept an orphan into his family. It would embarass him, challenge his manliness, I believe, though I hope to be proven wrong. While I spoke the truth when saying he loved her, I doubt he is ready or even willing to make such a sacrifice. With these thoughts churning in my head, I somehow manage to drift off into a dreamless slumber.

A crow is sitting on the uppermost branch of a tree below my window, croaking nastily and dragging me unwillingly from my sleep. Yawning and stretching my arms toward the heavens—or rather the plaster ceiling—I climb out of bed. Making my way to the window, I rub the remnants of sleep from my eyes. There it is, blue-black and loud, its head with beady eyes turned pointedly towards me. Surely, this is symbolic of something dire. A black crow at dawn, or, as I am surprised to observe from my bedside clock, at eight in the morning, cannot be a good omen. Perhaps I should simply crawl back into bed. A tempting thought.

With a sigh I abandon it and think instead of the plan Briony has drawn me into. An orphanage. I am an orpahn, too. I have a strong desire to stay here, rooted, not moving, to pretend I am ill, to feign a cold as unlikely as that would be. I do not want to go. I do not want to meet these parentless children. I do not want to feel helpless and small as I know I will. But I told her I would go with her, and so I must. Only for Briony.

I open the wardrobe, and after some rumaging decide on a plain white dress with thin blue stripes running down its length. An attached belt in the same fabric ties low on my hips. There. I look into the mirror, seeing a familiar young woman looking back at me. Slim and on the tall side, a wavy auburn bob that could use a trim, tense shoulders, a wary look in stormcloud gray eyes. That'll do. No jewelry. No adornments. Only me.

As I come down the stairs, Jeffrey rushes from the library, clutching a stack of creased and disorderd papers. "Oh, Evie, morning. I must dash, late already. There's a meeting of museum directors I cannot miss."

"Have a good day."

He nods and hurries past me, out of the door. Moments later, I hear the now familiar rumble of the Delage's engine and the sound of the tires running over the gravelly drive.

Briony is still at breakfast, a very old copy of Vogue spread over Jeffrey's empty space on the table.

"Hello," I say, gently squeezing her shoulder as I enter and take my usual seat.

"Good morning." Briony looks up from the paper, excited anticipation putting a glow into her cheeks.

As I pour myself a cup of the strong and fragrant coffee, Niobe bustles in, carrying an empty tray. Her face is pale, her skin waxy. I have heard pregnant women can suffer from ill-health, perhaps she is one of them. Briony still doesn't know.

"Can I get you anything else, Miss Carlisle?" Niobe inquires, attempting a smile, but only managing a pained expression.

"No, nothing at all. There is so much here, it could feed a small country."

With a distinctly relieved expression, she disappears again.

"Shall we leave in an hour?" Briony asks, handing me a plate of warm rolls and following it with a tub of butter. She is clearly in a hurry to get me fed and ready.

"Yes, that sounds fine." I butter one of the rolls and drizzle it with a generous stream of golden honey. "Where is Daniel? Has he left with Jeffrey?"

"No, he called the police again this morning, quite early, and was told he could begin arraging the funeral. I believe he is going to talk to Caspar's father and sort things out."

"Oh." I do not know what else to say. Poor Daniel. Hopefully though, a funeral will give him some closure, so he can move on with his life. Will he leave Crete afterwards? I wonder. The idea stirs in me a distressing sensation, and I am quick to push it aside.

"It is awful, to be sure," Briony goes on, dipping the edge of her toast into her tea, a habit she has fostered since childhood. "But he is not alone, at least."

"No," I agree, taking a small bite, "he isn't."

Breakfast passes, during which we speak of nothing of much importance, unless the topic of acquiring the "simply darling" little Chanel jacket found in Vogue can be classified as such.

Claiming it will only take me a moment to wash up and grab a purse and hat so we can be on our way, I dash upstairs, brush my teeth, grab my things and am out of the door when I nearly collide with Daniel. as he emerges from his room.

"Oh! Sorry," I cry. Sorry indeed. He looks drained; his handsome face hollow as the faint stubble of an unshaven chin casts further shadows.

"My fault." He tries a faint smile with little success.

"Briony told me you spoke to the police." My eyes search his, but they reveal nothing.

"Yes," he nods, hands in pockets. "I'm arranging the funeral."

"I hope you know you can depend on us for any help you might need. I understand he was your friend, but you mustn't shoulder this alone."

His mouth remains impassive, but his eyes crinkle ever so slightly at the edges. "Thank you, I will."

"Good."

"Evie!" Briony's shout is a boulder thrown into a placid lake, and both Daniel and I startle.

"Coming," I call back. "Briony is waiting for me," I quickly explain. "We're going out for a few hours."

"I won't keep you."

"Right, goodbye." I nod quickly and squeeze past, perceiving the aura of sadness emanating from him and feeling a pang of guilt for leaving.

Downstairs, Briony is fully dressed in a blouse and wide white trousers. Her shoes are flat, peeking out from the hem of her pants.

"Ready?" She asks, impatience in her voice.

I secure my wide-brimmed hat atop my head as we take out the bicyles. "Ready."

Zaros is only two miles away and slightly inland in a surprisingly green valley. The ride is pleasant, the day still cool, and a breeze gently embraces us while we make our way along the dry dirt road.

The orphanage is located on the outskirts, and we have to pedal down the main street through town to reach it. The buildings have suffered from greater wear than those in Miklos. Crumbling stones and chipped paint a common sight. Still, it possesses its own sort of charm, in the same way old places everywhere do. The people we encounter look friendly and pay us little heed. It is Monday, market day, and two women on bicycles, foreigners though we may be, are not a very exciting distraction.

The orphanage is marked by a single sign in Greek, which I am pleased to note I can read, "Orphanage of St. Christopher". The gates are rudimentary at best, and we glide over much-trodden ground without being questioned. Only at the front door, a massive and sturdy set of oakwood planks, a voice asks for our names.

"I am Mrs. Farnham, and this is Miss Carlisle. You may remember me, I—"

The door swings open, and a tiny woman in a nun's habit stands before us.

"Mrs. Farnham, how good to see you again!" She graces us with a welcoming smile. I am so surprised by her clear and fluent English, it takes a moment for this to register. Briony has been here before.

"Sister Sybil," Briony smiles broadly, "how good to see you again. How have you been?" She bends over slightly, though not particularly tall herself, and clasps the older woman's hand in a familiar gesture.

"Oh, well enough. I cannot complain." Her eyes, a pale blue so striking in her deeply tanned brown face, drift over to me. "And this is your friend?" Her smile does not diminish, and I immediately feel included and accepted, a sensation so precious I can entirely understand why my cousin would visit here.

"Yes, Sister, my name is Evelyn Carlisle, Briony's cousin."

"Wonderful! Family, it is so important. I have a large family here, all my children around. Please, come in, come in. You have journeyed here to meet some of them, of course. Follow me." With that, she steps aside, ushering us into the cool interior of the building. It is darker inside, and my eyes take a moment to adjust. The nun turns and leads us down the wide hallway. Our heels make faint tapping sounds on the worn tiles. The inside of the orphanage has a distinctly lived-in appearance, which is not to say it is lacking in comfort.

The walls are painted an earthy shade of orange, tiny bits of plaster crumbling here and there onto the floor. A spiral staircase of dark wood appears to our right. Sister Sybil passes it, and leads us toward the only significant source of light, a large set of doors thrown open at the end of the hall to reveal an inner courtyard.

As we approach, I can already hear the sound of high-pitched children's voices mingling with the gurgle of water from a fountain nearby.

"Have you been here often?" I whisper to Briony, bending my head, but raising an eyebrow in a gesture of surprise.

"Only once," she whispers back, and before I can ask anything else, we step into the sun again.

For all the darkness of the building, the courtyard compensates with light and air. It is large and rectangular, with potted greenery and even a small herb garden in one corner. A group of children are engaged in various activities as we enter the little sanctum. Two of the small, black-haired heads look up upon spying us. Sister Sybil gives them a wave.

"Visitors," she says, turning halfway toward us, "are quite a treat, so please forgive their curiosity."

The two children, a girl and a boy, both around four or five years old, approach us cautiously. Big black eyes unblinking, they hold hands in a heart-wrenchingly sweet way until standing before us uncertain what to do.

"Please children, you must greet our visitors," Sister Sybil instructs. The children keep staring. It is the little girl who lets go of her companion's hand and offers a tiny wave.

"Hello," Briony and I say almost at once. The girl smiles, twisting her little arms behind her back and rocking back and forth on the heels of her feet. The boy, having decided we are probably quite harmless, gives us a grin, one even more toothless than that of Sister Sybil.

"These two are Areta and Timon," the nun explains, nudging them forward.

"What lovely names!" Briony is glowing as if by some magic, their presence makes the sun reflect her skin more luminously.

"Ah, and here come the others." Sister Sybil waves at the three other children making their way towards our little group. Leading them is a thin girl, likely the eldest, with a long braid of thick dark hair cascading down her back. "Iona, Leah, and Deke." The three stand before us, curious expressions on their suntanned faces. The girl, Iona, is the first to speak.

"Hello." She does not shy away, her eyes meet mine as she takes my hand, and I observe the same confidence when she takes Briony's.

Sister Sybil looks pleased. "Shall we have something to drink?"

We sit around a circular stone table at the edge of the herb garden where a lemon tree, its branches heavy and stretching towards the cloudless blue sky, provides some welcome shade.

Another nun, Sister Agatha, enters the courtyard, bearing a tray of glasses and a jug of lemonade, along with a small basket of oranges. Setting them down, she smiles at us, uttering not a word before disappearing again indoors.

"She speaks no English and is quite shy," Sister Sybil tells us, pouring lemonade into our glasses, the sunlight making it glimmer and glint crystalline as it runs from the wide lipped pitcher.

I observe Iona looking at the nun and then at the basket of oranges. Sister Sybil nods slightly. The girl takes one and begins to peel it, filling the air with its unmistakable fragrance. Once peeled, she splits the fruit into exact segments, and places them into to the eager hands of the other four children. At ten, she is probably too old to be adopted, people preferring an infant to a child whose character and life have already been molded without the new parent's influence and guidance. I reflect again, how fortunate I was to have had people willing to take me in after I lost my parents. I really ought to write Agnes another card. She is a difficult woman, or perhaps we simply never understood one another, for surely she thought of me in much the same way. I was a child she could not comprehend, from a sister she did not connect with. We were incompatible from the start. Still, I had a home, and I was safe and well looked after.

Seeing these children though, much the same can be said. They appear healthy and happy, even educated to a certain extent. Sister Sybil and her order have done good work, and I resolve to make a generous donation, whatever Briony decides to do.

"Why have you come here?" Iona asks, her face revealing the openess of youth, mingled with suspicion born of hardship.

Before either of us can reply, little Timon, making big eyes at Briony answers, "They came to visit me, didn't they?"

The adults at the table smile at his cheek, and Briony bends down. "Yes, of course, we did. We wanted to see all of you."

Taking an orange she hands it to him, an offering he accepts eagerly, his small pudgy hands enveloping the fruit and drawing it to him possessively.

"Do you live here?" Again, the older girl makes herself heard, her voice clear and surprisingly low for such a young child. Her face betrays nothing beyond distance and indifference. This hardness toward us outsiders saddens me. I want to reassure her, to breathe ease and laughter into her. Childhood is over much too quickly as it is. I believe she is treated well here. Whatever armor she is wearing, she has carried it for a long time and will be loath to part with it.

"Yes, I live here with my husband. My cousin, Evelyn," Briony gestures at me, "is here on a visit. I am hoping she will decide to stay longer."

We sit together peacefully, the slender branches of the lemon tree sway and rustle above our heads, and more than once I fear one of the fat and juicy lemons will drop on our heads. After a while, Sister Agatha returns, fetching Deke and Leah who have been yawning impressively, to come inside for a nap. Sister Sybil excuses herself to help, and we are left alone with the three remaining children.

"I like your hat," comments Areta, her head bent to one side, masses of glossy curls tumbling over her shoulder. Oh, to have hair like that! I would never wear a hat again. She evidently thinks otherwise, so I take mine off and place it gently on her head.

"Don't you look lovely, although you have such beautiful hair, you should never cover it." As I say this, the odd thought strikes me, should she stay here and become a nun, she would most certainly have to cover it, or cut it even.

"Do I look like a fancy lady?" She asks, sitting up straight and folding her hands elegantly in her lap.

"Like a princess," I reply, gratified to see her mouth widen in a toothy grin.

"It's too big for you!" Timon points a stubby finger. "Iona, you try, you have a bigger head." Ah, the honesty of youth. Areta is reluctant to part with the hat, so Briony unpins hers and hands it to Iona. The girl hesitates at first, then even she cannot prevent a hint of childish glee to flash across her pretty features as she settles it reverently on her head. It suits her.

"Very nice."

"Are you going to take us home with you?" Timon has been uncorked and will not be stopped. Briony shoots me wide-eyed, amused look, which I counter with raised a brow.

"Well, not today. We wanted to visit and meet you all."

"I am a good boy."

"Of course you are," Briony beams at him.

Before Timon can so much as open his mouth again, Iona intervenes, "Timon, Areta, why don't you tell Mrs. Farnham and Miss Carlisle what you have been doing today." The youngsters perk up, apparently their day has been a fruitful one.

Timon immediately embarks upon a vivid tale regarding the orphanage's cat, Dionysous, which Areta considers too long a name for such a little cat. As it happens, Dionysous climbed into the lemon tree and would not come down.

"I stood there," Timon says, getting up and demonstrating most effectively, "and I called, 'Dionysous! Dionysous!'" He shouts the name, and I observe, with some amusement, the score of terrified birds lifting themselves from the branches and taking flight. "But," the boy continues, wearing an incredulous expression, "the cat did not come. Then I threw lemons at it." He picks up one of the lemons from the ground to show us how this may be done and is fortunately prevented by Iona from pursuing this wild endeavour. "Still, the stupid cat—"

"Timon!" Iona shakes her head.

"The cat," he corrects himself, "it did not come!"

Briony and I are a rapt audience.

"Then Sister Sybil came and she said we had to stop throwing things at the cat," complains Areta.

"Oh dear," Briony shakes her head, and I do not know whether her reaction is prompted by the intervention of the kindly nun or the actions of these rather wild children.

"She said we scared Dionysous." Timon looks unconvinced. "We only wanted to play!"

I imagine all to well what "play" can mean. Presumably it involved either tying the poor creatures tail in a knot or painting it with honey. Childhood games sometimes verge on the cruel.

"Did he come down?" Briony looks up to the leafy canopy, expecting the frightened creature to be cowering somewhere above us still.

"Yes," Areta nods, "Iona got him down."

"Did you?" I turn to the girl, who has remained quiet the whole time, allowing the younger children to sop up all of the attention.

She nods, the brim of the hat she is still wearing bobbing gently up and down.

"How did you do it?" Briony smiles reassuringly, and I see how deeply at ease my cousin is in this setting. She is made for a family.

"I brought a fishbone from supper last night, and climbed on the table." Thankfully Iona is less inclined than her small friends to demonstrate this. "I waved it about, and he jumped down."

"Straight into her arms," Timon adds with reverence.

"Quite impressive. Have you ever had a cat before?" Briony asks, and the engery shifts immediately as Iona pales under her wide hat.

"I had one once. When I was little." She falls silent, and neither Briony nor I know what to say. Fortunately, Areta and Timon have no sensitivity for such things as yet.

"I want to have a dog." Timon announces, puffing out his small chest, "a big black dog. Like a wolf." Startling us all, he lets out a loud howl. "Like a wolf," he repeats.

"Oh, no, a puppy, a little puppy!" Areta calls out excitedly, jiggling her head, making the curls bounce, reflecting her joviality.

"Do you have a dog?" Timon asks Briony.

"No, I am afraid I do not." Noticing his disappointment, she is quick to add, "But when I was younger my family had many dogs. Big ones and small ones." The children are hers again.

"Really?"

"How many"

"Did they bark?"

"Did they bite?"

"Oh no, they were very good. They belonged to my father. He liked to go hunting, and he always took the dogs along." Timon and Areta stare at Briony, who is basking in their attention.

"Did they have big teeth?" Timon bares his tiny ones in a growl.

"Well, yes, but they didn't hurt us."

"Only the animals they killed?" Iona suggests wisely.

"Er . . .indeed." Briony shrugs, and Iona takes another orange, this time for herself.

Conversation veers about from favorite sweets to games, to mice (yes, mice!), making it both hard to follow and oddly amusing. Iona keeps mostly silent, adding only an occasional comment here and there. She is a clever girl with a wild sort of energy beneath her placid surface. Areta and Timon stumble over their words, constantly interrupting and contradicting one another in their impulsive need to get out all that can be said, as though keeping parts untold will cause physical discomfort.

Sister Sybil rejoins our group, however the children do not allow her much more than an intermittent one-word contribution. As the shadow of the lemon tree travels, and the sun shifts above us, we decide to say our good-byes, to leave time to get back before dark.

Timon and Areta embrace us both enthusiastically, and even Iona, evidently too old for such exuberance, lets us shake her hand. We promise several times over to return, and at Timon's insistence and Sister Sybil's pink-faced mortification, assure him we will bring sweets.

As we push our bicycles up the sloping road, Briony turns to me her flushed face full of cheer. "It was lovely, wasn't it? Aren't you glad you came?"

"I am indeed. I have rarely had such lovely day in such amiable company."

"Areta is only four, you know, not old at all. Timon is five."

"And Iona?" I ask, thinking of the youthful seriousness she displayed, wondering what hides behind the wall from which so little laughter and childish fancy escaped.

"Nine or ten, though she seems older, don't you agree?"

"I do. Have you any idea why she is living in the orphanage? Is she from Zaros?"

"I do not know. I have only visited once before, and I met other children then."

"How many live there?" We have reached the top of the hill and mount our bicycles in silent mutual consent.

"Twelve. Four boys and eight girls. Sister Sybil and Sister Agatha strike me as very capable. They get support from donors as well from their order of Saint Christopher."

We begin pedaling. The road is even, pounded flat and hard by the traffic of carts and animals hauling heavy loads and the dry climate, which prevents dirt roads from becoming mud tracks.

"Will you tell Jeffrey?" I ask, as we turn the first bend, the thought a nagging presence in my mind since Briony requested my company for this excursion last night.

"Why should I?" Her tone is vaguely petulant child, and I tense instantly. She will not speak to her husband, nor, it appears, will he speak to her.

"Briony, how do you expect this to go on? You are not happy, yet you do not dare to disrupt the deceptive serenity at home, to allow Jeffrey to understand. He loves you, surely you know that. And you love him, don't you?" Briony hesitates and I wager a glance in her direction, only to see her tightening her jaw. "Briony! You have been married less than three years, have you gone off Jeffrey already?" My voice is a louder than anticipated.

"Of course not. I mean, of course I still love him. It's just—"

"What is it?" I almost shout. "I have been here less than ten days, and you have cried on more than one occasion about your unhappiness. Please, do not think me unsympathetic, you know the opposite is true, but it is frustrating to watch the two of you living alongside one another, your roads hardly intersecting." Right, there's that said. A wave of guilt washes over me immediately, and I wish I could take back my words. Alas, I cannot.

It takes a few moments for her to respond, and we hear only the rattling of the bicycle chains and the sound of birds shrieking somewhere beyond sight.

"I am sorry. You came here on holiday and—"

"Please, do not apologize. I am not complaining. I worry. You know I only want to see you two happy." I try to sound gentle, the reproach removed from my voice.

"I know and I am grateful. The truth is, I think Jeffrey is entirely content with his life. He has a job he is absorbed by, a lovely home, and if I do say so myself, a rather pleasant wife. It would be cruel to disillusion him."

"You must see it cannot stay this way? Sparing his feelings is a sweet thought, but the truth may not hurt or uspet him the way you think it will. He is a kind man, he will listen and I am sure he will understand." At least I hope so. In truth, what she says sounds uncomfortably accurate, and Jeffrey's life on this island fulfills his needs all too nicely.

We ride a while side by side, saying no more. I hope my comments did not spoil the day for her. The reason for my persistence has to do with my awareness of the frailty of our existence. I cannot abide this reckless wasting of time. We are all guilty of it, pushing worrisome or distasteful tasks to the next day and then the next, until facing them becomes more fantasy than reality.

My life in London, under Aunt Agnes' watchful and critical eye, was certainly an example of idle procrastination, I confess. I drew up plans, nearly packed my bags half a dozen times, then inertia or fear overtook conviction, and I remained rooted and frustrated where I was. Briony's invitation gave me the shove I needed, and in a way I want to offer the same to her.

Before I know it, we have reached the road to the villa, which is already visible ahead, pale and elegant in these natural surroundings. We reach the driveway and climb from our bicycles, the gravel surface making the ride terribly bumpy and rough.

As we secure them at the side of the house, Briony turns to me. "Evie," she pulls off her hat, the hat Iona had returned with a sad smile.

"What is it?"

"You won't say anything, will you?"

I shake my head, even though I would rather shake her. "No, I won't, but you should. What is the worst that might happen?"

"Jeffrey will think I am ungrateful and difficult." The words come out in a low rushed murmer, making me doubt, for a moment, what I heard.

"What do you mean?"

"He will regret marrying me. He'll think I am barren and—"

"Briony! Don't say such things! Do you have no faith in him at all?"

She digs her heel into the gravel, surely ruining it as she rotates her foot to create a groove.

"I cannot talk of this anymore. Please, don't say anything. We had such a lovely day. Let us leave it at that." She gives me a pleading look, her blue eyes moist, and turns toward the front door.

Knowing not what else I might do, I follow. As I reach the door, a fat raindrop spatters on my cheek. How very fitting, I think, shaking my head and entering the villa, pulling the door firmly closed behind me.

Briony disappears into the kitchen, probably with the dual purpose of running from me and of resuming her role as mistress of the house in one elegant sweep. Not wanting to disappear into my room, I saunter into the sitting room, which is home to a well-stocked shelf of what I take to be Briony's books, being wholly entertaining, and not wholly respectable, as far as it goes.

CHAPTER 26

I make my way to the bookshelf, hoping to find distract me from the dilemmas and anxieties that have taken residence in my mind when I am interrupted by a familiar voice.

"Hello."

I jump and twist around. Daniel is sitting in a low armchair near the window out of my sight when I entered the room.

"Heavens! You gave me a fright." I shake my head with a relieved giggle. My heart is beating so loudly, he must be able to hear it across the room.

"Sorry, sorry. I didn't mean to startle you." Daniel cannot prevent himself from grinning.

"It's all right. I didn't know you were home. Is Jeffrey back from town?"

He shakes his head, the rays of sunlight filtering in through the window draw out streaks of copper in his hair.

"I hope everything is all right at the museum. He was rather rushed this morning."

"Yes." Stepping closer I crouch on the arm of the sofa. "He mentioned something about pieces missing from the recent excavation. Hopefully only a misplacement and nothing to worry about."

"Hm, yes." he shrugs.

"What are you reading?" I ask, eyeing the book open in his lap.

He sheepishly holds it up for me to read the illustrated cover.

"The Adventures of Tom Sawyer."

"I'm a bit old for it, if it was up to Jeffrey, I'd be puzzling over Hawthorne or Homer."

"Then you are most fortunate he is not here to see you now, aren't you? And I happen to be rather good at keeping a secret."

"Is that so?" He raises an eyebrow. "What sort of secrets are locked away in that head of yours?"

Blushing at his question and at being the object of his green-eyed gaze, I am quick to add, "Ah, that would be telling. You are trying to trick me."

"Never." There is more in those two syllables than jest, and I cannot help but let a pleased smile spread across my lips. "Good."

We sit like this for a strange, not uncomfortable moment, contemplating the meaning of the other's words. It is Daniel who breaks the silence, his face taking on a different expression removed from our banter. "Dymas called."

"Oh." If I am honest with myself, I haven't thought about Caspar for some hours.

"He was able to speak to Darius."

"What did he say? He did not arrest him?"

"No, no he didn't." Two thin lines crease Daniel's forehead. "He said Darius denied it. He said, while Caspar and he were not friends, neither were they enemies. There are many called Darius on the island. It leaves us sadly none the wiser."

"I hope it's true, do not mistake my hesitation for disappointment." However, if I am entirely truthful, there is a tinge of the latter emotion in my skepticism. "If Caspar knew enough about another Darius to blackmail him, wouldn't he have met him quite a few times? He couldn't very well threaten the man, if he only saw him by chance pinching an orange off a fruit stall, or something like it. He would have been certain of the man's crime, and to be certain, he would have had to know him fairly well, would you not agree?"

The creases deepen, and Daniel folds his hands together in his lap, responding, "What you are saying may well be true. Darius or 'DARS' was being asked for a hefty sum, first 3500, and then 9000 Drachmae. Not an inconsequential amount. Caspar would need to be certain his method of exerting pressure would work, if he repeatedly demanded such sums. Further," he sits up, "if this had been a recurring event, then he needed to have met this Darius early on. We have been here less than three months and met Darius Calandra after the first week. I do not remember anyone else of our acquaintance with that name."

"It seems unlikely that many people would have had such sums to part with." I add, realizing, with a sinking feeling, murderer or not, Darius lied to Dymas.

"It must have been him." Daniel reaches the same conclusion.

"Do you think Dymas believed him?"

Daniel raises his hands. "I cannot say. I think he was inclined to. You saw his reaction to our suggestion that Darius had anything to do with the crime."

"Do you think Jeffrey spoke to him, warned him maybe?"

"Oh," he shakes his head, "it hadn't even crossed my mind."

"I doubt he would have, but hinting to Darius that Dymas might call on him in regards to the inquiry would have given Darius a chance to get his story right, to behave calmly when Dymas confronted him." Sighing, I add, "'What a tangled web we weave when we practice to deceive.'" I slide off the arm sinking onto the well-cushioned sofa itself.

"Indeed." Daniel's mood is dimming before my eyes.

"Even if Darius was being blackmailed, he did not necessarily commit murder."

"No, but his motive would be the most compelling of anyone we've come across."

"Excluding Nikolas."

"Perhaps," he concedes. "It is always love or money, isn't it. The driving forces are always love or money." He raises his eyes again, meeting mine. "And yet, no money can buy real love."

"No, it can't." I wonder what he is implying. My interpretations of subtlety and nuance are dubious at best.

"Evelyn, may I ask you a rather personal question?" His eyes are intently focused on mine, and I find myself nodding without a second thought.

"Are you happy? You've told me of your past, of what happened, and I suspect there is much more to be told. You know my own story, probably better than I do yours. I trust Briony has been more forthcoming than Jeffrey."

"Perhaps I do." I let my gaze drop to my lap where my clenched hands are resting.

"Forgive me," he says, "I should not—"

"No, it's all right. Yet you must allow me a question of my own." I raise my eyes again. "Do you think any of us are ever completely happy?"

Exhaling he lets his shoulders drop. "No, I do not. Well, no adult of my acquaintance, at least."

"Well, to answer your question, I am as happy as I have been in quite some time. I know that sounds odd, given what happened, but I feel freer than I have in a long time, add to that the good company I am in. I truly should not complain." He grins at this as I continue. "That is enough for me to be quite content."

"A good answer. Contentedness is not to be undervalued."

"It is not quite elated joy, but it is the next best thing. And I would feel ashamed, considering all the good fortune I have in my life, if I said anything else."

"Do you think people lie about being happy because they think others want to hear it? Or to convince themselves?"

"Surely both." I say, thinking of all the masks we wear, to disguise, to hide, to disappear behind.

"Yes, I believe so, too. Has it ever been otherwise, do you think?"

I lean back slightly, finding myself both at ease and unnerved by the philosophical turn this conversation has taken. "Probably not. I expect people when it comes right down to it are the same as they were a hundred, two-hundred years ago."

"Which is probably why we never learn from past mistakes either." His tone carries an edge of bitterness.

"Daniel," I bite on my bottom lip, wondering whether I ought to say what I am thinking.

"What is it?"

Well, I suppose he's asking for it.

"Daniel, are you very angry?"

The question clearly shocks him and he straightens in his chair, his expression hovering somewhere between surprise and dismay. "I . . . no, why—"

"Please, forgive my bluntness. I understand anger, I do, but—"

"No, I am not so angry as much as I am . . . I don't know, disappointed." He cranes his neck back, closing his eyes for a moment before opening them again and adding in a quiet tone, "Disappointed and exhausted."

"With life?"

He gives a quick mirthless laugh and shakes his head, a lock of dark hair falling onto his forehead. "Yes, no. I don't know. There are times when life is good, sunshine on your skin, the sweetest strawberries, laughter and friends, and times when it seems worth nothing at all, where blackness and bleakness hover like a thundercloud. Do I sound completely mad?"

The frightening thing is that he does not. Not at all. He mistakes my silence for judgement and continues in a more sober voice.

"I have shocked you. Unfiltered thoughts that course around my mind on occasion find their way out of my mouth."

"Don't apologize." The sun beyond the window hides behind a cloud, and I shiver. If he notices, he makes no remark. "Do you suppose we all feel that way?"

"You mean, do I think I am unique in this? No, but I also have not met many who admit to it. I suppose you have woken some dormant bravery in me." He smiles meaning to bring lightness to his words, but instead makes tears prick my eyes. I swallow, blinking them away.

"Do moments of goodness outweigh the others?" I ask, a lump at the back of my throat.

"Most days." Another smile, this time spreading to his eyes. "Most days."

"Good." For a moment we sit there, smiling at one another like the companionable fools we are.

CHAPTER 27

Dinner is a simple affair. Jeffrey calls ten minutes before to inform us tersely he has to miss it. Thus disappointed, Briony stares into her bowl of excellent cold soup and pushes pieces of roast chicken to the corners of her plate. After a dessert of honey cake, we retreat to the sitting room. Daniel is reading the last few pages of his guilty pleasure, and Briony is cutting a pattern for a new skirt, while I write postcards to Aunties Iris and Agnes. The first is easy, words flowing from my pen, natural and honest. The second proves more of a challenge.

Dear Aunt Agnes,

I hope you are well.

And now . . .? Do I tell her about Caspar? Does she already know? She claims not to read such "drivel" as the Mail, but perhaps she does. Jeffrey's name is mentioned, so it would take no great deductive powers to know I am somehow involved as well. I wonder, if she would even have me back, should I want to return?

Dear Aunt Agnes,

I hope you are well. The weather here is pleasant, the sun shining every day and little rain. The landscape is dry, though today I visited a village in a rather lush valley. I am well. Briony has an excellent cook, and we even had roast lamb for our Sunday luncheon. How are Harris and the rest of the staff? Have you kept Millie on?

So much has happened, yet I can only tell her about the weather. Perhaps I should be more blunt. She never expects much good of me, so why bother maintaining a façade? I continue writing, my hold on the pen tightening.

> *As you may have read, there has been a tragedy at Briony and Jeffrey's house. A fellow guest has fallen victim to murder. The police have been very vigilant and helpful, and you need not be concerned for my safety. I will write again when I know more. Briony and Jeffrey send their love, as do I.*
>
> *Yours truly,*
>
> *Evelyn*

There, not bad. I lay down the pen before I can scratch it all out again and add another line about fresh fruit instead. I wonder whether she will write back? She did not respond to the telegram. Am I disowned, punished for my disobedience? I wish these questions did not plague me so. My relationship with Agnes is what it is, and still, somewhere inside of me, the frightened and lonely four-year-old girl yearns for some sign of affection, though the woman in me, two decades later, knows it will not come.

Somewhere beyond the wall, we hear the heavy thud of a door slamming and then footsteps moving toward us. The sitting room is bathed in a pleasant light from the gaslamps and two candles on the low wooden table. Jeffrey's face, despite the illuminations he enters, is sallow and pale, the magic leaving him untouched.

"Jeffrey, dear!" Briony gets up in a hectic motion, having forgotten her anger. "What is it? Has something happened? Sit down." She guides him to the sofa. I turn around in my chair, and Daniel sets down his book, filling a heavy crystal glass with brandy before striding over to his friend.

"Have a drink. It will bring some color back to your face."

Jeffrey obeys, gulping a generous amount of fiery liquid.

"Better?" Daniel sits down on the chair across and narrows his eyes.

"Yes, cheers for that. I needed it after the day I've had."

"Tell us, darling, you're worrying me." Briony leans closer, placing a slender hand on his arm.

"Well," he pinches the bridge of his nose, wincing before he continues, "The excavation site was vandalized and robbed last night."

"What?" We echo in unison appalled and rapt at once.

"The damage is not bad. It looked more like an afterthought, the police say. A gold statue was taken. An invaluable piece! Can you imagine?"

"Surely there was a guard? Why was the statue not at the museum?"

"It was attached to the main structure. We did not want to cause breakage in the foundation, so Paul was going to visit the site with an architect today and see how best to sort it out. The guard was knocked out from behind. Barely anyone knew it even exhisted." He shakes his head incredulously. "The museum directors hinted very politely," he rolls his eyes, "that someone directly involved with the excavation or the museum itself must be the guilty party. We were interrogated! Can you believe it? In principal I understand, but still, no one on the team would damage our site, no one."

"What will happen?" I ask, leaning forward, my wicker chair creaking.

"I can't say. For now, they have halted all work at the site." He takes another hearty slip, setting the empty glass on the table. "Everyone was in a state."

Daniel and I exchange glances. It is unlikely Jeffrey found the time to talk to Darius about the investigation with all this troubling him. Dymas must have spoken to Darius before the museum meeting, otherwise the curator would surely not have had the presence of mind to think on his feet. Darius would be most upset at any violation of the excavation site. The way he spoke of the artifacts, even on the first evening we met, betrayed his utter fascination with them, and his devotion to maintaining and learning from them. Who would do such a thing? A statue of such value and repute could never openly be sold on the island without the thief drawing unwanted attention.

"How did Darius act today?" Daniel asks before I can.

"Darius? He was upset, of course, as we all were—still are." Jeffrey balls his left hand into a fist, clasping it with his right. "That statue was priceless, and now it's gone." He really does look very tired. I cannot help but notice that he is reacting with far greater agitation to the loss of a figurine, than to the murder of his guest.

"Is the guard all right?"

"What? Er . . .yes, fine, he is fine. Just a bit of a headache. He was taken to hospital."

"Well, that is good at least. The thief is no murderer."

"Small consolation." Jeffrey mumbles unsympathetically. I decide to be forgiving in view of his dilemma and offer no rebuke.

"Are you hungry? You must be." Briony jumps up. "I'll see what can be found."

Her husband sighs and gives her a half-hearted smile. Briony disappears through the doorway, and we can hear the light tap-tap of her heels on the polished tiles.

"Jeffrey," Daniel begins, "you may not be interested in this at the moment, but Dymas called earlier."

Jeffrey gives a low groan. "What now? Will we never have any peace?"

I notice the muscles in Daniel's neck twitch ever so slightly at this callous remark. Jeffrey has some way to go in the mastery of tact.

"He wanted to inform us that Darius denied the theft and the blackmail." Daniel's voice is harder now, matter-of-fact.

"Right," Jeffrey nods. He had clearly forgotten about that little concern. It is hardly any wonder he doesn't know his wife is unhappy. If he can forget the fact that his colleague and friend may very well have done-in his houseguest!

"We are quite skeptical," I say, my voice a hint too loud. "He is the only man named that Daniel thinks may fit."

"Nonsense, even I know another Darius. Caspar was a sociable fellow. He might have known five. It is utter nonsense to suspect that my friend has something to do with any sort of criminal behavior. Utter nonsense."

As he repeats the word, looking like a stubborn child, Briony breezes through the door, carrying a tray. Obviously the cook prepared it, but it is sweetly arranged by Briony. Her attentions rouse a slight strain of annoyance in me. He is showing his selfishness tonight, in words and actions, and I cannot stir up great sympathy for him.

"Here, darling. Some roast chicken, potatoes, and peas and some cake for pudding." She carefully sets the tray before him.

"Ah, good, thanks." He leans forward. "No bread roll?" he frowns ,and I could shake him.

"No? Let me fetch—"

"Surely you can manage without a roll, Jeffrey, dear." I hope my tone does not betray my rising irritation.

"Yes, I suppose." He tucks in, and I watch Briony as she watches him. She deserves to be appreciated. The more I think about it, the angrier I become. She has been crying to me, while her husband cares only for crumbling rock and relics of yesteryear. At none of the many meals we have shared, has he asked her about herself, always expecting to be heard, not to do the hearing. He is a tolerant husband and not unkind, but he isn't interested, and that, even I know is a vital part of any realtionship.

With more force than intended, I get to my feet, snatching the written postcards off the little table. "If you will excuse me, I am tired. It has been a long day."

"Shall I send Niobe up to help you with anything?" Briony asks, and I soften instantly.

"No. Thank you, I will manage on my own. Good night."

"Good night," the others echo as I make my way to my room, spine stiff, temples throbbing.

CHAPTER 28

My room is cool as the window is still wide open, and I shiver upon entering. Sinking onto my bed, I let out a deep breath, waiting for my thoughts to settle, the pressure behind my eyes to ease. The dimness is pleasant, and my eyes adjust quickly.

All around me swirls an eddy of misunderstanding and emotional turmoil, and I am powerless to do anything useful at all. Briony is depressed, Jeffrey is oblivious and Daniel remains an enigma to me. Still, we are forever connected because of Caspar's murder. I know the events that ocurred here have not left me untouched, yet looking into the mirror, the only change I see it the slight coloring of my skin and the circles caving out blueish hollows beneath my eyes.

Did I expect too much, coming here? I am not disappointed, rather overwhelmed. I go to bed every night with my head full of what is to come. It is so different from my other, past life when my thoughts centered largely around myself and my boredom and discontent. Have I grown as a person? Have I evolved to a higher level of maturity? One can only hope.

Right now, sitting in this dim room, afraid to enter the garden for fear of Caspar's spirit, I yearn for empty thoughts and silence in my head. For someone to sit down beside me, to hold my hand and take away the cold sting of loneliness that creeps under my skin like an English winter.

I close my eyes, painting the image of my mother as I have countless times before, seated beside me, warm and kind and protective, her strong, elegant hand covering mine. I can almost feel the warmth, the sagging of the matress under her phantom weight. She hardly ever speaks to me. I do not remember her voice and imagining one is too sad. She only sits with me, sometimes Father too, and I am no longer so lonely, no longer so lost in this world.

I told Briony once, and she nodded sweetly and made as though she understood, but I know she could not, nor would I wish such understanding on her. People think grief diminishes with time or so they say in the aftermath of bereavement, but it is a part of me. It lives inside me like a little demon, waking every so often, tugging at my heart, drawing forth memories. I have grown used to it in a way where losing it would almost mean a part of me was missing.

After the Great War, I saw it in others as well. People I knew from town who used to play with their sons, suddenly walking around like ghosts. Or the young men, the scarred and maimed, as well as those still beautiful and physically healthy, who carried themselves through their days, through life, with the images of suffering, loss, and despair, never to be outrun. Most days there is enough lightness and distraction to stifle the gloom, but only most days. A sign that we are human, at least. A sign that we can remember, even if we would rather forget.

Running my left hand over the smoothness of the bedsheet, I open my eyes. I do not know how long they were closed in my melancholy trance. The room has grown gloomy and even colder. As I stand up, rubbing my arms, I shiver.

I turn to close the window and catch sight of a flash of bright blue. Niobe is in the garden again. Is this a regular occurrance? Wearily and warily I am about to close the window when I hear the accented voice of Yannick. Unlike the last time I heard the two of them, this night they must be closer, for their voices are clear and seem to be coming from below my window. Perhaps in all the excitement, Niobe forgot that I am occupying the guest room?

I lean close, crouching slightly, to remain undetected, should they venture a glance in my direction. I feel only moderate shame for eavesdropping again. A murder investigation is in full swing, and a little spying won't hurt a soul.

"Do they know?" Niobe's voice is hard and accusing.

"No, I am certain." Yannick answers, rolling his r's.

"How can you be? Oh, how could you be so foolish! It will raise suspicion?"

Raise suspicion! What on earth are they on about? Am I to hear a confession?

"Do not worry." Yannick's voice is lower now, and I imagine him placing a calming hand on her shoulder. "Nothing happened. It was foolish, but nothing happened, and no one knows. We can forget about it."

There is some hesitation before Niobe replies. "Yannick, I do not want anyone to know the truth. It is enough that the English woman, Miss Carlisle does. I think she will keep quiet, but I don't want it going around."

"It won't, everything will be all right. I promise." Oh men, promises, promises. It would appear they are only speaking of the pregnancy. I wonder how much longer they can keep it a secret? If they do not marry soon, no one will believe the child was conceived in wedlock.

I crane my neck once more, trying to hear something else. There is only silence, and when I peak my head over the windowsill, the grove below is empty, save for a black cat, slinking away into the shadows.

I quickly undress, tossing my cotton sleeping shift over my head and depositing the blue silk dress I wore for dinner on the chair beside the dresser. Washing too fast to be very effective, I slip into bed, finding comfort in the soft, cool cocoon of freshly laundered sheets.

CHAPTER 29

The day of the festival of Saint George begins with the familiar screech of a crow, tearing me from a dream I cannot remember, though I know I was happy in it. What a pity! Oh well. I sit up straight at the sound, my head spinning for a moment from the abrupt motion. I wonder if the beast is the same one as before, and it has made it its mission to keep me from dawdling away the morning in bed? I climb out and walk to the window. Indeed, the creature is sitting on the highest branch of the tree, as yesterday, giving me an altogether critical look with those beady black eyes.

"I'm up, I'm up. You can stop this racket. You have won." I raise my hands, palms out. The bird is not familiar with diplomacy and continues croaking dismally.

The festival will begin in the evening, allowing people who work during the day to take part, since it falls on a weekday. I have plenty of time to find the most suitable attire. For now, I select a simple lilac skirt and white blouse with a lace collar. I would like to go into town later to mail the postcards. A weight is pressing on me for having been shamefully negligent in this area, and the sooner I have done my duty of communication, the sooner I will be lighter again and able to enjoy the festival.

At breakfast, I learn Jeffrey has already left for Heraklion. From Briony's tone of voice as she tells me this, I gather the tension between them has not eased. I keep reminding myself that Jeffrey is under significant pressure, and what happened at the excavation site is certainly disturbing. Still, my sentiments towards him are less than warm at the moment.

Briony, Daniel and I decide to walk into Miklos, instead of taking the bicycles. While the way down is enjoyable, the return trip is a trial, and we want to preserve our energy for the dancing this evening. Or at least I do. Briony tells me where the post office is located in the village, and within the hour we have put on our hats, rouged our cheeks (Briony and I, that is, Daniel, I believe, abstained), and begin our little trek down the dirt road.

The sun shines warm, but not burning, stroking my bare shoulders with its rays. I enjoy the walk, the hard, dry earth beneath my feet, the smells of wildflowers, which grow in abundant clusters by the roadside. Even the calls of seagulls, swerving, white and gray in the blue background above our heads, add to the atmosphere of exotic welcome I sought when I first arrived.

We chat about this and that, mostly what to expect from the festivities, rather than Jeffrey or Caspar or Darius. We are not so hardened that we no not need times of frivolity and distraction, even amid the turbulence we have faced these past days.

One positive outcome of this tragedy is the bond between us. Daniel and I, as well as he and Briony knew one other hardly at all. By now, we have reached a level of closeness and comraderie, which may never have been achieved had we not been thrown into this maelstrom together.

The village is abuzz with activity today. People all around are preparing for the party. Men on ladders are busy hanging colorful paper lanterns, women are tying bunches of blue and yellow flowers to the trees. The air is filled with cheerful chatter and a vibrant energy fueled by anticipation and happiness, which I hope is entirely infectuous.

Briony and Daniel also have letters to post, and the three of us are good business for the postmaster, who patiently stamps and marks every postcard or letter and adds the odd comment or question in his charming broken English about whether we like Crete, whether we like Miklos, and have we tried the figs this year? It is a small community, nothing like the London set I ran with, rather cozier and far more quaint. Life here could be so easy, couldn't it? If only it weren't for the cursed murder, blackmail, and domestic distress. If only, if only. If only it rained oranges, if only we could breath under water.

Alas, reality is upon us, and we run into Laria, colliding with our little group when we turn the corner. She is alone, no Kaia tugging at her hand. Her dark hair is piled on top of her head, a few curls tugged free by the wind frame her face.

"Oh, hello!" Briony greets her. Laria manages to plaster a half-convincing smile across her mouth.

"How are you?"

"Quite well, and you?"

"It is so busy here today. I am running some errands. It's taking longer than I thought. Everyone had the same idea."

"Will we be seeing you at the festivities tonight?" I notice the dark circles under her eyes.

"The festivities?" She looks puzzled for a moment, as if avoiding the preparations all around us were even a possibility. Quickly, she recovers and nods, smiling. "Oh yes, yes of course. We will all be there. You know Miklos is famous for the Saint George's day parties. You are in for a treat."

"It certainly looks promising." I return the smile and gesture at the bustle around us.

Laria nods again and glances down at her wristwatch. "Please do not think me rude, I have left Kaia with a neighbor, and I promised to be back in an hour."

"Of course," Briony exclaims. "We will see you all tonight."

With a quick goodbye, the doctor's wife is on her way. Briony pulls us in the direction of a small shop, a tinkling bell above the door. Daniel begs off, telling us he will wait at Hector's Café.

The inside of the shop is dimly lit, the only light filtering in from one open window. It smells faintly musty and dusty and all around us are bales and swatches of fabric.

"Look," Briony points to a roll of finely woven silk the color of ripe peaches.

"Lovely." I run a hand over the smooth material.

"Isn't it? I was here a while ago, and I thought it was the loveliest color, but it wouldn't suit me," she shakes her head, curls bouncing, before continuing, "not with my coloring. Someone with darker skin, however . . ." She hesitates, wearing a mischievous expression I know only too well.

"Yes?"

"Someone like Areta?" She turns the word into a question, assessing my reaction.

"Areta." I repeat the name quietly, thoughtfully. If Briony begins dressing the child, it is only a matter of time before she brings her home. Would that be so very bad? No, I decide, it wouldn't.

Briony lowers her gaze, brushing non-existant lint from the silk. "She has such a lovely complextion, don't you think? And maybe matching ribbons."

I can imagine of the little girl all dressed up, dancing around in her head. "Yes," I say carefully, "I am sure it would, but Briony—"

Her face tilts upwards in a show of defiance when she meets my eyes. Even in the gloom of the shop the determination that fills hers is unmistakble. "Don't talk me out of this, Evie. What hurt will it cause?"

"None, if you understand that giving Areta a dress is far removed from adopting her. Whatever step you take in that direction must be taken together with Jeffrey. I am on your side, but you cannot give a child a good home, if her would-be father is opposed to the plan."

"It is only a dress." Briony's voice is small with disappointment as she turns away, clutching the fabric to her breast.

The silk is bought, along with ribbons and a thin roll of white lace. What a child running around chasing cats should want with lace trimmings is beyond me. I make an order for a simple straw hat with a blue satin bow for Iona, who ought not be left out on account of her age.

Once in the sun again, we walk down a few of the wider alleys toward the café and Daniel. Briony speaks very little, and I am angry with myself for having allowed tension to creep up between us. Nevertheless, I can ease my mind knowing, what's done is done and will soon be overcome, at least in our case.

Daniel is sitting outside at what I secretly consider "our" table, sipping a pale golden nektar. I am immediately reminded of the dryness in my own throat and am pleased that Daion as soon as we are seated, rushes over with full glasses to quench our thirst. Excellent man.

"I hope you don't mind, I ordered for you." Daniel explains.

"Oh, I thought Daion was a mindreader," I smile and take a sip of the sweet juice. "It's delicious."

"Ambrosia of the gods." Daniel replies with a straight face.

"If that is so," I swirl the liquid in my glass, "ambrosia of the gods tastes suspiciously of orange juice."

Daniel shrugs and swallows the last of his drink, whatever it may be. "Did you find what you wanted? That shop was so small, I didn't think I would fit."

Briony and I glance at one another. She should know better than to think I would tell. I turn to Daniel with a smile on my face, masking the concern brewing inside me when I think of our trip to the draper.

"Oh, you were simply looking for an excuse to avoid shopping with us ladies, weren't you."

"Ah," Daniel lays a hand on hs heart in a dramatic gesture of defeat. "You have found me out. Still, I did not think my presence was required for your pleasure."

"As ever, your presence is most welcome and most pleasant." Briony says, the tightness of her face at odds with the humor in her voice. "We brought the owner good business." I gesture at the well-wrapped brown paper bundles beside our chairs.

"I expected as much. I was only worried I may have to comission one of the donkey carts to convey us homeward, should your excursion have proven too successful."

I roll my eyes at him.

"I am entirely serious, I assure you," he says, the sunlight making his eyes sparkle and his hair shine with a healthful luster.

"I am so looking forward to tonight." I glance around to where a man on a ladder is hoisting a flag of Saint George's cross up a makeshift pole. "It is all very exciting. I have been to many festivals before, but this different and new to me."

"They love festivities here," Briony explains indifferently. "It's always one Saint or another."

I ignore her lassitude and ask instead, "When will Jeffrey get back from the museum? Do you know? We don't want to be late tonight."

Briony sighs, crumbling a biscuit from the basket between her fingers. "He said he would be back by four. Who knows? It is bound to be a trying day. He may not even want to come along."

"Oh, he must!" I protest. "He needs some fun and distraction, besides his friends will all be there."

"We will convince him," Daniel replies with certainty. "Anyone for more ambrosia?"

CHAPTER 30

An hour later, we are back at the villa. We were held up for a while by a few of Briony's acquaintances who wanted to be introduced, and who then went on to tell us stories and anecdotes about past years' feast days before letting us go on our way.

The cool interior of the large house is pleasant after spending hours in the dry, dusty heat. I unpin my hat and follow Briony who was distracted and silent all the way home when Daniel catches my arm.

"Evelyn, may we speak for a moment?"

"Of course. Have you discovered anything new?" My mind immediately runs in the direction of Caspar's demise.

"No, nothing." He seems awkward. Gone is the joking, easy banter we shared all day.

"Is everything all right?" I ask, wanting to shout stop being so mysterious!

"Yes, it is only, the funeral." He swallows, looking very young, and very much a man who has been to too many funerals. Though of course, each one is one too many in any lifetime.

"Have you made arrangements? Can I help?" Without a thought, I take a step toward him.

"I've arranged it for Friday. A short service in Miklos and then to the cemetary."

I offer him a sympathetic smile. "It has to be done. Laying him to rest may grant you some peace."

He nods and runs a hand over his jaw. "You are right. It was only, it was strange and sad arranging this."

"I wish I could have been of some help."

"It was best that I should do it. The reason I am mentioning it is just, well, could you tell the others? I . . ." he trails off, shuddering ever so slightly. His reaction does not escape my notice.

"I'll tell them as soon as Jeffrey gets in. Don't worry. Would you like to have anyone else there? Nikolas or Laria, Paul and Rosie? Anyone?"

"I think Laria will decline an invitation. The mood Nikolas was in last time we saw him makes me believe he knows the truth, and her going to Caspar's funeral would only cause more trouble for them."

"Maybe you should ask her anyway, or I can. It is only right that he should have someone there who loved him."

"Yes, maybe. We will see."

"I won't suggest inviting Darius. I doubt he would come."

"Who knows?" Daniel raises his eyebrows. "If he is innocent in all of this, his relationship with Caspar remained relatively unsullied to the end."

I detect a hint of sarcasm, even anger in his voice, leading me to assume he is far from convinced of the museum curator's clean conscience.

"If Darius killed Caspar, it is only a matter of time before he is discovered. There are so few suspects, surely any one of them will be thoroughly investigated and any hole in their story pounced upon by the police."

"I hope so. Though in the end, what good will it do? If Darius is guilty, he will face the noose. It won't bring back Caspar."

"Nothing can do that. Occasionally, I catch myself wondering . . . Do you think sometimes an eye for an eye is justified?"

He looks at me in surprise, his head slightly tilted, "I hadn't taken you as someone in favor of such extreme measures."

I frown, "I hadn't either."

"I know what you are saying, at least I think so. In some cases, ultimate retribution seems the only punishment befitting the crime."

"That may be so, but retribution has many faces. Justice can become vengance, which can become murder. It can take on a vicious, cyclical quality."

"Let us stop speaking of such miserable things now." Daniel straightens. "Let us talk of the festival, the delightful weather and of how we may tease Jeffrey tonight." He smiles and offers me his elbow.

I take it and say, "Lead the way."

To my surprise and Briony's relief, Jeffrey arrives on time and in better spirits than the prior evening. It has been decided the museum will continue with the excavation, and it has hired additional security in the form of three guards in rotating shifts. Should anything worth stealing be dug up, anything that cannot easily be moved, more guards will be hired. Jeffrey emphasizes that he and Paul offered their services, but were told to wait until the time comes.

I have my doubts regarding Jeffrey's ability as a particularly competent guard . . . Paul on the other hand, with his Viking-build, may be of greater use, if only for the purpose of intimidation.

The house is abuzz with activity as the staff joins us in getting ready to enjoy an evening off at the festivities. Niobe looks better than she has in some days, her nose not so pale and her eyes not so tired. Perhaps she is finally deciding how to proceed with Yannick. Their secret trysts in the garden are probably for the purpose of making plans. I must confess, they do not act exceedingly romantic toward one another. Whenever I watch them crossing paths, they appear casually friendly, nothing more. Every so often, I catch Yannick gazing at her retreating figure, a look of longing adoration written across his features, and I feel a pang of pity. Their feelings are in all likelihood unequal. I am oddly defensive of the pale Pole, far from home and willing to take on another man's child because he is infatuated with the pretty Greek lass. It bodes for disappointment. But I will stay optimistic. Love can grow, especially from trust and friendship, so I may well be proven wrong. Hopefully.

In my room, dabbing on lipstain I hear a knock at the door.

"Come in!" I call out before asking who it it is. I am surely too trusting.

It is Niobe—speak of the devil—carrying my cream cashmere jacket, from which two of the dainty mother-of-pearl buttons had come perilously loose.

"I mended your jacket, miss. Shall I put it away?"

"Thank you. Yes, please, although," I put down the lipstain and glance at the window, framing the glowing blue sky. "Do you think it will grow cold? The evenings can be surprisingly chilly. Perhaps I ought to wear it? What do you think," I stand up and strike a pose. "Will it go with this dress?"

Niobe smiles one of her rare smiles and holds the jacket into the air as if I were a paper doll. "Yes, it will look nice. The gray buttons match your eyes."

"So they do," I note quite pleased.

"Athena is said to have had gray eyes." Niobe adds, gently arranging the garment on the bed, then strides over to the open wardrobe to hang up a pile of dresses I tried on and discarded on the back of a chair.

"And boundless wisdom. I should be glad of that, too. Alas," I tilt my head, "I must contend with what I have. Gray eyes it is."

"You have so many beautiful clothes." Niobe slides a blue charmeuse Lanvin dress onto a padded hanger.

"You don't have to clean up this mess. I can do it later."

"Later you will be exhausted. I don't mind. It's my job." She is speaking more than ever before. Could it be that she is warming to me? Or does she merely need someone to talk to? Someone who knows her sercret.

"Thank you. You are coming later, aren't you?" I crouch down on the edge of the bed, folding up a cardigan, to have something to do while she does her work.

"Yes, Mrs. Farnham gave all of us the evening off. She is a good employer."

I smile. "Do you like working here? You can tell me the truth, I can keep a secret." Instantly her face falls, and I realize I chose the wrong words. "I only meant—"

"No, it is all right, I . . ." she breaks off, continuing her task, not meeting my eye.

"Niobe, are you well? How are you coping?" I feel selfish and foolish for having neglected to inquire before.

"I am fine. I was ill for a few days in the mornings, but I am told it is normal."

"Are you excited?"

She pauses, her face as ever, betraying little of what goes on behind it. "Of course."

"Have you made plans for the wedding? Is there anything I can do to help?" I let the offer hang between us, hoping she will grasp it.

She presses her full lips together and swallows. "We are going to have a small ceremony this month. Only my family. It is best that way."

"Hm . . ." the muscles in my forehead tighten. Niobe looks stolid as ever, but her voice betrays her. She does not sound happy, and whether it is because of the child or the possibly unwelcome wedding, I cannot say. "Is it what you want?"

Her hesitation lasts a moment too long to lend her answer credence. "Yes, of course. I want to be married. I want my baby to have a father, a family."

Just not Yannick.

"Niobe, forgive me if I am being inquisitive, but the father, the real father—"

"Yannick will be the father." Her tone hints at deep stubbornness, and I fear she is trying harder to convince herself than me.

"Then I am happy for you both."

She smiles, though faintly. "I am certain. Yannick is a good man. He will be a good husband, a good father."

I nod, not wanting to cause her further distress. "Then it is all very good. Now," I stand up and step towards the wardrobe, "this dress," I tug at a draped Paquin in a startling pink, "would suit you beautifully. The color is made for someone with your complexion. Or would you prefer a different one?"

She looks startled. "I-I can't—"

"You must! I insist. You will look lovely in whatever you wear, of course." I add hastily, not wanting to offend the proud woman.

"I don't know . . ."

"Here," I pull the dress out of the wardrobe, holding it up to her. It is made of a loosely draped silk that ought to fit, though her figure is more voluptuous than mine. "You don't have to decide now. Take it with you and see if you like it when you try it on."

"This is very kind—"

I hold up a hand. "Nonsense, it is selfish of me, really. I would love to see worn by someone it suits. I look absurd in the color, and it would be a sad waste it was never worn."

"If you insist." She is not convinced, though I observe the pleasure in her face as I thrust the dress into her hands, the fabric smooth and soft to the touch.

"You had better get ready. And I must try not to spill anything on myself before we leave. Go on, enjoy your evening."

"Thank you, I hope you like the feast. It is always good fun."

"I am sure I will. It will doubtless be an evening to remember."

CHAPTER 31

Later we assemble in the entrance hall. Niobe, I am happy to see, is looking resplendant in the pink dress, which drapes elegantly around her body, the modern version of a toga, although I suppose that description hardly does it justice. Lacking Niobe's curves, I have done what I could for my appearance this evening. The occasion is not formal enough to warrant the silver crepe-de-chine Worth I brought for a special occasion, so I decided on a subtle, far more comfortable, pale rose silk dress with a dropped waist and silver beading at the hem. Briony glows in a vibrant green skirt and a blouse of a darker emerald green. The men are equally dapper, wearing freshly pressed trousers and shirts, without ascots or ties. It is to be a party, after all.

"Are we ready?" Jeffrey asks, though he makes it clear by his taut expression, he is the least eager to be going.

"Yes," Briony settles her hat in place, casting a glance at the ornate hall mirror leaning against one wall. "How do I look?" She does a little twirl.

"Lovely, as always." I loop my arm through hers as we stride to the door.

Yannick, who is waiting outside, stands proprietarily beside the gleaming Delage. He will drive us first and then come and fetch Cook and Niobe in a second run. We could have walked, but later on, when it is dark and we are weary, a car will be a nice luxury to have at our disposal. I have the sneaking suspicion Jeffrey intends to creep away earlier. He is in no mood for a feast, obviously joining us as a favor to his wife. It might be for the best, if he absented himself, should his face continue to reflect the woes of the world rather than the merryment of his fellow revelers.

In no time we are bundled in and whisked down the drive towards the village. From a distance, the bright garlands streaming from the ancient gate are already visible. Yannick is forced to leave us here as the road is blocked by a rush of revelers. From somewhere to our right, cheery music is wafts through the air, accompanied by the mouth-watering aroma of cooking.

"Let's follow these people," Daniel suggests, and we join a throng of men and women, chattering happily. What they are saying is a mystery to me.

Briony points up at a St. George's cross, made entirely of red and white carnations. "Oh my, they have gone to a lot of trouble. What a scene!"

The alley is crowded, and people are merry. Men let their little ones sit on their shoulders, and women laugh merrily, white teeth gleaming in generous mouths.

As we reach the village square, we find a large animal roasting over a spit and a five man ensemble playing a jaunty tune on a low, make-shift stage. A barrel-chested man, no taller than myself, is pouring out a song in a rich barritone, all the while tapping his feet on the wooden planks in rhythm to the music. Small groups or couples are dancing before him, black curls and colorful scarves swirling through the air.

It has grown cooler already. As I turn my body to look around, I catch sight of Laria and Nikolas not far off, talking to Paul and Rosie. Paul looms large, a protective presence as Rosie peers unblinkingly into the distance. He is holding her hand, but she doesn't seem to notice. How hard it must be for him, and for her, if she is at all aware.

"Briony," I gesture at the group, "should we say hello?"

"Yes! Jeffrey, Daniel." She tugs at her husband's sleeve. "We've found our friends. Let's go over to them."

Jeffrey perks up ever so slightly. Probably he anticipates an opportunity to talk to Paul about the museum or some such matter. Oh well, whatever makes him smile this evening will do. Like his friend, Daniel also gravitates toward the tall Dutchman, who breaks into a toothy welcoming smile.

Laria, facing us, breaks into a smile and waves her hand. "You've found us! We were wondering whether we would be able to pick you out in this throng. There are more people this year than any other I can remember. Are you enjoying yourselves?"

Laria is in better spirits than the last time we met. Nikolas has lost the tightness in his features and chats amiably, breaking off occasionally to accept a kiss or an embrace from a neighbor or friend, who recognizes him in the crowd. He proves to be a popular man and a well-respected doctor. At one point, an older woman tugs at his sleeve and gives him a creased smile, whispering some words in a raspy voice and disappearing after he gently pats her hand and whispers something back.

"Nikolas saved her grandson's life years ago." Laria explains, more bemused than impressed, leading me to believe this story has been told many a time. "The boy had climbed onto a set of shelves to reach a jar of honey when the whole set fell on him. He might have been killed, but Nikolas was next door with a patient and was able to save him. The woman, Ilia, she always thanks Nik, every time she meets him." Laria points at a boy of about eight or nine. "There is the grandson. Hale and healthy!"

"What incredible luck to have a doctor so close by," I say, and Nikolas nods bashfully.

"It was a coincidence. I did what I could. He will always have a bit of a limp, but—"

"But he is alive." Laria squeezes his arm. He looks at her, and in that moment I see forgiveness. His rough face relaxes, and his mouth widens into a grin.

"He is alive."

"Why don't the two of you have a dance," Briony suggests, gesturing at the growing mass of people hopping and swaying to the wild rhythm of the music. "If I can tear my husband away from Paul for a moment, we shall join you."

Nikolas gives his wife an uncertain glance. She ignores it and pulls him away into the crowd. I follow them with my eyes, hoping he also understands that she is trying. Still, one must consider, forgiveness is one matter, forgetfulness another entirely.

I turn around again, and find myself beside Dymas, almost unrecognizeable in a loose cotton shirt and casual trousers.

"Miss Carlisle, how nice to meet you here. How are you enjoying Cretan hospitality?" He pushes a dark curl behind his ear and plants his hands on his hips.

"It's wonderful. I had not expected so many people . . ." I wave my hand in a sweeping gesture, "and the music and the dancing."

"Would you care for a dance?" He asks without preamble, and I answer without hesitation.

"Certainly. Though I must warn you. Slightly below my atrocious embroidery skills are my abilities as a dancer. If you value your feet, you can beg off."

He laughs, an open-mouthed laugh showing his white teeth to advantage. "I am a policeman, risk and danger are no obstacles for me."

"In that case, lead the way."

He takes my hand, dainty in his bear-paw and pulls me into a gap in front of the stage. The dance is energetic and follows no set of rules where feet ought to be placed, which works to my advantage. Dymas doesn't even wince when I accidentally kick his shin on a lofty turn or when I step on his right foot as I am jostled forward by an even more excited dancer behind me.

It is nice to be here. Nice to be spinning, the energy and joy from the strangers pulsing around me. I sense color coming into my cheeks, the muscles in my legs springing and straining. It is nice to be alive.

Dymas is an excellent dancer. Despite his height and broad shoulders, his movements possess surprising grace as he whirls across the floor, never stepping on my feet, nor bumping into the people around us. Even

Briony and Jeffrey are dancing, her blond head bobbing, curls boucing. Jeffrey appears less enthusiatic, but not miserable, which is something.

I crane my head to search for Daniel and meet his eyes as he stands on the fringe of the crowd. His arms are folded across his chest, his face sternly impassive. Surely he cannot be jealous? No, surely not.

Dymas twirls me around again to face him, and Daniel's woes are pushed away. Tonight is meant for laughter, dancing, and cheerful company. The musicians break, and the song ends, the singer accepting cheerful applause and a goblet of wine to moisten his throat. Dymas leads me back to the others. Laria and Briony and their husbands are flushed as they congregate near Paul, Rosie, and Daniel.

"Ah, inspector, fancy seeing you here!" Briony has a question written on her face. I shrug ever so slightly, the universal sign to ward off judgement or curiosity.

As everyone begins to chat about this and that—the smells, the sights the sounds—my eyes dart over to Daniel. He is regarding Dymas with something akin to dislike, quite unwarranted as far as I can tell. But then, men will be men, Aunt Agnes would say. Greater wisdom was rarely spoken.

"Look, Darius has come." Briony's eyes widen.

"He has not been proven guilty of anything," Jeffrey comments sternly. "I would advise everyone to remember that." His point made, he strides forward, holding out his hand to the smaller man. Darius clasps it gratefully.

"Darius, we meet again," Dymas greets him with a smile, dulling the suspicious implication.

"Good to see you all." He is nervous. I have said before, my skills of perception are not impressive, but that much I can say with certainty. He is visibly tense, his narrow frame tight and his face drawn. I am still convinced he lied to Dymas about the blackmail and thus must be lying about the theft as well. Murder is such a ghastly, cruel affair . . . I somehow can connect him neither with such concealed villainy, nor a particular skill as an actor.

"Is your family here with you?" Briony's training as a lady shines through. Innocent until proven guilty. Good manners never go amiss. Or something like that.

"Yes, my parents are here. They have lived near the village their entire lives. They are always part of these events," he speaks quickly, his tongue tripping over his words, his accent more pronounced. Somehow, I am sorry for him. He may well have stolen something, and perhaps Caspar caught him, but theft is not murder.

I offer a small, hopefully reassuring smile. "It is quite a treat, all the people, the music, the smells . . ."

"I am glad you are enjoying it. Yes, one would not think a small village like Miklos capable of staging such an event." He meets my eyes. Something in his gaze makes me take a tiny step back.

"I think villages are the heart of Crete, or of any place." Jeffrey chimes in, and Darius turns his head, releasing me from his stare.

"Is everything all right?" Daniel's voice whispers behind me. I swivel around. The evening has grown into night. We are standing at the edge of this well lit square, and his face is half shadowed. There is comfort in his presence, and I am relieved for a reason I am yet to discern.

"Would you . . ." he swallows and glances at his shoes before tentatively looking up again, "would you care for a dance?"

The eagerness in his face pleases me enormously, and I smile in agreement.

He takes my elbow and leads me back to the dance floor where couples are spinning and swaying to the melodious sounds of the music, wafting through the night like whispy enchantments, enveloping us, pulling us closer.

This dance is over much faster than the first, I am certain, and in no time we are united with our group again. Darius has disappeared, and Paul and Rosie are standing a way off with another couple. Paul is easily found in a crowd, his gleaming blond hair standing out among the dark curls, his height making him a tree in the landscape wherever he goes. I wonder what he thinks among these groups of people, families, friends, lovers, with Rosie mute and impassive at his side. Does he want to scream at the injustice of it? Behind this open joviality, is there a man who feels trapped and alone with a partner who is no partner at all? If only I could ask these questions. Even if Aunt Agnes had not taught me manners, I know how improper such behavior would be. Nonetheless, with all these thoughts whirling about in my mind, I cannot help but wish I knew, just occasionally, what was happening inside the heads of the people around me. If I knew though, would I be disappointed or hurt or angry? We all deserve privacy; our secrets, locked in our minds, the ultimate treasure chests.

"There you are!" Briony waves and comes toward us, Jeffrey trailing behind, yawning in her wake. We cannot have been here much over an hour, and he is already yearning for the sweet silence of his home. Alas, tonight he must suffer some more. Briony looks in no mood to settle her well coiffed head on her pillow yet.

"I am starving!" Jeffrey states dramatically.

"Well, food can be had, my love," Briony rolls her eyes at me. "Let us see what they are roasting on the spit." She lowers her voice and whispers into my ear. "If he yawns one more time it will be him."

I chuckle. "But my dear, you must get used to early bedtime. Pretend Jeffrey is a child, patience is the key." She chuckles as I pull her and Daniel to a large table.

The table is set for a banquet. Mounds of pastries filled with spicy meat, spinach and cheese, cubes of lamb on wooden spikes, olives of all varieties, blocks of creamy white cheese and on and on it goes. No one needs to go hungry tonight. We make our donations. The money is intended for the repair of the church roof (church roofs, it seems, are perpetually in need of repair, a universal dilemma) and fill our plates with all sorts of delicacies. Soon Jeffrey is sated and crouches on an upturned barrel, looking like a pleased child.

The food, as I have come to expect here, is wonderful. However, I keep finding distractions all around me, before I know it, it has all gone cold. As have I, now that I think of it. My arms are covered in goosepricks.

"Briony, did I leave my jacket in the car?"

She furrows her brows. "You may have, I don't think I saw it once we left the car."

"Is Yannick around? I am feeling a bit of a chill."

"Yes, I saw him a while ago," she glances around. "There he is!" I follow her gesture and find the pale young man at the fringe of the crowd, speaking with an older man and a boy of about sixteen.

"I will quickly dash over and ask where he left the car."

"Shall I go with you?" Daniel offers, already lowering his plate.

"No, no," I shake my head. "Stay, I will only be a moment."

I squeeze my way through the throng of people. Everyone has been gripped by a monstrous hunger and is swarming to the buffet. Still, I manage to push through and meet Yannick and his group of friends.

"Yannick," I call out as I reach them, "would you tell me where you left the car? I need my jacket."

"It is only around the corner. I will get it for you."

"You are very kind, but I will not take you away from your friends." Nodding at them, I take off before he can protest. Get my jacket, indeed. I am not a child, I can manage this much. Fortunately, I have dropped the habit of speaking to myself, at least in public.

CHAPTER 32

The alley is well lit, and the occasional reveller comes my way. My heels make a soft tapping sound on the cobbles, an accompaniment to the music filling the night around me. As I reach the end of the lane and turn the corner, my eyes find the hulking form of the Delage a few houses away. The street is deserted here, dipped into shadow, a contrast to its light and bustle during the day. I am calm, the small crouched-together houses emanating a sense of cozy comfort rather than concealed menace.

The roof of the Delage is down. Yannick probably saw little chance of rain on a clear night such as this. I tilt my head back. The sky is blue velvet with tiny diamonds twinkling in a random pattern. I never learned the constellations, I should admit, I never felt much inclined to. Now I wish I could say, ah, there is Orion and isn't Pegasus ever so bright tonight? Even so, this natural spectacle is enough to make me pause for a moment to admire. A chill tingles down my spine as the cool evening air fills my lungs and feeds my body. How many others are looking at this sky right now, at this very moment? In England it may still be lighter; in London it will never be as clear. The sky and the sea surround this lovely strip of land, and I feel very small, enveloped in realms of blue beyond measure, which have been forever and may be forever more. My grandchildren or theirs will be looking at this same sky, at these same stars. I stand quietly for another moment, the world so large and uncontrollable around me, a force to be feared and revered. Suddenly, there is a sound farther up the road. My head snaps forward, and I am back on earth, back in a dark, empty street.

Pricking my ears, I identify the sound as that of footsteps. Light steps. Quick steps. Someone is searching for a loo probably, considering the vats of wine on offer tonight. The footsteps do not stop, and I peak around the car, shielding my view. Squinting in the low light, I make out a figure about fifty meters ahead. There is something familiar . . . Darius? Is it him? As if on cue, the figure turns. Instinctively I duck down. It is him. What to do? What to do?

Should I ignore it? He may be dashing off to relieve himself or to go home. Maybe he is meeting someone? A secret lover? Should I follow him? No other choice, really. At least none my feet, already stealthily creeping along the shadowed side of the road, will permit.

Darius does not turn back. His stride is quick and purposeful and nearly silent. I am walking on my toes to avoid my heels giving me away, an effort, which is costing me a fair bit of concentration.

We are nearing the end of the main street, and I speculate what to do if he simply enters a house and disappears. Probably walk back to the others and never say a thing. This really is quite improper of me. Despite this insight, I cannot shake off the suspicion that there is something amiss, something Darius is hiding. As he reaches the gate, he steps right through it. Blast! He is leaving the village. Oh, what should I do? Briony will have a fit if she discovers I am gone, but I can't give up now. Gnawing on my lower lip, I am jittery with indecision. I will have a quick look where he is going and then return to the others. I will be careful. Besides, all of this may very well be completely innocent. I am probably making a fool of myself.

Deciding to chance, it I follow. I could not have hesitated a moment longer, for Darius is a distance ahead of me now. It is difficult to keep my eyes on his shadowy form, away from the bright light of the town square. At least here, on the dirt road, I can walk properly. My toes are aching like anything. You are no ballerina, my body reminds me.

The museum curator walks on for a few minutes before turning right, apparently intent on hiking up the mountain. It is not a proper path at all, and I debate following him to the certain ruination of my freshly soled kidskin shoes, or turning back.

Again, curiosity is the stronger force, propelling me onward. The going is not easy in the dark and I tread carefully, aware of dangerously protruding roots or worse, a snake! Are there snakes on Crete? Heavens, I hope not. Ruined shoes and a snake bite! And the evening started out so well. I allow myself a quiet sigh. In for a penny, in for a pound. Soldier on, Evie.

Darius is moving alongside the mountain wall. Occasionally he runs his hand along the cracked rock, perhaps to steady himself. What is he doing? I am too far away to observe anything clearly and do not dare to move closer, lest he should become aware of my presence. Perhaps it is all quite harmless, and I am being irrational. Yet my instinct tells me to remain concealed.

The dark is growing even darker, and in the open country the night is colder. Luckily, I remembered my jacket before setting out on this fool's errand. In spite of the extra layer of fabric against my skin, I am shivering and sure to catch a monstrous cold. Was it maddness to come out here following a man, who may well be a murderer? The answer, now that I take a moment to think on it, is a resounding YES!

Before I can give up and hurry back along the road to Miklos, a flash of light glimmers in the near distance where Darius stood a moment ago. With nervous caution, I take a few quiet creeping steps forward, shielding my body as best I can, against the uneven rock wall and scraggly bushes.

Ahead, I see him more clearly now, his face illuminated by the white glow of a torch. Where did that come from, I wonder. Was he carrying it all along? Again and again the question runs through my mind, What is he doing here?

He walks on even more slowly, as if expecting something or someone up ahead. Suddenly, he stops, the waning moon casts a meagre light upon the scene, but it is enough. Pausing a moment, he disappears inside the mountain! A cave? He is entering a cave. Quickly, without much sense or thought, I scramble forward. Soon I have reached the mouth of the cave. It is a small black hole, not in the least inviting. Couldn't he have snuck off to meet his mistress or to sit in a garden? A cave? He had to choose a blasted cave in the black of night, and I had to be the one to see him.

Nothing to do now but follow. His beam of light flickers up ahead. He is making slow progress. Taking a deep silent breath, I sincerely hope ruined shoes are the only sacrifice I will have to make this night. Into the mouth of the beast.

The air inside the cave smells of dust and damp. Somewhere above me or beyond, I hear the monotonous dripping of water. The ground is sandy and soft, and my steps make no sound as I follow the man with the torch. He appears completely unaware of my presence, which I sincerely hope will remain so. I decide to count seconds to measure how long we walk from the entrance of the cave, realizing I will have to wait inside until he decides to return, for I have no chance of safely finding my way out without the guiding light of his torch.

After about three minutes, he stops again. He is standing before a flat rock wall. Maybe he has taken a wrong turn. Yet he doesn't search around as one who is lost may do. Instead, he passes the torch from his right hand to his left and slides his free hand along the right side of the wall. He presses against something and takes a step back.

Now, this sounds as if I have read the tales of Ali Baba one too many times, but the wall begins to move! It is tossing up a great swirl of dust, which dances thick and yellow in the light of the torch. Heavens, what is this place! Darius waits patiently, covering his mouth and nose to avoid the worst of the clouds of earthy air.

The dust settles and Darius steps through the opening in the wall. A cave within a cave. A secret lair. I rub my eyes, and hold my sleeve up to my mouth, carefully sliding around the rock I have been hiding behind and in the direction of the newly revealed portal. I must not cough or sneeze! Something very dubious is happening and—

He is speaking. Is there someone with him? What if he is keeping someone locked away in this place? For the first time this evening, I am afraid. I try to listen. He is speaking in rapid Greek mixed with the local dialogue. He may as well be speaking Chinese for all the good it does me. After a few moments, I have to believe he is the only one in there. No one answers. No other voice joins his. The glow from inside the cave intensifies, and I peak my head a fraction around the corner.

I almost gasp aloud. Darius has lit at least four torches within the chamber, revealing what he has been so careful to conceal. The room is full of relics. Not crumbly terra-cotta pots either; gold and marble statues, chalices and urns. And that is only my first impression. A treasure chamber? Or maybe a tomb? One thing is crushingly clear: Caspar was right about Darius' theft. But how? How could he make such a hoard vanish. It is obvious now, he must be the one who took the statue from the excavation. He has a car, after all. He has easy access and easy transport for whatever he deems worth having. Why though? He can study these objects as much as he wants. Why the need to hide them away, to deprive the world of such glorious finds? Is he driven by desire or by greed? Does he sell these pieces? Is he a smuggler, too? So many questions, and no answers.

Darius is still talking, not loudly, but I can hear him well enough to give me chills. His voice is as calm and measured as ever. I wish I could understand what he is saying, but I only make out the odd, meaningless word. He is moving around, the echo of his voice carries into different directions.

My fingers and feet are beginning to grow numb from the cold, and I yearn to move or cozy up safely under my soft blanket and forget I was ever such a fool to come here. I refrain from sighing. Instead, I lean closer against the wall. Please, Darius, finish whatever you are doing and lead me out of here!

As I shift my body to fit into a crevice in the rock, I hear a light tapping sound right above me. Horrified at the thought of nasty little creatures lurking in the dark, I look up. The light emanating from the opening in the wall is enough to show me that not a bat, but a long, dripping stalachtite hanging above me. Where then did that sound—

Before I can finish the thought, a monstrous rock detatches itself from the ceiling and crashes to the floor only fingerwidths from my feet. I cannot stop myself. I give a startled shriek, which echos like a cruel reminder of my folly. Then utter silence. In a panic, I make myself fit tighter into the crevice. My legs are aching, and a jagged rock bites into my back. Darius has stopped talking to himself, and I hear footsteps drawing closer.

If I am lucky, he may think it is an animal? What sounds do bats make? No, it is no use. He is coming, and he will find me and then . . . What will he do? Will he hurt me? What can I say? What explanation can I offer for being in this obscure place?

I hold my breath, my heart is thumping so loudly against my chest I may as well call out: Here I am!

The beam of light from the torch grows brighter and finally Darius' figure emerges, framed by the lit chamber behind. "Hello?" His voice is tentative, and he is speaking Greek. Might it be wise simply to answer back? Better than prolonging this misery. I cannot find my voice. A lump is lodged in my throat, and I feel the suffocating fear that I will not be able even to scream.

Darius calls out again, moving out of the make-shift doorway. He is only steps away from me now. The torch beam dances through the cave, light cutting into the darkness with the sharpness of a blade. And then . . . my face glows. The ray falls upon me.

"You?" Darius sounds more puzzled than angry, although it is difficult to say with the shadows blackening the contours of his eyes.

"I-I . . ." I stammer amid the flutter of hysteria rising within me, grateful to find I can still make a sound. This relief passes quickly as the realization dawns on me that nobody at all can hear us.

"What are you doing here?" His voice is calm. He is already overcoming his initial shock at finding me. He takes three quick steps closer, and before I can say another word of pointless explanation, he takes hold of my arm and yanks me forward.

"Please—"

"You should not have done this. You should not have done this." he repeats himself, pulling me towards the entrance of the chamber. He is holding the torch tightly in his right hand and has his back half-turned as he drags me along. I cannot see his face, which frightens me even more.

"Darius, I am sorry. It was foolish of me. If you will let me go, I won't say a word." I realize my mistake as the words pass my lips.

Darius whips around. "You won't say a word? So you know!" His dark eyes grow wide behind his glasses, light reflecting eerily in those small round lenses. I see my own reflection in them. My face is drawn into a terrified grimace.

"I only meant—" I try, but he gives my arm a forceful tug, and we are in the treasure hall. All around us are urns and vases, chalices and chests, statues and votives worthy of museum treatment. The torches positioned at various angles gently illuminate these treasures, casting everything in a pale golden glow. There is gold aplenty as it is.

"Why did you follow me?" Darius demands, his voice taking on a higher pitch, and his short, neat nails dig into the skin of my arm.

"I am sorry. Truly, I never meant any harm—" I break off in horror as my eyes fix on the empty ones of a skeleton in the corner. My jaw falls, and I stumble backward. There is a dead person, a long dead person, feet away from me.

"He turns his head wildy, following my gaze. When he looks at me again, his expression is bland and unreadable. "Oh, it is only Andros." He shifts again and begins addressing the dead man. "This foolish girl, Andros! She should not have come here," he shakes his head. "No, no, she should not."

My breath is stuck in my throat, and I feel a wave of nausea washing over me. I am not built for this. I am not brave or strong. I want to be safe and alive, not staring into the empty eyesockets of a dead man. But I am here, and I must try somehow to stay at least outwardly composed, in the hope that it will calm this mad-man as well.

"Darius, could you . . . could you let my arm go, please, you are hurting me. I can't run. I don't know the way."

He gives me a curious gaze, his eyes narrowing. To my surprise, he releases his grip entirely. Angry pink marks are imprinted on the pale flesh of my forearm. It is such a relief to be out of his grasp, I hardly care. Darius has begun pacing, casting both Andros and me strange looks in turn.

"You know. You know now, and you will tell. You will ruin everything." He shakes his head, twisting his hands together.

"I won't," I attempt meekly. "I won't say anything, I don't know anything, please, Darius, let me go. I am only visiting. I will be gone soon."

Darius doesn't show any sign of having heard me. His forehead is creased, and his specs sit crookedly on his nose. He doesn't seem aware.

"You didn't understand either. You, you—" he points an accusing finger at the skeleton, "you would have betrayed me, too! Would have betrayed this!" He gestures wildly at the opulence surrounding us.

What in heavens name is he raving about. If only I could snatch up one of the torches and make a run for it, but I am afraid to attempt anything that may startle him. He is clearly out of his right mind, and I am convinced he must be Caspar's killer. The thought makes me shudder, and my thoughts drift to the unpleasant possibility of no one else ever finding out. I could disappear like this poor Andros, and no one will ever know what happened. The possibility is so unbearable, I force it from my mind.

Darius interrupts my thoughts and pulls me back to the present. He is standing, feet apart, in front of the skeleton. I see his profile, but the light is low and his expression again is hard to decipher.

"What will I do with her, Andros? Tell me brother, what will I do?"

Brother? Brother! I swallow and take a small, slow step backwards. Andros is his brother. What devils are at work in this place?

"Answer me, you fool," he sounds angry now, jabbing a finger into the air. "You don't know. Ha, you don't know anything. I was always the intelligent one. I—" he pounds his chest in a primitive gesture, "I knew you would be too greedy, too selfish. You only wanted me to come along so I would help carry, so I would be impressed by you, big brother. I wasn't though, was I?" He lets out a high-pitched giggle. "I got you. And now it's all mine. Mine, mine, mine. You wanted to sell it, be rich, leave Crete. Stupid, stupid!" He swivels around, and I nearly fall back at the shock.

"Don't think I forgot about you. I followed him and look at him now," he points at the figure of his brother. "You followed me. You are trying to steal from me. You are trying to stab me in the back. Well," he steps closer, and I instinctively shrink back, "you will not trick me, silly girl. I know the tricks. I created the tricks." His eyes are wide and mad. He runs a hand through his hair, making it stand on end. Within the stretch of an hour, a neat, dignified man has turned into a raving lunatic. Or was the lunatic only disguised as the museum curator? Which mask fits?

"Darius, you don't understand. I was simply curious. I do not want to take anything, I swear it. It's all yours. All yours"

"Yes," he says slowly, like a child, "all mine." A flash of confusion appears on his face. He narrows his eyes and strokes his chin in a gesture reminding me oddly of Daniel. If only he would come and find me. If only anyone would.

"Now," I say echoing his tone, "if you lead me out of here, we can go back to the village. Everything will be all right. This will be our little secret. I am good at keeping secrets."

Is he actually considering this? His shoulders hunch forward, and he sighs tiredly before looking at me again. His eyes meet mine.

"You do not understand," he says. "They will take it away from me. All my treasures, all taken away. Andros tried and . . . " he breaks off, looking over at the broken body of his brother.

"What happened?" My voice is very low, almost a whisper. I hope it calms him somehow. He turns back to me, a lone tear slides down his cheek.

"Andros, my brother . . . he heard some tale of a treasure in the mountain. He found it, and he took me with him. He said we would share the profits, the spoils. He said, 'We will be rich men'. Crete had just declared union with Greece, and Andros wanted to go to Athens. 'We will be rich men, we could begin life anew in Greece', he told me. We could become merchants, buy a ship. I didn't want to go. I wanted to stay. I wanted the treasure not the glory, not the rewards."

Darius is suddenly somewhere far away. He is lost in his world. Should I pity him? I need only look at the skeleton of Andros Calandra, leaning with his bony back against the wall, to know that pity for this man means closing my eyes to his deeds, and that I cannot do. Theft I could overlook, but murder... murder is unforgiveable. And irrespective of such philosophical meanderings, I may well become his next victim! No, pity is out of the question. Only survival counts now.

"All of this is mine. My heritage," he waves forlornly at the pieces placed neatly around us. "I could not let him take it, let him sell it." He runs a hand over the head of a small gold statue, tenderly as if he were stroking the head of a child.

"You killed him." The words come out before I can stop myself, but he doesn't seem alarmed, not even shifting his gaze to find mine.

"I had no choice." His hand is resting on the statue's head, as though the touch, feeling the cool gold against his skin, justifies his action. Gold and marble in exchange for a brother. Disgusted, I want to move away. I stop myself, afraid any abrupt motion will alert him and draw him back into his state of manic raving.

"What about your parents? What did you tell them?" I ask, not knowing where the words come from, grateful for the small space of clarity left in my head, keeping me from running and screaming; keeping me from joining him in madness.

"Father was at sea, and mother was visiting her sister in Chania. When they returned, I said Andros had gone to away," he chuckles. "I even wrote a letter. Everyone believed it. Andros was always talking about leaving."

I have to swallow, the lump in my throat will not move. He robbed his parents of a son, and laughs at his ingenuity in deceiving them.

"A-and Caspar," I nearly choke on the name, still I have to ask, "was he blackmailing you? Is that why you killed him?"

Darius turns his head, his expression betraying his surprise. "He blackmailed me, yes, the filth, but I did not kill him."

Now it is my turn to be shocked (though, admittedly, I must have looked rather shocked for the better part of an hour now, so the expression does not alarm Darius).

"What do you mean?" I ask. "You didn't kill him?"

"No. I would have, probably," he shrugs as if taking a life is a trivial task. "It was a great relief someone did it for me. He was a vile man, you know." He wrinkles his nose and shakes his head again.

"I-I see. Do you know who—"

"No. Not a clue. Whoever it was did a very nice job. Poison is a good way to kill, I couldn't use it, unfortunately. It is much better. Much cleaner."

"You used—"

"Oh, a knife. Only sensible thing. On that day I was behind him; Andros always leading the way; Andros always in charge," he grimaces. "And then," he mimicks, drawing a daggar and perfoms a high stab in the air, "done. Very quick. He did not suffer. Not much, anyway."

He did not suffer. I am certain those few last moments of his were pure agony. If the physical pain was not horrendous, the pain of knowing his own brother, with whom he had shared his greatest secret, had stabbed him in the back, had betrayed him, would certainly have been unbearable. Darius talks so easily as if he has been waiting to tell someone. He has to get everything out. I dare not think why else he is so open with me.

"Has your family never wondered why he never returned? Why he hasn't kept in touch?"

"No. I write the letters."

"They are not post-marked?"

"It does not matter, they believe it. Or they want to believe. I write, 'I am very happy in Athens.' or 'I have found good work here,' and they are happy."

I wonder whether they really believe him or need simply wish to? Darius has been careful thus far. There is a chance he has truly mislead even his parents. He falls silent and lets his eyes bask in the glory of what surrounds him. Does he fear it is finally over? Or does he think he can go on as he has? Oddly enough, Caspar's death, of which he insists he is innocent, may be his undoing. A question, gnawing at me all this time, pushes again to the forefront of my mind, and I am too drained to fight it off.

"What will you do now?" What will you do to me? The question hangs heavy in the air, and my muscles tense awaiting his answer.

When he finally answers, he does not look at me, but at the body of his brother. "You know there is only one thing I can do." A chill runs down my spine, and I shudder.

"Please," my voice is hoarse, "Darius, I won't say a word, please. I'll leave. Go back to England. Truly, only—"

"No," he takes a menacing step toward me, his eyes glinting like burning embers. A predator's eyes. It is not his eyes that make me tremble, but the smile twitching on his lips. An inhuman smile, cruel and cold.

I have to buy time. If I can somehow immobilize him, knock him over with one of his little treasures, I can try to make an escape. Anything is better than complacently waiting for execution.

"Before," I swallow, the words clinging to my throat like sticky honey, "before you do it, at least tell me whether it was you who stole the statue from the excavation." A silly last request, but I need to buy time, and this seems the only option.

His grin widens and he shows his teeth. "Of course it was me! Do you think I would let anyone else have her? Do you think I would leave her outside in the cold night? No," he shakes his head emphatically, "I saved her. I rescued her. She is with me now where she belongs." The way he speaks of the statue is unsettling. Nonetheless, it spurs me on in my quest to convince him that I am harmless.

"Is she here?" I play along, hoping he does not see through my feigned sincerity.

He is obliviously immersed in his world, nodding vigorously and rubbing his hands together. "Where else would she be? She is here, among her brothers and sisters."

I feign a smile. "I don't know if I believe you. Perhaps you are only boasting. Perhaps, as with Caspar, someone else is responsible." His eyes grow wide and his mouth straightens into a thin line. I hope I haven't pushed him too far. This may be the only chance I have.

"I am telling the truth! You-you," he points an angry finger at me. "You don't know anything, English woman!"

"Show me." Two words. Simple enough, the two words my plan hinges on, my survival plan.

He wavers, narrowing his eyes at me. I try to look unaffected, all but impossible as one might imagine.

"You will not touch her!" His tone is sharp, warning a naughty child.

"I promise."

He licks his lips and nods. "Come."

Yes, turn your back on me, Darius. Trust me. He begins to lead me across the chamber. Lights flicker, casting eerie shadows on the wall, armless, headless figures like the ones I pass. He has created a strange sort of order. The pieces are striking, none very large. I keep searching for anything within my reach I might reasonably lift to hit him with before he understands what I am doing. Easier said than done. Everything is just a bit too far to touch, and I am afraid to alarm him by making any sudden moves he might sense even with his back turned. I haven't much time, and this opportunity will pass quickly.

"Here, come, come, be careful. Don't touch anything."

He leads me to the left side of the cave, and I see my chance. Ten steps away from me is a golden votive statue, no larger than a bottle of wine, I can easily wield it. My heartbeat races as I draw closer. Five steps, three, one—

"Look!" Just as I reach for it, he turns around, pointing upward. I drop my arm as innocently as I can, fixing an interested expression on my face. We are standing in front of a small female nude. He has set her atop a blue velvet sheet like a crown jewel. She is beautiful, that much is true.

"Very nice. Yes, very nice." I try to cover the fear in my voice.

"Nice? She is beautiful! My lady, my princess." Darius stares dotingly at the figurine, his eyes hidden behind the reflection in his glasses. This is the moment. He is in her thrall.

In one swift motion, I take a tiny step back, swipe up the votive and bring it crashing down onto the back of his neck. He makes a gurgling noise and doubles over. For a moment I stand frozen to the spot, the crumpled body of the museum curator on the ground. Have I killed him? Oh God, I hope not! I cannot bring my trembling fingers to touch him, to feel for a pulse. Dropping the statuette, I grab one of the neaby torches. Out. Out, out, out, is my only thought now.

CHAPTER 33

In quick strides, I am at the chamber's entryway. Glancing back to reassure myself no angry lunatic is pursuing, I climb through the opening. For a second, I close my eyes, trying to remember which way to go. Right. It was right, because coming in we turned left. Good.

Holding the flickering torch in front of me, I make my way. At the next intersection of two pitchblack tunnels, I am less certain. Wavering, yet afraid to wait too long, an idea strikes. Might not Darius have left some marks to show himself the way?

Frantically, all the time awaiting his pursuit, I hold the light up to the walls, searching for a sign, a symbol to show me the way. Carefully, I run my hand over the rough stone. There is nothing unusual on its damp, cool surface. What am I to do? My breath is ragged and my heart frantic, ready to burst from my chest, desperate as I am for escape. Taking a few steps toward the tunnel to the right, I am almost certain it is the one we came from.

Nervously, I plunge into the darkness. The light emanating from the torch is weak and small, barely enough to guide the way, though hopefully enough to keep me from plumeting into some hidden depth.

I move quickly, all the time afraid any wrong move may send me tumbling, or worse. After some time, I reach another crossroads. A few minutes have gone by, and if I am moving in the right direction, the exit of the cave ought to be nearing soon. Unfortunately, it is night outside, and sunlight won't be beckoning me forth. Still, I sense it is the correct path. Darius did not make many turns, and the tunnels I have chosen led only in a slight curve off the central way. I would have remembered any drastic bends, but cannot be certain. I only hope not to be heading too deeply into the wrong direction, farther and farther into the mountain. I push down my swelling sense of panic, building inside me. One way or another, I have to get away from Darius.

Walking on, the torch heavy in my damp hand, my arm is growing weary, and rough stones poke through the thin soles of my shoes. Every few moments I stop, holding my breath to listen for sounds of pursuit, but as yet have heard none. I wonder whether Darius has woken up, and, if so, what he will do.

Onward it goes. I must be reaching the mouth of the cave soon. The dust in the air is making my eyes sting and water. I cannot dally. Wiping away the tears with the sleeve of my jacket, I push on. Rounding a slight bend, I feel a chill. No, not a chill, a breeze! Air! Fresh air is coming from somewhere ahead. My feet pull me forward faster, the lure of freedom a magnet my whole body cannot resist.

Yes, I see it! I want to scream with relief. Vague outlines of a hole in the wall. My escape. Thank heavens, my escape! I almost fly the next few feet, so fast am I at that most welcome, perfect, beautiful portal. Sticking my head out first, I suck in a welcome lungful of fresh air. Casting a quick look around, I make certain Darius hasn't come by some other route to intercept me. No one in sight. Quickly, with all measure of lady-like decorum abandoned, I scramble out into the open. Taking a moment to steady myself, I turn to the right side of the mountain and break into a run.

The cool night wind bites my cheeks. It is a good pain, a sign of being alive and free. In moments, I reach the dirt road. The torchlight is growing dim, and I hope it will last until I see the village. The slight shimmer of the moon will be enough to guide me on the last stretch of the way. It doesn't take long. Like Hermes with his winged sandals, I fly over the dusty road, my feet barely touching the earth. Desperation and fear burn inside me, fueling me until I can finally collapse in safety.

My lungs are stinging as I discern the village gates in the distance. Without a motor or bicycle, Darius would be hard-pressed to catch me now, and if he did, I could scream and would likely be heard. My throat is dry from running as I stumble through the gates and into the village.

A hum of cheerful music still fills the air, and it smells as it did before, salty and delicious. Everything has remained as it was, while for me, everything has been turned upside down and quite roughly at that. Slowing to a walk, my pulse is still pumping rhythmically in my neck. I cast my eyes around. Where are the others? Where is Dymas? Yes, Dymas. I have to show him the cave so they can find Darius, not least to tell me that I haven't killed him.

With quick steps, while my legs feel like jelly after the frantic run, I rush towards the town square. At the sound of voices, I sigh with immense relief. People, I am amongst people again. Leaning momentarily against the high wall to my right, assailed by exhaustion, I force myself on. The music grows louder and the lights brighter, such a welcome assault on the senses. Finally in the square, I sweep my eyes around, searching for a familiar face. Where are they? The Delage was still parked by the road. They wouldn't have left without me.

I start to feel dizzy. There are so many people. So many faces and noises and smells. Dancing and laughing and drinking. Where are they? Where are they?

Summoning the last of my energy, I shout, "Briony! Daniel! Jeffrey!" My voice is not as loud as I had hoped, instead it comes out raspy and ragged from the run. I call out again, people around me regarding me with puzzled expressions. Please, please be here somewhere! All I want now is to sit down somewhere warm and quiet and have a good long cry. Perhaps I will. I don't want to be here anymore. I want to go home, wherever that is. I want to be safe.

"Miss Carlisle?" I feel a hand on my shoulder and for an instant fear it is Darius, come to finish what he began. Twisting around, shaking off the hand, I recognize with tremendous relief the hulking figure of Dymas.

"Oh, thank God!" I collapse against the unsuspecting man. I cannot describe the relief at having escaped, and it ebbs out of me in choking sobs.

"What happened? Are you hurt?" Dymas takes a step back, his hands on my shoulders, eyes scanning me up and down.

"N-no," I sniffle, "Darius, h-he is mad!" I wipe at my eyes, a twinge of shame for having allowed myself this outburst in front of a near stranger.

"What do you mean? Where is he?"

Before I can answer I hear the most welcome voice of my counsin. "Evie! Oh, Evie, there you are. We've been looking all over for you!" I turn around and see Briony, Jeffrey, and Daniel approaching. Briony's steps quicken when she sees my tearstained face. She knows I never cry in public and rarely in private. Besides, I must be filthy, covered in ancient dust.

"What happened?" Her voice is steady and she takes my hand, looking suspiciously at Dymas. "Did he hurt you?"

"What? No, no." I swallow a hiccupping sob. "It's Darius."

"Come," Briony leads me to an empty bench next to the crumbling side of a town house. The others follow, their expressions ranging from shock to relief.

"Now, take a deep breath and tell us what happened." Briony sits down beside me, leaving no room for the men who position themselves awkwardly around us, blocking the light. Their presence is so comforting, and with a tremor in my voice, I manage to recount the events of my evening.

When I finish, the others are silent. Dymas is the first to find his voice again. He clears his throat before he speaks.

"Andros Calandra." He shakes his head. "His poor parents. They go around saying he has important work in Athens. This will be a terrible shock. Terrible."

"Oh Evie, what have you been through!" Briony places an arm around my shoulder.

Daniel nods. "We ought to go and find Darius. He has to be arrested before he can escape."

"Yes, of course. I will summon a few of my colleagues. Hopefully, I will find some who haven't been too liberal in sampling the wine tonight. Darius is not exactly a menacing figure of a man. A few of us should manage to frighten him into submission." Dymas' voice is somber and resolute.

"Miss Carlisle, you have been very lucky tonight. It was dangerous to follow him, though I believe none of us imagined him capable of violence." Dymas shakes his head again, still at odds with the truth, and makes his exit. I have told him exactly where to go, and with any luck they will be successful in locating him.

"I was a fool." I pull my jacket a little closer to me. Here, with the fires and people, it should be warmer, but I still feel the creeping cold of the cave deep in my bones.

"The important fact is that you got away." Jeffrey steps forward, patting my shoulder in a brotherly manner.

"Come, let us take you home. Or do you want to see a doctor? I am sure, I can find Nikolas somewhere." Daniel looks around, scanning the crowd for Laria's husband.

"No, no. I am all right, just tired and—"

"You don't have to explain." He holds out a hand to pull me up. "The car isn't far away. Yannick is waiting."

In a slow procession, made slower by my battered feet, we make our way down the alley to the Delage. I thank the heavens—whoever rules them—for Yannick is indeed leaning against the gleaming motor, smoking a cigarette. Upon noticing us, he quickly tosses it aside, crushing it with the toe of his shoe.

"Miss Carlisle!" Even in the dim light, I see his blue eyes widen in surprise at my appearance. "Are you all right?"

I must look ghastly, if this is everyone's reaction. I put on a brave smile for him. Best not say too much yet. If Darius told the truth, Caspar's murderer is still at large, whoever he or she may be, and revealing what I learned tonight may only cause further complications.

"I am very tired, Yannick." I catch him glancing at my ruined shoes, the heels caked in dirt. "Too much dancing," I offer as explanation.

Yannick opens the doors for us. Silently, we squeeze in. With weak effort, I think: Should I not be at the police station, making a statement? With the events of this evening still in motion, there is probably no one there anyway. All out celebrating or chasing down the mad museum curator. Jeffrey is sitting in the front beside Yannick, and I am cocooned between Briony and Daniel, safe and sound for now as we, at last, drive home.

CHAPTER 34

We reach the villa in no time at all, or at least it seems that way to me. The misadventure of the evening has left me drained, and I may have dozed off for a while during our journey. The image of that withered body, the skeleton with its empty stare, claws its way back into my mind, forcing me to wrench my eyes open to escape the vivid memory.

When Yannick parks the motor and turns off the engine, the night suddenly turns terribly silent, the world outside our metal cage so large and confusing. I mustn't brood now. Darius is not a well man. I must focus on all the kindness I have been shown, help I have been offered this evening. The world is terrible and terribly good; darkness and light, always shifting. There have been many times in my life where this simple truth has been so difficult to remember.

Getting out of the car, I am carefully assisted as though I am a fragile creature not to be trusted to hold herself upright. If this night has taught me anything, it is that I am not as weak as I may have believed myself to be. Gently escaping the helping hands, I climb out. The cool air whips at my hair and makes me feel cleaner again. I want all the dust and misery of that horrible cave to wash away, restoring me to how I was before. I know it cannot be. I will always remember the suffocating fear for my life, saddened and frightened by the dead figure of a man I never knew. It is as if invisible fragments have crept under my skin and will not leave, no matter how hard I scrub. Memories are like tattoos. They are etched into us, and we are never rid of them. We may cover them up, yet they remain, always threatening to reveal themselves and to pull us back again.

"Evie? Come," Briony beckons me forth, and I draw out of my trance to see them all staring curiously, creases on their foreheads, eyes narrowed.

I worry them. I have happened upon two dead bodies in the span of ten days. Am I some sort of reaper?

No. No more stupid, silly thoughts!

We enter the house. It is silent and pleasantly warm. The stones of the building retain the day's heat enough to provide comfort on a cool evening.

"I will draw you a bath." Briony says.

"Can I get you anything? Tea? Brandy?" Daniel looks wretched, or perhaps I am only projecting my own turmoil.

"No, a bath is enough. Then I will sleep." I hope. Will I sleep? Will those empty eyesockets haunt me in my dreams? Will I be doomed to running and running even in my unconscious hours?

"Sleep well then." I have the strong impression there is more he wants to say, but Briony bustles me up the stairs, and whatever is on his mind is left unspoken.

"You must wake me when Dymas calls. Tell me if he caught Darius. Promise me, Briony." We enter my room, and she walks into the bathroom to begin filling the tub.

"Of course. I am certain he will catch him. How long can Darius hope to hide in the cave? He must know it is over." She returns to my room and perches on my bed as I sit on the stool, unbuckling my shoes. There are no words for the liberation of taking of painful shoes. Men may never know it. It is quite incredible. I toss the offensive foot-traps to the side with relief, wiggling my tired, cramped toes before returning to the seriousness of the situation.

"You didn't see him, Briony. He was mad. Confused, manic, I cannot explain it better. He was most certainly not thinking rationally. To my fortune, otherwise he surely would not have been so easily duped."

Briony shudders and wraps her arms around herself. "I cannot believe it. To think we were having a pleasant picnic with him a few days ago, and all the time—"

"It is terrible. You know what makes it worse?"

"What?"

"If he was honest in the cave, and I trust he was since he had not reason to lie anymore, he wasn't responsible for Caspar's death. Whoever killed him is still at large, living a normal life. We may well have seen him or her at the festival. Will we ever discover who is responsible?"

Briony shrugs. "I have to believe so."

"We will see."

"I am so sorry you have had such a horrid time, Evie." She bites her lower lip, a telltale sign tears will soon follow. Too tired to give much consolation tonight, I only shake my head and offer a weak smile.

"It is not your fault, as you know. I am glad I came. Darius did what he did so long ago, and Caspar would likely have met the same fate if I had been thousands of miles away. It is as it is and cannot be undone, I am not broken by either event. These tragedies are just that, tragic, but we have to learn to live with the fact that they invaded our lives and are part of our history."

"I suppose that is true, Evie. And for what it's worth, I am glad you came. You have been a good friend, and now I will be a good friend, too."

"You are always a good friend."

"Despite whining all the time?" She frowns at her lap.

"Briony." I pull myself off the chair with effort and walk over to her. "Everything is well between us. As it always will be. Now," I sink onto the bed, "be a friend and see if the bath water is ready. I am filthy and exhausted, and you will not want me falling asleep on your precious linen in this state."

Once in the bath with Briony dispatched to find out whether there have been any news, I close my eyes and lean my head against the small towel at the nape of my neck. I exhale deeply, but the tightness in my chest does not ease. Was it all a dream? I cannot help but wonder, floating here in this scented tub. Can it really have happened? It seems a lifetime ago I was in that ghastly cave, but the memories are so fresh and potent these events cannot have been mere figments of my imgination.

Darius killed his own brother—his own brother—and left his body to rot while he went about his life, returning to the cave all the time, stealing and lying. His parents. Oh, his poor parents! Will they believe their own child capable of such a horrendous deed? He was the only son they had left, even before knowing why Andros could never return. Now, they will lose their only living child, too. What horror. What senseless tragedy. There are no other words for it. Four lives are ruined, if not more. And for what? A madman's obession.

Our little world has seen too many mad, careless, cruel people. I shudder of what else is still to come in my lifetime, my children's, their children's . . . It goes on and on, and we follow along, living and dying. How will history judge what we do? Darius will be forgotten, despite the pain he caused. His evil was not grand enough to be commemorated in the books and stories of our lives. The people here and now will cry and mourn, grieve and shout, yet in ten years, twenty, who but his parents will remember? Our stories are so small, and the few of us who make them big are often the worst of the lot. Is it not enough to be, to simply be? Cannot goodness be our highest aim, or is that a thought even children are not long able to sustain? For some perhaps it is, still we are none of us perfect, and distraction, whether it comes disguised as love or reward, is often our downfall. Will I resist? Will I end my life without regrets? If Darius had succeeded, if he had killed me, what would my life have meant? Briony would be shattered, and I could not be there to comfort her. Jeffrey would feel responsible, and Agnes . . .? Would she blame me for having run away in the first place?

I open my eyes, my face wet from bathwater mingled with tears. He did not succeed, and I am here. Battered feet, gangly limbs, pruny fingers. All still here. Life is a fragile thing, but we are resilient, too, and this I must remember. Daniel has suffered terrible losses. He has seen death, lived with it hovering over his trench in the mud of France. He is coping and moving on and so will I.

The water has grown cool and my fingers wrinkly. I clamber out, wrapping myself in a soft towel and then a sky-blue robe, which Briony has draped over a small stool beside the washbasin.

I glance into the mirror, wiping away the fog. There I am, just as before, maybe a bit pinker. Sometimes our scars are visible on the outside for everyone to see, a reminder that we have been harmed. When they are on the inside, we learn to dress those wounds well enough to appear as undamaged as we do on the outside. People tend to believe what they see, and black holes in your heart are rarely visible to others.

Smiling encouragement at my weary reflection, I walk back to my bedroom. As I enter, I hear a knock at the door.

"Evie? Evie are you—"

"Come in!"

Briony enters, her face flushed with excitement. My heart quickens.

"Dymas called. They found him! They've arrested him. He's at the police station right now."

I inhale slowly, relief and an unexpected melancholy coursing through me. "Thank heavens!" I drop onto the edge of the bed.

"He was not violent. No one got hurt. They are questioning him now. Dymas sounded rather frustrated. Darius is talking only to himself saying, 'mine, they are mine' or something similar over and over again, maybe a bit addled from the blow you dealt him. I am so relieved."

"Yes," I smile weakly, "he is unwell, of course. It is a very sad story."

"He is a murderer, Evie. He killed his own brother, and he would have—"

"I know. Still, I cannot help feeling a little sad, for him and his brother and his parents. Imagine, their remaining son killed his only brother, and now he is too far gone to recognize the evil nature of his deed." I shake my head. "All that misery might have been avoided, if he had only spoken to his brother, tried to come to an agreement."

"Men are brutes," is Briony's simple answer.

CHAPTER 35

I am lying in bed, watching the shadows of tree branches dance across the walls, the curtain swaying everytime a soft breeze enters the room. Bone tired, and still I cannot sleep. Tossing and turning, too hot, then too cold, I cannot be comfortable. Counting sheep proves a complete waste of time as I disover at number nine-hundred and seventy. I try to clear my mind, to think of the blue sky, soft and gentle and . . . No, still awake. It is hardly surprising, but I had hoped to disappear into a dreamworld for a little while, to stop my mind from haunting me with images of dead men, of which I have seen two too many of late. Perhaps I should accept it. Allow myself to think about it, acknowledge reality and move on. It is never so simple.

Troubling me, beyond his obvious villainy, is Darius' denial of responsibility for Caspar's murder. I believe him. He was too far gone to bother denying the truth if he had done it. The question looms in my mind: Who else might have done it? Of the innocence of Jeffrey, Briony, Daniel and myself, I am certain. Who remains? Yes, Caspar was a blackmailer, however, the sums listed in his journal were not ruinous. Then again, some people will only be pushed so far before they do something regrettable.

Initially, Nikolas was my main suspect. He does have a good alibi, and he and Laria were in much better spirits at the festival than before. No, most likely, it was not him. Beyond all else, he is a doctor, sworn to ease suffering and not to be the cause of it. But he is human . . . I cannot fully discount him. Laria's alibi is her mother, and mothers are known to protect their children. On the other hand, she appeared genuinely shocked when we told her what had befallen her ex-lover that I cannot in good conscience consider her a suspect. Who else, who else?

The curtain flutters at a gust of wind as if aiming to tell me something. Right! Niobe and Yannick. Our secretive couple and their garden trysts. They appear, if my observation can be trusted, not particularly romantic. Certainly any amorous feeling is not two-sided. Niobe is plainly using the poor chap, and he is infatuated. He may do whatever she asks. Including murder? What if . . . I sit up in bed, what if Caspar is the child's father? What if he was going about romancing a number of women and when Niobe presented him with the result, he rejected her! What if she told Yannick that Caspar had seduced her and ought to be punished? Oh dear, oh dear!

As the thought crosses my mind, I remember they have alibis, too. I sink back into the pillows. How strong are their alibis? If I trust Laria's mother to vouch for her daughter, I ought to believe Niobe's as well. And Yannick . . . He might have slipped off, he had the car after all, done the deed and gone back to have cheese and olives with his soon-to-be family. Possibly, possibly. Very worrisome indeed. For a moment, I toy with the idea of waking the others, then decide it will keep till the morning. The police is overworked with one criminal tonight, and a fair number of them will go to work with throbbing heads from tonight's festival.

So, Yannick and Niobe are possible suspects. Anyone else? There are many people whom Caspar knew, people I have not met. It may be anyone of them. Within the circle of our shared acquaintances, Yannick seems the most obvious choice, if indeed the child is Caspar's.

The cook can be dismissed from my list of suspects. Her alibi is tight as Dymas assured us the day after the murder. Further, she has no apparent motive, though it would certainly have been easiest for her to poison him as she handled all of his food and drink. Too obvious. No, I cannot think it was her.

Paul and Rosie? Why? Rosie is a very unlikely candidate. She is not physically or mentally able to set into action such an elaborate plan. What if her condition is a front? No. The poor woman has been dealt a terrible fate as has her husband. What motive could either of them possibly have? Paul may have been blackmailed by Caspar for something or other, but his name does not appear in the journal. Further, they are unlikely to have ever met before coming to Crete. Paul and Rosie are from Holland, and Caspar lived in England before going to France during the war. I have to yawn. While my exhaustion takes over and my eyes drift shut, I have the faint idea that I am forgetting something terribly important . . .

CHAPTER 36

Despite the fear of never sleeping again or being haunted forever by the spindly hands of ghosts and spirits, I was able to drift off into a deep, dreamless slumber, waking at the respectable hour of nine in the morning. Initially, I believe yesterday's events were only a frightening nightmare. It does not take long to realize this is, unfortunately, not the case. My crippling shoes are lying dirty and ruined on the floor beside my dresser, a potent reminder of the truth.

As are the blisters on my feet.

I am faced with conflicting emotions of wanting to stay in bed and wanting to find out whether there have been any developments. Allowing myself the private luxury of a frustrated groan, I climb out of bed. The wooden planks between the two rugs that cover much of the floor are delightfully cool, and I stand for a moment, stretching my arms. I wonder whether the others are already awake? It is Wednesday, so Jeffrey may even go to the museum. It will be quite an ordeal for him to explain that their respectable curator is a murderer and thief. I do not envy Jeffrey this thankless task. Cretans are protective of 'their own' and will almost certainly find it difficult to believe the mild-mannered man they knew and respected capable of such villainy. It is a frightening truth. Anyone might be capable of evil doings, if even a man like Darius was. I pad over to the wardrobe. After some internal debate whether I should wear black, I instead decide on an emerald green dress with a square neckline and large buttons I can easily do up without Niobe's help. What happened to her last night? Either Yannick picked her up later, or she went home with her parents. Contemplating this, my semi-conscious suspicion bubbles to the surface again. I must speak with someone about it. Time is running, and all this must be resolved.

Doing up the last button, I slip into a pair of soft leather sandals, a relief for my still blistered feet, and decide to ask Daniel about his thoughts on the matter. He is in possession of a clear head, and I do not want Briony to come to the wrong conclusions regarding her household staff. Besides, I cannot tell her about Niobe's pregnancy. Not yet. And I cannot explain my suspicion without revealing her secret. I feel guilty towards Niobe. On the other hand, motive for murder trounces a promise of discretion.

Leaving my room, I happen upon just the man. Daniel looks pleased as he notices me in the hallway.

"Good morning. Did you sleep after last night's ordeal?"

"Disturbingly soundly, I must admit."

"I am hoping Dymas will come and tell us his news."

"Yes, I am quite certain he will. I still have to sign my statement."

He gives me a sympathetic smile

"Daniel," I touch his arm when we reach the bottom step, "might we speak in private a moment?"

"Yes, of course. Are you all right?"

"As can be expected. This is about something else. Last night I went over all that happened and . . ." I explain to him my suspicions.

He stays calm throughout, only raising his eyebrows and widening his eyes when I tell him of the pregnancy. Then he rubs his chin and frowns. "If Caspar knew of this, I believe he would have told me. He often felt the need for a confessor regarding his affairs, and he did not attend church."

"Maybe you are right. I hope so. I wouldn't want—"

"No, wait." He stops me. "Obviously, there was much I did not know about him. Maybe he was worried I would push him into assuming responsibility, if he was the child's father."

"Would you have?" I ask inspite of myself.

He hesitates a moment, meeting my eye when he answers, "I would have tried. Not for him to marry Niobe, heaven knows what misery may have resulted, but at least to provide for the child. He was certainly profiting enough from his blackmailing business to afford it." His voice carries a bitter note. He was badly hurt when faced with proof concerning the depth of his best friend's unsavory guile. Yet, Caspar is no longer on hand to be confronted with it. Discovering who is responsible for his death is the only way Daniel will find closure.

"What do you think?"

"I do not like to encourage your detective work. Our hypothesis hinges on whether Caspar is the father of Niobe's child. If not, gone is her motive, and Yannick would have none we are aware of either."

I lean against the wall. "Do you think I might simply ask her about it?"

"I—"

"Oh, here you are!" Briony chooses this moment to rush out of the kitchen. Did she hear our conversation? I do not think so. She would be shocked to discover her maid's pregnancy and surely unable to hide her emotions from us.

"Yes, we are coming in for breakfast. Have you eaten?" I speak too quickly to disguise my discomfort at having been caught.

"I have. Jeffrey was up early, and we ate together," she says, and I detect a hint of a smile. Could such a new crisis bring them closer together?

"Is he gone?"

"Not yet. He is still in the conservatory, reading something or other. Yannick is getting the car ready. He is terribly nervous. He will have to explain Darius' absence to his colleagues. Dymas suggested last night to be very vague if asked, so he has been formulating his explanation half the night."

"Oh dear, poor Jeffrey. Are there been any news?"

"Nothing yet," Briony leads the way to the conservatory.

"If Dymas doesn't—" Daniel is interrupted mid-sentence by a loud knock on the door.

From the corner of my eye, I catch Niobe hastening from the kitchen to answer it.

"Inspector Dymas," she says upon opening, "come in."

"Good morning," he greets us.

I want to be kind, but the man looks wretched as though he has not slept a wink all night, which may well be true. His eyes are red-rimmed and framed by dark circles, emphasized even more by the shadowy dark stubble on his face.

"Inspector," Briony smiles. "Please, will you join us for breakfast?" Allowing him little choice in the matter, she gently leads him forward and Daniel and I follow, giving each other a quick glance.

CHAPTER 37

Once settled in the sunlit conservatory where Jeffrey is waiting, pale-faced. Briony plies us with food and drink, and not before our plates are full and our cups steaming, is Dymas able to speak.

"As I said on the telephone last night, we were able to arrest Darius—Mr. Calandra."

"Has he confessed?" My hand is clenching my butter-knife in a white-knuckled grip.

"Well, yes," Dymas drags out the word, perhaps unsure of what it means.

"Yes? That is good, isn't it?" Daniel holds his teacup in the air, forgetting to drink.

"It is," Dymas nods, wearing a slightly befuddled expression.

"So?"

"He is raving. He has been talking and talking, and while somewhere amid his stream of words he admitted to Andros' murder, it is difficult to piece everything together. I do not know exactly how he will be prosecuted. He belongs in an asylum, not a prison, really."

"What?" I am unable to hide my indignation. "He as much as told me he would kill me!"

"Yes, of course." He sounds placatory. I will not be so easily silenced.

"What he did to his brother happened nearly two decades ago, surely he was not as unhinged as he is now. He has been able to hide his deed for so long, convincing everyone of his even temper and harmlessness."

"That is true," Daniel agrees, finally taking a sip and wincing as the tea scalds his tongue.

Dymas concedes. "Yes, it is. However, another problem lies in the fact that we couldn't go into the cave to find the body last night. It will have to be done today, and we were hoping Darius could be swayed to lead the way. As it is," he frowns and shakes his head, "he is in no state. He has completely dropped the mask we all knew, and I cannot get through to him."

"I wish I could show you the way, but I cannot remember. It was a great stroke of luck I got out last night."

"I understand. We will manage."

"And his family? His parents? Have they been informed?" Daniel asks.

"His parents, yes." Dymas falters and rubs his temples. "It was very difficult. They could not believe it. I think, they still cannot."

"Oh, those poor people. What a shock it must be for them." Briony clasps her hands together.

"Does anybody else know?"

"A few people. We have tried to contain it for the time, although it is difficult. Everyone knows everyone, and news travels quickly."

"Inspector," Daniel has lowered his cup and stares intently at the weary man, "Evelyn said Darius denied any involvement in Caspar's death. Did he mention anything about it? Anything at all?"

"Nothing. That is why we are inclined to believe it is true. His mind is too muddled to filter out what he ought not say and what might get him into even greater trouble. He has not mentioned your friend's name, not once. Admittedly, I am strangely relieved that he was not involved in that crime as well. Then again, I fear a murderer is still somewhere among us. Be assured, we are working intently on discovering his or her identity." Dymas' speech has left him exhausted, and I am tempted to tell him to go home, take a nap and then have a shave.

Propriety demands I do not. Instead I ask, "Do you have any new ideas?"

Before the harried man can answer, Jeffrey chimes in. "Really, Dymas, we know what Darius is capable of, why not suspect him of pretending, of putting on an act? He fooled us all. Conceivably, in a moment of lucidity, he decided to deny any involvement in Caspar's death."

"I have to agree with Jeffrey," Briony adds. "If Darius was blackmailed, he is a logical suspect. If he could," she falters, swallowing nervously, "if he could kill his own brother, he could certainly do the same to a strange man he felt was a threat to him and his treasures. He was clearly cunning and would have no difficulty in planning this whole wretched affair"

"That is true," Dymas admits at once. "We are holding him on charges of theft and one case of murder. He will be no further danger to anyone. Once he has calmed down, we may have a chance of finding out more definitively whether he is telling the truth or simply acting to avoid even greater punishment."

"I believe him." My voice is calm, in spite the nervous eddy stirring inside me. "He told me he would have done it, but someone else came before him. Why, when he so readily admitted to fratricide, would he have denied responsibility for Caspar's murder. He was calm when he told me, not raving. I believe it, and I believe a second killer is still free." My voice grows louder, the more empassioned my speech. It really has been a bit much these past few days.

Everyone is silent for a moment, staring at me. Daniel is the first to speak.

"The funeral is in two days. I cannot have his murderer attending, whoever it may be."

The thought sends a chill down my spine. Everyone else has a similar reaction, judging from their pained expressions.

"I will do my best," Dymas says finally. Getting to his feet he adds, "I will keep you abreast of developments." And when Briony rises to see him out, "Thank you, I will find my way. Good day."

As he leaves, I try to catch his gaze, but his eyes are lost in shadow and exhaustion. Then he is gone.

CHAPTER 38

"Well . . ." Jeffrey begins, deep lines around his mouth. "Well, indeed." Daniel says. Briony and I throw each other helpless looks. Thankfully, Yannick chooses this moment to enter through the glass-paned door.

"Mr. Farnham, Sir," he hesitates as eight eyes are turned on him, then finds his voice or his courage or both and continues, looking resolutely at Jeffrey. "The car, it is ready."

Jeffrey gets to his feet. "Thank you Yannick." He turns to us. "I had best get this over with."

"Good luck, my dear," Briony plants a chaste kiss on his cheek, and Daniel and I offer words conveying the same sentiment.

His wife on his arm, accompanying him to the door, and Yannick at their heels, Daniel and I are left alone for a moment.

He wastes no time, "Evelyn, I hate to ask this of you but—"

"I will speak to Niobe presently. You are right. This situation must be resolved before the funeral. It will be ghastly enough without being forever marred in your memory by later discovering the murderer was present." I scrape back my chair. "Tell Briony I had to speak to Niobe about a gown which needs mending. I am loath to keep this from her, yet for the moment—"

"For the moment, it will not harm her."

"Yes," I add, though with weak conviction and with knot of guilt inside me. I smooth the front of my dress and go my way. Briony is still not back. Passing the sitting room, I see Niobe with a dusting rag near one of the bookshelves.

I enter. The room is bathed in the yellow light of the morning sun, and Niobe's long, dark braid gleams. Careful not to cause alarm, I slide the door almost closed and call out in a cheery tone.

"Oh, hello!" As though our meeting is entirely coincidental.

She spins around, an expression first of alarm then of surprise crossing her features.

"Miss Carlisle. Good morning."

I stroll over to the bookshelf, not failing to notice the tiny step backward the maid takes.

"Can I help you?"

"I am only looking for something to read." I pause, tapping my chin contemplatively. "I did want to have a quick word with you, if you can spare a moment."

"With me?" Her eyes narrow ever so slightly. Her expression tightens.

"Yes." I tilt my head and smile. "How are you?" Her face relaxes. She was clearly expecting something else. Interesting.

"I am well."

"Are you? Good. So much worry lately, I was concerned."

"That is kind. You need not worry about me."

"Oh, but I do," I assure her, stepping closer. "Niobe, I understand now why you have been so unhappy."

"Unhappy, I—"

I hold up a hand. "It is all right. It must have been so difficult to find out the father of your child had been killed." There, blunt and blatant. Niobe's face turns ashen, and her dark eyes widen.

"But, oh . . . no!" She shakes her head, strands of hair tumble from her loose braid. She is a vision of loveliness. Even in distress.

"I understand, Niobe dear," I say with honey in my voice. She does not, to her credit, look like someone concealing a murderous secret, perhaps just an ordinary one.

"No, you do not." Her voice has regained firmness. "He is—was not the father. Never could I—" she shakes her head as if disgusted.

While this is not entirely unexpected, my theory is weakening and so is my conviction in its validity.

"He isn't?" I venture to ask, leaning slightly against the shelf.

"No," she shakes her head again. Her braid is now nearly undone, so vehemnt is her denial. "He was a cad! I would not have fallen for him. He may have charmed poor Laria, but not me."

"You know about Laria?"

Niobe makes a dismissive gesture. "Her mother told my mother who told me. It is a surprise Nikolas hasn't thrown her out. He is quite confident in himself. He would not think his wife could ever betray him." She rolls her eyes. Her arguments are too plausible to be denied, but having come this far, I must plough on.

"If Caspar is not the father, who is? I will be honest with you," I decide on a rather loose definition of honesty. "Caspar left behind a journal."

"So? What concern is it to me?" She crosses her arms over her ample bosom.

"Well," I begin, not quite certain what will come out of my mouth, "in the journal he claims you were the mistress of other men of his acquaintance. You must not blame me when I come to the conclusion—"

Her mouth gapes for a moment, before she gathers herself, quickly bursting out, "That is a lie! He was a bad man, a liar!" She is fuming now, which is exactly what I intended. I keep my face relaxed, not to show her the relief I feel in having evoked this outburst. Someone so deeply insulted will be eager to defend their honor, hopefully by a plain confession of the truth.

"I did not mean to insult you," I lie. "I felt it was necessary to tell you the truth."

Her brows are creased, her jaw set tightly. "I am not a whore. This child was conceived out of love."

"Of course."

"You do not understand," she bites her bottom lip, all angry tension ebbing away.

"You can tell me, Niobe," I take her by the elbow and lead her to a low settee. She sits down with me beside her. Her eyes are suddenly swimming, and I experience a stab of guilt in view of my manipulation. I push it aside. Finding out who is behind Caspar's death is vital, and Niobe clearly needs to unburden herself. So there is really no harm . . .

"Caspar made his advances, of course, he did with everyone. He even flirted with Eleni, the cook, and she is married with six children!" She sniffles, and I dare not interrupt. "He backed off quickly. Caspar and Laria were quite fond of one another. We grew up together, though she is older than me, and we were never close friends. Her marriage has not been very happy, I think. Nikolas is a good man, but he can be selfish at times, and Laria married him so young. Then they had Kaia, and she might have felt trapped or lonely. I do not blame her for the affair. I would not be surprised if Nikolas had a few of his own. Still, you will understand, it is never the same for a man." She looks at me for sympathy and I nod, no longer play-acting.

"Caspar and I were never a couple."

I nod again, and my mind flashes to the image of her and Caspar on the night of the dinner party, whispering away from the group. I decide it is now or never, and say, "Niobe, since you and Caspar were not a couple, why did he take you aside on the night of the dinner party? You remember, I am sure."

To her credit, she does not deny it, instead exhales sharply and wipes a tear from her cheek. "It is true. It was nothing important. He was drunk and upset. He wanted me to give Laria a message, wanted to meet her alone later that night."

"And did you?"

"No."

"No?"

"I did not want him to make a scene. Not for Laria and not for Mrs. Farnham. He was in a bad state, and it would have been an embarrassment."

"I understand." While I am not entirely certain I believe this explanation, instinct tells me it is not important at the moment, and I encourage her to go on.

"The father of my child was at the dinner party that evening," she continues, and for a moment my stomach clenches at the thought it might be Jeffrey or Daniel.

"He was?" I mutter for lack of anything useful to say.

"Miss Carlisle, I must have your promise of discretion. You cannot tell anyone."

"Niobe, I have to be truthful, I can't make such a promise." I do not want to betray her, not outright. But I must know the truth. "I will only tell Mr. Harper. He can be trusted. He is very discreet."

Niobe wavers, though now she is too far into her confession to stop. She has been keeping a great secret, and I am near enough her age to qualify as a potential friend, who under other circumstances may be in the same boat.

"You will not tell anyone else? Mrs. Farnham? I would not—"

"Soon you will have to tell her about the child yourself. We can do it together, if you like." I put a hand on her arm.

Her resolve breaks and with a tiny sob she utters, "It is Paul. My Paul. He is the father of my child."

I can feel my eyes widen in surprise. Paul! Of course. I am so stupid. He was the only real choice, beside Caspar. I thank heavens it is not Darius. That would create even more trauma. But Paul? Paul who is married. Married to Rosie. Oh, Rosie with that permanent, innocent smile, those empty eyes. Oh no. Poor, poor Rosie, and poor Paul and poor Niobe. What a mess I have stumbled into!

As these thoughts course through my mind, I make an effort to remain outwardly calm. Niobe is searching for a reaction, her eyes are fixed on me in anticipation, her mouth open slightly, hardly believing her own disclosure.

"Er . . ." I stammer, searching for something, anything useful to say. "Paul. I see." Well, I have never claimed to be a poet.

"Yes, Paul. Oh, Miss Carlisle," she touches a hand to her chest, "it is such a relief to tell someone. I have been so worried and—" a plump tear rolls down her cheek, and I rummage for a handkerchief to press into her hand.

"I am glad you told me, Niobe. I confess, I had not expected it."

"No. Still, you must not think badly of him. He felt so guilty, so miserable. We were—we are in love. He was lonely and always here with Mr. Farnham, talking about their work. I saw him all the time, and then, one day when Mr. Farnham was late and Mrs. Farnham was out, we began to talk and—" she swallows, and wipes away another tear, "and we fell in love. He is such a good man, kind and clever and handsome. Don't you think, Miss Carlisle?" She casts me a beseeching look, and I manage a nod.

"How long did your affair last? You do intend to marry Yannick, do you not?"

At this her face falls. "I must. Yannick is a good man, too, and I like him. He is not Paul, though."

"Paul is married already," I state dumbly, altogether out of my depth.

"I know." Niobe makes a vague gesture with her hand. "But she is only a shell. He told me so. He said she does not speak to him. Her mind is broken. They can never have children, because he cannot . . ." she trails off blushing slightly.

"Indeed."

"He loves me, but he will not leave her. He feels a responsibility toward her. Such a good man. They can never be happy together. He could take care of her and live with me. I would not be jealous, I would understand. We could have a family . . ."

"Does he know of your condition?" I ask, adding at her confused expression, "your pregnancy?"

"No."

"No? Why in heaven's name not?"

Niobe twists a curl around her finger as she answers. "I only discovered it a few days after he ended the affair. I was angry and sad ,and I couldn't bear him knowing of the child and still choosing her; or him only choosing me out of his sense of responsibility. I do not want to be another burden to him. You understand, don't you? Then Yannick was there. He has always liked me. I know this."

"So you encouraged his affections."

"I do not want to be alone and unmarried with a child. Don't you understand?"

"Certainly. Does Yannick know who the real father is?"

"No. I said it was a sailor. I said he is long gone."

"And your parents? Your family?"

"They do not know. My mother suspects the pregnancy, I believe, though she does not doubt Yannick is the father. My family would be scandalized, if I had the child out of wedlock. You are modern, from a big city. I live in a small village on a small island. I have no means to leave, and I do not want to, though for Paul . . . No, there is no choice. I will make Yannick happy, we will all be happy." This speech, while empassioned, is not convincing. I observe the quivering of her bottom lip.

"Yes, I am sure you will. Yannick is a kind man and reliable. You will be all right."

Her dark eyes light up, and I am happy to give her some small comfort, though not wholly believing it myself. Yannick is second best. Her child will not be his. One day, bitterness will rise to the surface. I sympathize with Niobe, but cannot fault Paul for his decision. As I contemplate this, my mind turns back to the scene I witnessed between Niobe and Yannick in the garden. Suspicion, was a word they used. Were they speaking of the child? I decide to play my final card, bring it what it may.

"Niobe," I opt for a low, intimate tone, "I am glad you trusted me. I hope to repay your confidence in some manner. However, there is something you are keeping from me, isn't there. Something Yannick has done?" I lean forward conspiratorially.

"Oh, well, it was only a foolish mistake." Niobe says in an off-hand manner, too blasé to be disguising something truly awful.

"He should have told Mr. Farnham," I counter, with confidence I do not possess. Jeffrey is the authority Yannick should report to on most any matter.

"He probably should have told the police. Really, it was nothing though, and he was afraid he would be sent away, and I was afraid, too." She rests a hand on her abdomen.

Controlling my eagerness to discover the truth I go on. "Surely he would not be sent away, it was harmless, after all, wasn't it?" I hold my breath, waiting for her to volunteer more.

"Yes," Niobe waves dismissively, "he only hit him once. He was well when Yannick left him. We worried the police would not believe it."

I digest this information quickly. If I understand correctly, Yannick hit Caspar? I must clairfy. "Caspar bore a small bruise, the police said . . ."

"Yes, we hoped they would believe it happened when he fell off the bench." Niobe shrugs. "Yannick is a man. He was upset because he thought Caspar was making advances at me again. He was jealous, not murderous."

"No, I understand. Still, if he was here at the time of Caspar's death, there would be little to prove he did not poison him."

"But he was not here then."

"Not?"

"No, Yannick hit him the night of the party. After you had gone to bed, Caspar came downstairs for some matches. Yannick and he got into an argument. I saw it. Caspar was angry and very drunk. He simply went back to his room. He said something about Yannick paying for what he did, nothing more. Yannick was worried. But he was not at the house when Caspar was killed."

Not willing to explore the idea of Yannick leaving Caspar a bottle of poisoned wine, I decide to save this information for Daniel. I must not alarm Niobe in any way, lest she warn Yannick.

"Thank you, Niobe. You have been most helpful." We get to our feet. I am at least three inches taller than her, which makes me feel oddly safe. Despite Niobe's candor, I cannot trust her. She possesses a shrewd nature, and I should not like to be her enemy.

"I am glad to have been able to tell someone, Miss Carlisle."

"I am glad you trusted me. Now, if you are in need of anything, please do not hesitate to come to me. You should not be alone with all your worries."

"Thank you." A small smile tugs at her lips.

We part company. Going up to my room, I am hopeful that Daniel is near at hand. Niobe returns to her tasks in the kitchen.

I am in luck. Passing Daniel's room, I catch sight of him through a slit in the door, seated on a wicker chair in front of the window, scribbling something into a notebook.

Gently, I knock against the frame of the door.

"Yes? Come in!"

I push open the door and step inside. "Am I disturbing you?"

"Not at all." He puts his writing tools aside and pulls another chair to the window. "Please, take a seat. Have you been able to obtain any new information?"

I sit and take a deep breath, feeling wrong to come to Daniel right after speaking with Niobe. Still, I remind myself I am not betraying her in in recounting her admission to Daniel, which I promptly proceed in doing.

"Paul?" he interrupts half-way through my narrative, an expression of astonishment on his face.

"I was as surprised as you, though when I think about it, it makes sense."

"It would have been too clichéd for the cad to woo the maid, wouldn't it."

I go on, ending my tale with Yannick's supposedly mild assault on Caspar the night of the dinner party. "What do you think? Could he have given Caspar a poisoned bottle?"

Daniel's brow creases in thought. "Poisoning is a planned, careful act. Yannick's anger was fueled by a bout of passion and jealousy. It is unlikely he would go on to prepare a wine bottle and sneak to Caspar's room. Further, on purely practical grounds, he would have had to steal a bottle, as well as the rat poison from the kitchen, which is where it is kept. Both the cook and Niobe were there throughout the evening, especially after the meal to clean up. Yannick could not easily go in and fetch these items without stirring up suspicion. Even if Niobe did not oppose Yannick's murderous interference, the cook surely would not have kept such an unusual occurance from the police."

"Yes, I see the logic in that, though I will admit disliking the idea of Yannick as the guilty party."

Daniel's eyes wander to the window for a moment where the sky is the purest blue, and a pair of excited brown wrens are flying in circles, a little lover's dance.

"What of Paul." It is not a question. When his eyes meet mine, I understand his insinuation.

"I thought of him as well, but it makes little sense. What motive would he have? If he wanted to remove a romantic rival, it would have been Yannick, would it not?"

Daniel nods. "Yes, I think so too. But we cannot be certain. There may be more to the story. You said yourself Niobe gives the impression of being not entirely trustworthy."

At that I cannot help but wince for fear of doing her an injustice. "I only meant she may be slightly more manipulative than she makes herself out to be . . . She has to protect herself in this situation. I understand. I sympathize with her. Sometimes there is no other choice, but to be a little manipulative. She has been dealt a difficult card."

"It's all right, you need not defend her. I am not accusing her. Her alibi is strong. There were neighbors at her parents' house when she visited them on the day of Caspar's death. Everyone saw her. Part of me wonders," he taps his finger against the arm of the chair, "whether her alibi is too sound."

"Perhaps. Nonetheless, I cannot truly imagine what motive she could have to take such drastic measures. Caspar was a nuisance to her, nothing more, so far as I can tell. Yannick already knew of the child, so with what could Caspar have threatened her. No, I do not believe she is behind the murder." I lean back in my chair.

"I will trust your intuition." Daniel remarks without a hint of sarcasm or condescension, which pleases me greatly. He must have at least a modicum of respect for me, for my mind, which is gratifying at a time when women are still, despite having finally won the vote, seen as the intellectual and physical inferiors to men; at times overtly and at others by innuendo—equally insulting.

"Thank you," I reply, a small smile curving at my lips.

"I would like to speak to Paul. I sympathize with the man. I cannot help it. Especially, if he is unaware of the trouble Niobe is in."

"What would you say to him? Would you confront him with the truth?"

Daniel contemplates this suggestion for a moment, then replies. "I will not betray Niobe's confidence. It is for her to tell him of the child, if she will at all. It may be best, if no one knows of Paul's paternity."

"It is good to hear you say so. I would not support such a confrontation either. I gave Niobe my word to tell only you. Let us not make matters harder for her. She is still infatuated with Paul, but she is acting very strong about accepting his decision to separate, and I think she can move on with Yannick to lead a happy life. I hope so at least."

"It will be hard for Yannick once he realizes she still loves another man."

"What makes you think he will? For that matter, what makes you think she will not love Yannick?"

He gives me a wary look. "I don't, you are right. For all their sakes I hope they will have a loving marriage and family, yet I am not convinced. The child will be a constant reminder of the man Niobe loved, and Yannick will have a constant reminder that he is not this child's father. What if they have more children? Will Yannick resist the temptation of loving his own more than their first? Will Niobe love her second as much as the one she had with her true love?"

"Really Daniel, you are quite the romantic."

"Not romantic, realistic."

"No. You credit our sex with too much sweetness. Niobe is a shrewd girl. She will be able to move on. In time, she will learn there is much to life beyond a man who will not stand by her."

"Hopefully you are right. However, I still want to speak to Paul and confront him with our knowledge regarding the affair."

"He will probably be at the museum now."

Daniel leans back in his chair, then continues, "Yes, you are right, and I wouldn't want to disturb him at work today. On the other hand, it will be difficult to speak at home when Rosie is about."

"We can hardly ask her to leave the room," I agree.

"We?" He raises an eyebrow.

"I certainly won't be sitting here twiddling my thumbs while you're off interrogating—"

"Not interrogating!"

"Questioning then, questioning Paul at his home. Do you even know where he lives?"

"I do, as it happens. I have been there before. It is very close by, past Miklos, in the next village, Prinias."

"Let us call on him after work. You can telephone and ask whether Paul will see us."

"I don't know . . . " he looks unconvinced.

"You don't want to waste more time, do you? I'll even volunteer to drive, if Jeffrey will loan us the motor."

Daniel gives a defeated groan, yet refrains from further argument. I am pleased. Our relationship is progressing as I hoped it would, with me getting what I want, naturally.

CHAPTER 39

The next few hours pass quickly. Daniel goes to Miklos on one of the bicycles to finalize the funaral arrangements at the church. Briony and I spend much of the afternoon hours reading. Briony has chosen Leaves of Grass by an American named Walt Whitman. Having myself read this volume of poetry, I am surprised she chose it and am quite keen to hear her thoughts on the, shall we say, rather incendiary verse. I am working my way through A Passage to India, which sounded so exotic, I could not resist. It started out slow, but after some hours I am entirely absorbed by Dr. Aziz and his fate. I barely register Jeffrey's arrival, or for that matter, Daniel's.

Briony, dutiful wife and hostess, leaps from her chair and hurries toward her wan and weary husband. "Jeffrey, dear, how did it go? You look exhausted! Shall I fetch you a drink, and you, Daniel? Sit, sit." She bustles about, practically pushing the men into empty armchairs and pressing generously filled glasses into their hands.

Daniel gives me a curious look. I only shrug. I expect Briony is preparing to tell her husband the heap of fabric on the table in the corner is part of a dress she is making for the child she is planning to adopt. A drink or two may come in useful.

"So," she finally sits down, cheeks flushed, "how did it go?"

"It was tiring." Jeffrey takes a long sip of the two fingers of Brandy sloshing about his glass. "I had to explain in as vague terms as possible what had happened and why we ought to start looking for a new museum curator."

Briony shakes her head in sympathy.

"As you can imagine, there were a lot of questions. I claimed to know very little, only that Darius had been arrested, which opened up a floodgate. Why? When? What for? On and on they went. I tell you," he gestures at us, "I have never been so glad to get away."

"And Paul?" I ask innocently . . . or not so innocently, truth told. "Was he any help?"

"You know Paul." Jeffrey ignores the fact that I hardly do. "He tried, but he knew even less than me, so what could he say."

"Did he go home as well?"

"What? Yes, yes he did." Jeffrey shoots me an odd look, and I smile innocently.

"Jeffrey, would you mind if Evelyn and I borrowed the motor for an hour or so?"

"You and Evelyn?" Jeffrey furrows his brow and Briony glances curiously from me to Daniel, doubtlessly thinking up all sorts of unspeakable scenarios, especially after spending the whole afternoon with her literary marvel of intriguing influence, Mr. Whitman. Heaven knows what is going through her mind!

"Yes," Daniel continues, "I need to drive to the cemetary and find whether—"

"Oh, poor you!" Briony cries out, "Of course, you shall use the car and take Evelyn along . . . for support," she adds with a completely mortifying wink in my direction. I must speak to her at the nearest convenient occasion, to inform her that her skills in subtlety are in dire need of adjustment.

"Support, yes, right." Daniel responds enthusiastically, and I supplement this by nodding vigorously, all the while guilty of this act of subterfuge. I soothe my troubled conscience by reminding myself of some not insignificant facts. After all, if we were completely honest about our reasons for borrowing the car, we would have to reveal Niobe's condition, or, at the very least, the affair, which, at this point, may cause further trouble and confusion. Best to speak with Paul and discover what can then be left to his and Niobe's discretion.

CHAPTER 40

Thankfully, we are spared further awkwardness as Jeffrey decides he is in need of a hot bath to rid himself of the day's dust, figuratively speaking I assume as he looks clean as a cat. Briony is left to finish her poems or possibly the hem of Areta's dress as Daniel and I fetch our hats and depart.

With myself seated, quite naturally, in the driver's seat of the Delage, we laugh as we realize our mutual relief at having been spared further quizzing by our friends.

"You must direct me," I request, raising my voice to best the roar of the engine.

"It is very easy to find. Follow the main street through Miklos, and then we will turn right and drive up the mountain road."

"Off we go then."

The sun is still lighting our world, beautiful streaks of orange, pink and purple are paint the sky, hinting it will soon turn inky blue. There is little traffic, only a few carts and one other motorcar driving so slowly, I am eager to overtake. This, however, is not a wise idea, since it would mean skirting a good two feet off the road and the edge of the mountain. To my great relief, the rickety contraption remains on the main road right after Miklos where we turn, making our steep ascent.

"What will you say to Paul?" I ask, keeping my eyes firmly fixed on the narrow winding lane.

"First we will have to suggest a private conversation, if Rosie should to be present. I know she has a nurse, for when Paul is out or at work, so there is a chance she is with her."

"And then?"

"Then, I think it will be best to simply come out and tell him we know of the affair."

"He may think we are ganging up on him? Ambushing him in his own home. Maybe this is a mistake."

"No." Daniel's tone is calm and resolute. "I do not plan to attack him, yet my friend has been murdered, and all these secrets may very well be reated to his death. I must know the truth, and if that upsets a few people I can live with it."

I wait a moment to reply, not certain I should have come. Still, it would have been misery waiting at home, reading and rereading the same sentence again and again with anxiety about the events happening only a few miles away. "What do you expect Paul to say?"

"He will hopefully acknowledge the truth. It could be embarassing for him if he did not. Besides, people like to free their minds of guilt. Telling us may be helpful to him."

"Daniel," I venture, my stomach tightening, "what if Rosie is not really . . . well, not—"

"Not as ill as she seems, you mean?"

I nod. "Most likely I am wrong, but if she knew of Paul's affair, she may have been very angry."

"Certainly." Daniel agrees. "There are two questions immediately arising out of such a possibility. Why would she go on pretending? Her husband is obviously still devoted to her, he would surely be overjoyed if she regained some of her old self."

"That is true. I suppose the situation has been very difficult for Paul."

"Indeed. Even if she was better and knew of Paul's indiscretion, what motive might she possibly have for killing Caspar?"

"What motive would Paul have?" I turn the question around as I drive through the gates of the village of Prinias.

"I cannot say. Nor do I claim he is guilty. Still, we cannot deny there is something altogether wrong in this community, and Caspar's death was the result. If we tell him we suspect Niobe is guilty—"

"But—"

"Just Listen. If we tell him we consider her to be guilty, perhaps he will be more forthcoming. He will not want her to be in trouble. Little does he know, in a manner of speaking she already is."

"Hm . . . it's rather deceptive, don't you think? He may know nothing."

"Maybe not. Should that be the case, I confess, I am running out of ideas. Niobe's affair with Paul must be important in all of this."

Before I can react, he points to a narrow lane, which barely holds the impressive mass of the Delage.

"Don't pull in," Daniel advises as I slow the car to make the precarious turn. "Park it here on the side of the road. The house is second on the left."

I let my eyes wander to an elegant townhouse with a slightly faded ochre exterior and boxes of bright purple flowers gracing the shuttered windows.

"Do you think they are out?"

"No, I see Paul's bicycle. They close the shutters on the lower levels in the evening to prevent crime."

Turning the engine off, we spend the next few minutes sitting in silence. A growing sense of tension and dread is mounting inside of me. Is it right to do this, I wonder? Is it right to disrupt a man's life by confronting him with his mistakes? He has been through so much, and now . . . What do we even expect will happen?

I glance over at Daniel. He needs to do something. To keep moving, to remain involved. Caspar's funeral is in two days.

"Let's do it." He offers me a weak smile.

"Right." Climbing out of the car, we pull up the roof. Daniel's mention of neighborhood crime makes me feel acutely responsible for the safety of this lovely gleaming block of metal.

Walking to the ochre house, I can hear sounds of a gramophone from beyond the walls. A slow, sad melody fills the air with an atmospheric hum. A breeze whips around the corner, tugging at my skirt. It is cooler up here in the mountains, and I suddenly yearn to be back at the villa. This confrontation, peaceful as we want it to be, worries me and has my stomach in knots. Before I can say I've changed my mind, I'll wait in the car, thank you very much, Daniel has clasped the brass knocker and rapped it against the solid wood of the door.

The music continues humming beyond the walls. After a moment, we hear the faint tapping of nearing footsteps. Then the door swings open to reveal a stern-faced woman of about forty, wearing a plain gray cotton dress and flat shoes.

"Yes?" She asks, not disguising her distaste at our disturbance.

"Daniel Harper and Evelyn Carlisle. We are here to talk to Paul, Mr. Vanderheyden. Is he home?"

She narrows her eyes and reluctantly opens the door to let us step in. Without another word she then leads us down the narrow corridor to the back of the house. Paul is sitting on the terrace, smoking a thick cigar and reading in the last of the evening light.

"Mr. Vanderheyden," her tone is flat and sharp, and Paul immediately swivels around in his seat.

"Yes, Miss—" his face tightens for an instant as he registers Daniel and me standing in the woman's shadow. "Oh, Daniel, Miss Carlisle, what a surprise." He stands, unable to hide the fact that this suprise is not of the entirely welcome variety. I cannot blame him.

"Paul, I am sorry to impose on you at your home," Daniel begins and is immediately interrupted by Paul, who has recovered and is friendly as ever.

"Nonsense, I am always happy to receive guests. Please, sit down. Would you like anything to drink, to eat?"

Daniel and I politely decline. Paul turns to the woman who is staring at us, framed in the light of the hallway behind her. "Miss Holm, thank you. You may go." She frowns, then follows his instruction and disappears.

Paul takes his original seat beside Daniel and across from me. "Now, if you are not here to share a drink with me, tell me what is on your mind. Has anything happened? Are Jeffrey and Briony all right?"

"They are well, thank you." I say, hoping Daniel will take the lead in this conversation and come to the point quickly. I cannot stand the thought of sitting here in Paul's friendly presence when we have come to place another burden on his shoulders.

"Paul," Daniel begins, "is Rosie at home?"

"Rosie? Why yes, she is resting."

"That is good. We must speak to you in private."

Paul's forehead creases in puzzlement, but his face still wears the amiable expression I have grown accustomed to. "You are worrying me, Daniel. Tell me, what is the matter?"

"I," Daniel swallows, "we, I should say," nodding in my directon, "we have discovered something concerning you."

"Me? Well, out with it." Paul's tone is light-hearted, though his jaw is tightening.

"All right. We know about your relationship with Niobe."

For a moment, there is silence and I think Paul will deny it; he will laugh and say she lied. However, and to my dismay, his friendly face falls and turns pale.

"Paul," I say gently, "we are not here to condemn you. We understand—"

"No!" He shakes his head, and I observe his hands clenched in fists in his lap. "With all due respect, you do not understand, Miss Carlisle.

And you should be glad you do not." He shudders and runs a shaky hand through his gleaming blond hair.

"I am sorry."

"No," his voice, when it returns, is thick and low. Tears are collecting in the corners of his eyes. "Don't be sorry. Did she tell you? Yes, she must have. She is your maid, is she not?"

"She is."

"I thought so. She is so young. She should not have been expected to keep a secret like that. I confess, I hoped she would."

"She only told me the truth, because I made a terrible accusation."

"Accusation? What do you mean?"

"I though Caspar had been her lover. I suspected her of having been guilty of his murder."

"Proposterous!" Paul's eyes grow wide and he looks genuinely stunned.

"Is it?" Daniel probes.

"Of course it is. She would never, could never . . ." Paul takes a deep breath to calm himself. I feel wretched for causing him more misery.

"Anyone can be capable of anything," Daniel throws in speculatively. "Poison is said to be a woman's weapon."

"Nonsense. Complete nonsense. Caspar liked to flirt, but Niobe did not care about him, certainly not enough to harm him."

"No?"

"No, and she had an alibi, or did you forget that?"

"Calm yourself, Paul, Niobe is an unlikely suspect. Although, we have discovered Caspar was blackmailing people. He might have blackmailed her. Niobe, as you know, is set to marry Yannick. If it became known she was—" Daniel breaks off, the truth now too clear to avoid. He turns pale and stares at Paul.

"What?" Paul glares in confusion. "What is it?"

I notice Daniel's hands shaking ever so slightly when he clasps them firmly together in an attempt to steady himself. "Caspar might have blackmailed you." His voice is hoarse, almost a whisper.

"Me?" Paul's eyes grow large, two big blue orbs of sweet innocence. "Don't be absurd! I did not like the man. We had little to do with one another. He most certainly was not blackmailing me."

"But he was." I add, playing along, trying for confidence. "He kept a diary of his exploits, using abbreviations for his victim's names. 'PV' was among them. Isn't that right, Daniel?" I ask, hoping he will play along, and wondering whether we are completely wrong. PV was not noted in the journal, nor anything like Paul's name.

"I'm afraid it is."

"So? There are many men with the letters 'P' and 'V' in their names. It proves nothing." He is still calm. Despite the chill in the air, I notice tiny beads of perspiration dotting his brow. What if Daniel is right? What if all this time . . .

"Not men of Caspar's aquaintance," counters Daniel, a vein pulsing in his neck. I can see more than hear anger beginning to boil inside him, though his tone is still even, the effort to remain calm now as agonizing for him as it is for me. I am itching to squirm in my seat and make a dash for the door, all the while obliquely grateful that we declined Paul's offer of food and drink.

"Daniel, Miss Carlisle, I understand your frustration, but to come to my home and make these accusations, unfounded accusations . . ." Paul shakes his head.

"Niobe knows, doesn't she?" I say with a burst of clarity. "About the blackmail? She knew Caspar had threatened to expose you, both of you. Her alibi is solid but yours is not, is it Paul? You were in the museum. The museum is large. You could easily have snuck out for an hour, driven to the villa and returned."

"Madness, this is madness! I want you to leave, both of you. Please, get out of my house." Paul jumps to his feet, his cheeks an angry shade of pink, and he is pointing a finger at the door.

I look at Daniel for an indication of what he is thinking. He stays glued to his chair, staring at Paul with undisguised contempt.

Emboldened I plough on. "Yes, it's true, is it not? You slipped out of the museum, knowing from Niobe, the villa would be empty but for Caspar. You drove there with your bottle of wine, probably to convince him you would pay the blackmail money and to seal the transaction with a glass. Caspar thought he had won and didn't notice when you did not drink." I do not pause to let him offer an explanation or defense. "Then he collapsed, and you left. You left him there to die. You murdered him and drove back to work as if nothing had happened!" I have grown loud, my voice carrying a hint of authority I did not know I possessed. My eyes are sharp and focused, probing his.

He does not speak, but runs a trembling hand through his already tousled hair. A droplet of perspiration drips down the bridge of his nose. For a moment, the air is thick with silence, with the impact of the terrible words that have just been spoken ringing in our ears.

"Paul?" Daniel sounds almost afraid. "It is true, isn't it? All of it. You killed him?" I watch him as he inhales deeply, wide eyes fixed on the hulk of a man in shambles before us. Will he confess? Will he admit what is now obvious?

"You wanted to protect Rosie and Niobe as well as yourself," I mutter quietly, hoping to coax an admission from him by disguising his deed with some veil of selfless valor.

Another moment passes, his silent frozen expression a confession in itself. Finally, as I am about to speak again, his mouth opens and he licks his lower lip.

"It was for Rosie. For Rosie, she has suffered, suffered so badly. I could not have her humiliated."

I am eager to say that he, too, would have been humiliated, and so would poor Niobe, though I now wonder whether she is as innocent in all of this as she claims to be. Did she not perhaps alert Paul about Caspar being alone in the villa? Even if she did not know what Paul was planning, she would have understood that he was likely the last person to have been alone with Caspar. She told him he could be found at the villa that day, thus making him the likely suspect.

"You admit it?" Daniel asks in a grim voice.

Paul slumps down in his seat. His long, large frame suddenly collapses like a fallen soufflé. "I had no choice." He whispers.

"You might have come to me!" Daniel shouts desperately. "You might have told me. I would have helped. I would have spoken to Caspar! You did not have to kill him! You never had to kill him." He shakes his head, his eyes swimming.

"I could not come to you, Daniel, you know I could not. I would have had to betray Niobe. I would have paid, you know. I care little for money, but he asked so much. So much. I need to pay a nurse for Rosie. I need to provide for her. I could think of no way out. There was no reasoning with Caspar. I tried." Paul gestures, palms stretched outward like a helpless child, "I tried to plead with him, told him I could not pay what he demanded. He would not listen. He laughed at me. Threatened me. He would have taken what little I had and never stopped asking for more."

He is pleading with us, and I am shocked how well he has hidden his desperation for so long. Shocked, too, by the stab of pity I feel for him as he crumbles apart in front of us; such a solid man reduced to teary-eyed pleas for understanding.

Daniel is unaffected. "You expect compassion? You murdered my oldest friend."

"He was a horrible man, Daniel. He was no friend to you, as you well know. Death makes us remember the departed through rosy glasses, but we cannot deny that he was a bad man."

True as this may be, it is entirely the wrong line to take with Daniel, gripping the armrests of his chair with angry white knuckles, his jaw tight, his forehead set in deep lines.

Worried he will either implode or explode, I say, "Paul, whatever type of person Caspar was, he was still a person. You took his life, Paul. It was not self-defense, it was calculated murder." There seems nothing more to say, so we sit together in miserable silence, watching each other's shock-frozen faces.

Finally, it is Paul who finds his voice again. "After the war, even before, but especially after, I loathed violence. My father had been a violent man until I grew too big to be bullied. I never fought back, never raised a hand to him in my defense. Then the war began. I read about the horrendous acts of violence men committed against other men, and I thought I could never be such a man. I could never betray my species so horribly, so permanently. I know you fought, Daniel, and I am not criticising you, truly, I didn't see the front, so I cannot judge what one does as a soldier in the heat of battle, in a struggle to survive. I am sure you did what you had to do, and I can tell, it pains you to this day."

I glance in Daniel's direction. He will not meet my eye, staring instead at some place in the distance with a passive expression, hollowed out.

Paul continues, "When I met Rosie, I knew almost instantly I had to marry her, and she felt the same." A soft smile appears and vanishes again in an instant. "Then the accident happened, yet I remained hopeful. Hopeful she would improve, and things could be as we always wished them to be. I took this position, thinking it would do her good. Nothing has changed. She nods and smiles, but there is nothing left of who she was.

"Six months or so after we arrived here, I met Niobe. At first, well, at first I never imagined . . . never intended . . ." He rubs a tear from his eye with the side of his thumb. "We fell in love, or at least into a sort of passionate liking for one another. She was so alive and real and aware, so unlike Rosie. It went on for months. It was too easy, really. I was heavy with guilt. Every time we met, I said to myself it must end, nothing good will come of it. Then it did end. Niobe wanted me to leave Rosie, to marry her. Of course

I couldn't do that. I am married to Rosie and will remain so. I didn't want to give Niobe false hope, or steal more of her affection when I knew I could not fully return it. She is so young and beautiful and kind, she deserves someone real, not a shadow like me."

"You ended the affair." I comment, knowing the story and more.

"Yes, but not before Caspar discovered it." He shakes his head wistfully. "I often think, 'if only we had not met that day', but we do that, don't we? If only this, if only that. It doesn't change a thing. Not a thing. It just made my guilt and fear grow. He waited another two weeks before coming to me for money. I was even more upset, because, by then, Niobe and I were no longer in a relationship. I tried to reason with him. I told him it was over, begged him to keep quiet. The humiliation would have been terrible for all of us. I was afraid Rosie, if she understood somehow, would retreat further into herself, lost forever."

His story truly does sounds very sad, although I fear Rosie has been gone too long for her to come back now. Each time I have met her, there has been little more than a faint glimmer of life. It must have driven Paul nearly to madness, watching her this way day in and day out. I cannot forget what he did, and I cannot justify it, though I confess, a part of me understands.

"I did the only thing I could in my desperation. I went to the villa and told him I would give him the money. I brought the poison, not the wine, not truly trusting I would do anything, still hoping I could somehow convince him to change his mind. As you now know, I failed. It was he who suggested we seal the agreement with a toast. I was so repulsed by his glee at my expense that I agreed. I know where the kitchen is, since I have been to the villa often. I fetched a bottle and two glasses. I had no intention of sharing even a drop of wine with this man. Instead I tipped the poison into the bottle. When I went outside he gloated and insulted me, saying he never understood what a pretty thing like Niobe would see in me, saying that he would have her next. I watched him as he drank the poisoned wine. I tipped my wine into the grass when he wasn't looking, so he never even noticed I did not touch it. He did not offer me any more either. Then I left, though not before cleaning my own glass and replacing it in the kitchen.

"I was in disbelief of what I had done. Halfway to Heraklion, I was almost convinced it had not happened, or that he hadn't ingested enough, that he would survive. I felt relief, truly I did. But then . . ."

"Then he died," Daniels says flatly.

"He died." Paul concedes, pressing his lips together in a pale line before looking up and asking, "What will happen now?" His tone suggests he already knows, and from his slumped shoulders and weary expression I presume he has resigned himself to his fate.

"You will be formally arrested and tried and . . ." even Daniel can hardly bring himself to speak the words aloud.

"And hanged." Paul finishes the morbid thought.

"It is a possibility," I somehow hope it will not come to this. Paul did something ghastly and irreperable, yet . . . Oh, I should not think it, but I am sad for him. Sad for what he has lost, what he has become. He is not a monster, though his action was monstrous indeed. I find myself wanting to separate the man from the deed, which cannot, of course, be done.

"What will happen to Rosie?"

Daniel and I look at one another, unease written across our features. Rosie. Rosie, who is at this moment so close at hand; Rosie, who will be parted from the person who most believes in her, who most loves her.

"Is there family? Is there anybody who can take care of her?" I ask cautiously.

"She has a brother. He lives in Amsterdam."

"He will be contacted. For now, Rosie will have her nurse to take care of her needs."

From the stricken expression on Paul's face, I believe this gives him little comfort. Indeed, for the first time this evening, he looks consumed with pain, closing his eyes tightly as if a wave of agony is passing through him.

"Paul," Daniel slowly gets to his feet, "You must come with us now. It is early enough. We will take you to the police station in Miklos where you will confess."

Paul hovers for another moment in his chair, and a shiver of anxiety that he may try to resist runs through me. To my relief, he pulls himself up with great effort and nods. He is such a large figure of a man, taller even than Dymas and Daniel. He could probably fight his way past us and attempt escape. Somehow though, I know he will not. He and Daniel walk beside one another, both in their own way broken tonight. As we near the stairway across the door, the stern-faced nurse appears from a small sitting room facing the street.

"What is the matter? Mr. Vanderheyden? Are you leaving?"

Before Paul can reply, Rosie appears at the woman's shoulder, confused but not alarmed.

Infinite sadness flashes across Paul's face. He is quick to replace it with a pained smile. "I have to go with my friends, Rosie, you will be all right. I promise." He reaches out and takes hold of her hand. She looks at him with such innocence, it is enough to cause tears to pool in my eyes. Rosie does not speak. Paul releases her and without another word, walks through the open door into the pink and purple onset of night.

CHAPTER 41

It takes no effort to guide him into the backseat of the motorcar where Daniel sits beside him and I, shaken though I am, reassume my place behind the wheel. The drive passes in utter silence. I focus resolutely on the road, on driving, getting us to Miklos, bringing an end to all of this. With a heavy heart I realize, whatever happens tonight, it is far from over; not for Paul, with his uncertain fate, or Rosie and her loss of protection and love, or even for Daniel, who despite of what has been said about the man's character, loved Caspar as a brother and will have to do without him for the rest of his life. So much finality caused by one angry impassioned deed. But it will happen again and again; it is happening right now somewhere at the hand of someone else. Another person who has forgotten we are all meant to be brothers and sisters of a kind, connected by the very species we are part of. All of us, flawed, foolish, wonderful, and intricate human beings. All of us temporary owners of the fragile gift that is life.

Within moments, we roll down the hill, negotiate the trecherous bends in the unlit road, and arrive in Miklos. The gaslight outside the police station is burning bright, and I bring the Delage to a stop in front of it. Without the hum of the motor, it is suddenly very quiet. From somewhere nearby, we hear the faint cry of a child. It fades quickly, soothed away by a gentle voice, a soft touch.

"Come." Daniel says, and we climb out of the car and ascend the steps to the station door.

The desk clerk yawns, observing our little group and raises a wary eyebrow.

"We need to see Inspector Dymas." Daniel's tone will broke no argument.

The man frowns, grudgingly getting to his feet, a sign, I hope, that Dymas is on the premises.

"Wait here." He points to a shabby bench leaning against a wall on the far side of the room.

None of us make a move. We will be sitting for some time when Paul makes his official confession, and my nerves are too overwrought to suffer immobility a moment sooner. Will Dymas allow us to remain while he listens to Paul's story? Part of me wants to get away, never to set foot in this wretched place again. Another, understands we must stay. Only knowing Paul has told Dymas exactly what he told us will allow me to believe it is real. If we are leave, Paul may deny everything and make a run for it. No, Dymas will be suspicious. He will understand. He—

"Miss Carlisle!" He is coming down the narrow hallway, spotting me first, the others hidden from the inspector's view for a moment. His face falls slightly and the familiar lines on his forehead appear as he takes in our dismal troupe.

"Inspector," I manage a brittle smile, "Paul has come to make a confession."

The lines on his brow deepen as he raises an eyebrow. "Am I to understand . . ."

"Yes," Paul nods and swallows with a bob of his Adam's apple. "It was me. I am guilty."

Dymas runs a hand across his mouth and stubbly chin. "Then you better follow me."

Without asking permission, Daniel and I tag along towards the inspector's office. The hallway is dimly lit, and the large bodies of Paul and Dymas cast enormous shadows, like werewolves or giants rambling alongside me. Werewolves and giants are not real, but monsters are. They are not confined to the pages of children's books. They roam among us, live inside of us or, in some dreadful cases, devour us entirely, until man and monster are one and the same.

The office is well lit by a large lamp beside the desk. There are only three chairs for "guests". Dymas drags in another from an office next door for the desk sergent who must write everything down and act as witness. We are packed closely into the small space, and it is with tight-chested relief that I watch Dymas opening the window. We shall not suffocate from close proximity at least.

Dymas takes his seat and leans his elbows on the desk, hands in a contemplative steeple.

Paul swallows as though the words are obstructing his throat. Finally he begins. "I am responsible for the death of Caspar Ballantine."

Dymas does not interrupt nor change his expression throughout Paul's long narrative. Hearing it again, spoken clearly without denials, without tears or raised voices, it chills me to the bone. I shrink farther away from Paul, though we are already separated by Daniel, who, without question, has taken the seat beside him.

"And that is all." Paul ends his confession with a resigned lowering of his head.

Dymas lets out a slow breath and nods. "I see. You know what must happen now?"

Paul only nods.

Dymas straightens in his seat and stands up. "Paul Vanderheyden, I am placing you under arrest for the murder of Caspar Ballantine. You may have legal council and can make a telephone call in the morning. Please," he turns to the desk sergeant, who is sitting rigidly in a wooden chair, "Sergeant, take Mr. Vanderheyden to the holding cell."

With a nervous twitch of his left eye, the young man gets to his feet, pulling a set of slim metal shackles from his jacket. Paul, who dwarfs the sergeant by at least a head and a half, holds out his hands. The smaller man, relieved to find compliance, claps the shackles onto his wrists.

As he is being led from the room, Paul turns his head and focuses his gaze on Daniel. "I am sorry. I never wanted to be a cause for pain. I am sorry, Daniel."

Those are the last words we hear from him. Then, there is only the heavy shuffling of feet on the worn floor, moving away from us.

Dymas clears his throat and sits down again, slumping in his chair, tension drawn out of him. "So it was Paul. I must confess he was very low on my list of possible suspects."

I cannot think what to say in response.

"We are free to leave now?" Daniel asks, already getting to his feet.

"Of course," the inspector replies, "and thank you for your assistance."

On our short walk out of the station, Daniel remains silent. The desk sergeant has not yet returned to his post, and the hallway is entirely unattended. We climb into the car. The leather seats are cool in the night air, a relief after the stuffy warmth of the inspector's office.

I start the motor. The engine howls to life, and we begin our short drive back to the villa.

When the silence becomes too much, I finally say, "Are you all right, Daniel?" Regretting my words almost instantly. Are you all right, indeed! These are the helpless words we use time and time again in situations so utterly out of the ordinary.

"I don't know." He sounds surprised, turning the phrase almost into a question.

Concentrating on the road, I try to maneuver the large vehicle along the baked dirt path, fainly illuminated by the car's lights. I see, from the corner of my eye, Daniel turning toward me.

"Are you all right?"

"I don't know either."

We chuckle in confused and overwhelmed unison. This eases the tension ever so slightly. and Daniel goes on in a tone more akin to normalcy.

"Jeffrey will be miserable on two counts. He will have lost a friend and another colleague."

"Heavens, you are right. Both of them worked at the museum. Perhaps it is a bad influence? Or a bad omen?"

"Best not mention such speculation to Briony."

"No," I agree, catching a glimpse of the villa at the end of the road. "Best not. She will be distraught enough."

"I dread having to go over the story once more, but we must of course tell them."

I turn into the drive, letting the Delage come to a rest in front of the pillared entry. "Daniel," I hesitate a moment to gather my thoughts, "how far do you think Niobe's involvement in this matter went?"

"From the way Paul described the situation, she had no knowledge of his plans. Yet she knew he had come to the house before Caspar died. So she must have suspected Paul at the very least. She is no fool, after all."

The thought of her crying to me while having a notion of who had murdered the man whose body I found is highly disturbing. "We will have to tell Briony and Jeffrey about the child. Under these circumstance, I must say, I do not feel a great deal of guilt breaking Niobe's confidence."

"Nor should you."

We sit silently for another moment, until, as if by spoken agreement, we climb out of the car and walk to the door.

CHAPTER 42

It turns into a very long night. Jeffrey and Briony are shocked and appalled, constantly interjecting, "This cannot be!" or "He seemed such a kind man". Needless to say, it takes a fair amount of time to fully enlighten them of our adventures, or misadventures, however one might interpret the events of this fateful night.

When we reach the part about Niobe's pregnancy, Briony pales noticeably, and Daniel and I quickly move on as though this fact is very minor indeed.

"First Darius and now Paul," Jeffrey shakes his head. "How will I explain it all?"

"It is hardly for you to explain, Jeffrey, the police will do that."

"That may well be. But what a scandal it will cause. I need something strong for the shock." Jeffrey gets to his feet and walks to the cabinet with crystal decanters. "Anyone else?"

"A drop of sherry might not go amiss," Briony leans heavily against the cushions in her back.

"Whatever you're having," Daniel adds and I agree. "Make that two, please."

"Here we are," Jeffrey hands out drinks. I take a fortifying sip.

"What shall be done about Niobe?" Briony wonders aloud after nearly draining her glass. She sounds bewildered, and I slide closer to her on the sofa.

"What shall be done? We will have to dismiss her, if Dymas won't arrest her, that is."

"Jeffrey! She is pregnant, we can't—"

"We can and we must." Jeffrey states firmly, setting his crystal tumbler on the low coffeetable with a clank. "I will not have some plotting Jezebel—"

"Come now," Daniel stops Jeffrey, aware of Briony's distress. "We are all exhausted, and angry threats will do one one any good. Let us get some rest. You had a difficult day at work and now this."

"He is right." I stifle a yawn. "Let us try to sleep, and we will find a solution in the morning. Caspar's murderer has been caught at last, that is most important."

Jeffrey frowns while he gets to his feet, holding out a hand to Briony.

"In all probability, you are right, though I do not take pleasure knowing a complicit to murder is sleeping safe and sound under my roof."

"We cannot know how well she was informed. It will be best if Briony and Evelyn confront her tomorrow. One way or another, a decision will be made."

Amidst general agreement, we go to our rooms. Briony and Jeffrey sleep on the western side of the house, Daniel and I on the eastern side. Thus, Daniel and I are left alone upon the landing.

Unspoken words hang heavily in the air between us, but before I can encourage elucidation, he swallows them and only wishes me a weak goodnight. When I close the door of my room behind me, I hear his footsteps growing fainter as he walks away.

So much has happened in so little time. It was really only a moment ago I snuck out of Aunt Agnes' house in Eaton Square. Recalling my rather underhand action, I remember the envelope, which arrived in the post today. A letter from the very woman. I didn't open it when Briony gave it to me, but instead left it on my dressing table, almost afraid of the harsh words and accusations it might contain.

But now . . . I walk to the dresser where the unassuming envelope is still waiting in a puddle of yellow lamplight. I pick it up gingerly with the tips of my fingers. The paper is smooth, yet heavy in the way of high quality stationary. Her prim and precise writing is instantly recognizable on the back. I gnaw on my bottom lip. I faced two murderers in as many days. Should I not be able to open a simple envelope? Reaching for a hatpin, I slice it open.

The letter is longer than expected, two sheets filled with delicate boarding-school handwriting. I can picture Agnes at her Chippendale table in the blue parlor overlooking the square, scribbling away to that thankless niece of hers. I crouch down on the end of the bed and, with a tightness around my heart, begin to read.

> *April 20, 1925*
>
> *12 Eaton Square*
>
> *Belgravia, London*
>
> Dear Evelyn,
>
> *I received your telegram two days ago. The letter you left at least informed me that you had not been abducted. I am glad you are well. Long voyages can bring on all sorts of illnesses, not to mention the inherent perils. Briony is a sensible girl and will see to it that you do not disgrace yourself. I was sorry to hear of the death of the Englishman and hope it has been resolved.*

A slight change in the color of the ink here leads me to believe she wrote the following at some later time.

> *Evelyn, your low regard of my person has not escaped me. You have made your disdain for my way of life, for my attitudes, clear on many occasions. I am not so obtuse as you may imagine, and you not so talented an actress. I will not make accusations, for I do understand. I understand I am not your mother. You have never viewed me as such, and perhaps I am to blame. You have resented me for not being my sister, either sister, I should add. You have always loved Iris much more than me. Maybe I am not a particularly warm person, nor do I make my sentiments known to those around me. We all have our faults, do we not? A fault I will not own, however, is that I do not love you. After the fire, Iris and even your father's family wanted charge of you, but I would not hear of it. Brendan and I fought for you, and we never regretted it. I am set in my ways, heaven knows, I was*

stubborn even as a child, but this one time, my determination bore fruit. We always regarded you as a daughter, our daughter. If I was cross or rigid in your upbringing, it was because I felt the need to protect you. To keep you, this fragment of my lost sister, alive and safe as I had promised I would. I am sorry you felt the need to flee home so secretively, though I will not deny I would have attempted to prevent such a flight.

When you decide to come back, you will always have a home here, whether you see it this way yet or not. Harris and Milly send their love.

Take care, my dear.

Yours faithfully,

Agnes

I sit motionless on the edge of the bed, the letter in my lap. The words drift through my mind. I faught for you . . . you will always have a home here. She felt the distance between us as acutely as I did. I wince at the unadorned truth behind her revelations. I did resent her, wanted my mother or Iris, anyone but her. I hated her rigidity, hated her conservative views, the way she was bent on crushing any thought of excitement or adventure. And she knew. She knew.

Putting the letter on my bedside table, I turn off the light. The room is nearly black now. This day, this long day is finally at an end. So many confessions, so many truths uncovered. Some can make the world better and some . . . only more complicated.

I close my eyes. Coming here was like dropping a stone into a pond, ripples forming all around, Caspar's death, Darius' breakdown, Paul's confession. Good as well though; being with Briony, visiting Knossos, meeting Daniel . . .

CHAPTER 43

I wake up early the next morning and remain idly in bed in a weak attempt to delay the conversation we must have with Niobe, dreading what Dymas will say about Paul. .

Just as I am convinced I can make out Pegasus in the rough plaster swirls of the ceiling, I hear a knock on my door and jolt upright at the idea of Niobe having come looking to brush my hair . . . or scalp me.

"Who it it?"

"It's me," Briony answers, and I breathe a sigh of relief.

"Come in!"

She does and the door swings open, revealing my cousin already dressed in a dark blue sheath.

"You look well." I pat the spot beside me. Briony crosses the room and climbs onto the rumpled duvet.

"I could barely sleep, Evie."

Indeed, upon closer inspection I notice the deep shadows under her eyes and experience a stab of guilt that I, oddly enough, was able to sleep like a babe. I blame it on sheer exhaustion and not on lack of compassion or conscience.

"Is Jeffrey awake?"

"Yes, he asked us to join him for breakfast in half an hour, so we may discuss how to proceed. I told cook we only want some toast, so Niobe won't enter while we are discussing her fate in this household."

"It has to be done, and so far we don't know if Dymas will charge her with anything. Nobody can prove she was in any way complicit. Paul wouldn't admit to it, especially if she tells him she is having his child."

"The morals of a murderer." Briony shrugs.

"Yes, it is still hard to believe two people of our aquaintance have committed such crimes, taken lives."

"Do you think Daniel has, too? He was in the war, in France, surely—"

"That is different!" I insist with more vehemence than intended. Briony raises a curious eyebrow, and I continue in a more even tone. "He was a soldier. In war . . . in war, I suppose, it's not considered murder."

"It is still killing. Don't misunderstand, I am not judging him. If not for men like Daniel, things may have ended very badly for us. I only wonder how he copes with it, especially now. He has dealt with a great deal of tragedy in his life, carries around so many ghosts, sometimes he himself seems like one. Still, he appears more alive than he did three months ago. Jeffrey agrees with me, as it happens."

While I am not deaf to the meaning of her words, I am not ready to embark upon such a discussion, so I only shrug and reply, "What will happen to Niobe?"

"Jeffrey insists we let her go. He assumes Dymas will arrest her, but as you say, there is little if any evidence and none, if Paul wishes to keep her out of it. Besides, she is an islander. The people here tend to protect their own against outsiders. It was bad enough Darius turned out such a bad seed. Dymas is probably relieved Paul is the person responsible for Caspar's death. He can dismiss it as a squabble between foreigners."

"Give him some credit. He has acted very fairly and even kept us informed all the while." I feel slightly defensive on the part of the inspector.

"Fair or not, you must admit Paul being the guilty one makes the situation significantly easier for him."

"Politically perhaps, though in no other way I can think of. Paul will never meet his child, and Rosie has lost the one person who had hope in her recovery. It is a tragic situation."

Briony nods in sad agreement.

"What do you want to do, about Niobe?" I ask. Mentioning Niobe and Paul's child has cast a shadow over her eyes. To her credit, she does not moan about the unfairness of it all. A woman—likely was complicit to murder—has exactly what she herself has been yearning for.

Briony leans against the headboard. "She and Yannick must marry soon. They will live with her family. Yannick can retain his position here. Niobe would soon leave us anyway, wouldn't she, when the child is born."

"This sounds like the most practical solution," I answer slowly, assessing her expression.

"It is for the best. There are many women who can take her place."

By some instinct, or simply the desire to see a smile upon her face, I ask, "Have you finished Areta's dress?"

The smile appears, though small and sad. "Yes. I will give it to her on Saturday."

"Have you . . ." I falter, biting my lip as I am in the habit of doing. "Have you spoken to Jeffrey? About adoption?"

"No, he has been under so much pressure these past days; first, the museum and then Darius and now Paul. It seemed best to wait. I will speak to Sister Sybil first."

"Oh Briony, you must tell him soon. You cannot make these plans with the Sister and not consult the would-be father."

"What if he refuses?"

"You must take him to meet the child."

"If he says no then, it will be even worse. It will mean he does not like her."

"Nonsense. If he says no, it shows he is afraid. He will be afraid. Taking on a child not biologically yours is an endeavour worthy of contemplation, for your own good and Areta's."

"Do you think he will agree to accompanying me?" Briony looks at me with pleading eyes, reminding of a much younger, no less vulnerable version of herself. I clasp her hand and give it a small squeeze.

"I do." Adding in a lighter tone, "and if he does not, I certainly will."

The smile touches her eyes, and I am once again reassured in my decision to come here.

"Shall we go to breakfast?" Briony is already climbing off the bed.

"In a minute, first I have to show you something." I reach over to the bedside table where Agnes' letter lies waiting. Unfolding the stiff paper, I show it to my cousin. "Aunt Agnes wrote to me."

"I know. I gave you the letter—"

"No, look." I hold it out to her. Reluctantly she takes the sheaves from my outstretched hands.

"I can't read this, it's private!"

"Forget decorum for a moment, Briony. I could just as well tell you what it says."

"Fine, give it here then." Reluctantly my cousin takes the letter and leans against the sturdy bedpost as her eyes dart across the pages. When she is finished, Briony places them gently on my bedside table.

"Are you pleased?"

"Pleased? Do you mean, am I relieved she doesn't hate me as I suspected?"

"Come now, don't be so dramatic. You always knew she didn't hate you."

"I never felt loved, never accepted. Why would she fight for me as she says, if she couldn't kiss me when I scraped a knee or hold my hand when I went off to school?"

"It's not her way."

"What an easy explanation!"

"I am not her greatest champion by any means. I just want to say, it was hard for her, too. In some sense, she probably assumed providing in other ways was more important, that it compensated enough. Perhaps she thought she was doing you a favor, hardening you in a way."

"Hardening me? Why should a child need to be hardened? I had lost my parents!" I notice the volume of my voice creeping up as I vent my frustrations, feel the heat in my cheeks as I put into words the pain that has dwelt within me for so long. I never liked speaking about it, only jokingly complaining about Agnes' shortcomings, rarely daring to acknowledge much more. There was always a barrier of guilt and necessary gratitude preventing me. I forced myself to remember the ways in which I was fortunate to have Agnes in my life. Those past years of unvoiced unhappiness building up inside of me created a bitterness I had not truly been aware of. I lean against the bedpost, self-conscious at my outburst and oddly relieved at once.

"I know." Her voice carries a hint of melancholy, and she takes hold of my hand. "What happened to your parents was so tragic. Agnes is not the sort of person to comfort with kindness. Her comfort was by being useful. She was probably under the impression that she was helping you, as well as helping herself by being useful. Jeffrey is the same. After we lost the baby, he buried himself in his work. I think that is why I sometimes so resent it. There are different people on this planet, countless different people, who see and feel and grieve differently. We cannot possibly understand it all."

I am stunned to hear her words, so commanding, yet spoken in a voice full of compassion and warmth. Briony has always been the cheerful one, and in spite of being older than me, always seemed the more youthful of the two of us, simply a consequence of her manner. It would appear she has matured. More than me, perhaps?

"You are right, of course you are. I am sorry, I shouldn't—"

"No apologies." She smiles gently and gives my hand a final squeeze before letting go and moving to the door. "Come now, make yourself decent and have breakfast with us. It will doubtless be a long day." She disappears, and I experience a sudden pang of loneliness.

Following her wise words, I get ready, washing and throwing on a mauve skirt and cream blouse with a print of tiny flowers. As I leave the room, passing the bed, I turn and tuck the letter into the drawer. It will keep a while.

Daniel and Jeffrey are seated at the round table in the conservatory. I take my chair when Briony enters with the newspaper.

"Is that the Mail?" Jeffrey sets down his teacup.

"Yes, yesterday's." She hands it to him, sits down beside me, and takes two pieces of golden toast from a platter.

Jeffrey scans the front page. "Nothing about Caspar. Not that I thought there would be. Frankly, I doubt even Paul's arrest will be much in the way of news. The paper is full of this Von Hindenburg fellow having been elected the President of Germany. That leaves little space for anything coming from a small island in the Mediterranean."

"Good." Daniel swallows a sip of coffee. "His father has telegraphed that only one reporter has approached him. He lives privately on our estate, so he should have little bother."

"Was he very upset about missing his son's funeral?" I want to know, spooning some of cooks' wonderfully thick blackberry marmelade onto a piece of toast.

"To be honest, I got the impression he was relieved not to attend. They had little contact, but of course he was sad and troubled by Caspar's passing."

"This way, he can almost pretend it didn't happen, if he isn't there to witness the final rites," I say.

"Maybe."

"It must be hard though, knowing his boy is buried so far from home, and he will likely never visit his grave." Briony adds.

"Undoubtedly it is, but as I say, they hardly spoke. The man I know him to be will cope, and what other choice does he have?"

We are all silent for a moment. Contemplatively taking bites and sips and stirring and buttering until Jeffrey puts down the paper. "Has Briony told you what we will do about that girl?"

It takes me a second to understand the meaning of this abrupt change direction in our conversation. "Oh . . . yes, yes she has."

"And? Do you agree? I told Daniel, and he thinks it is a good course of action."

I shrug. "In the circumstances, it is the best you can be expected to do by her."

"Well, I wouldn't mind Dymas coming by to arrest her. Briony believes Paul will not incriminate her though, and I suppose I agree."

"As do I," I say.

"That's settled then. I shall tell her after breakfast. We will have to find a new girl. You will see to it will you not, dear?"

Briony offers her husband a smile. "I will. If you don't mind, I would like to be the one to speak to Niobe."

"Alone?" I ask, stiffening with concern.

"She will not harm me."

"You can't be certain of her! For all we know—"

"Evie," she adopts a calm, firm tone, which will serve her well with Areta or whoever her future child will be. "I can manage quite well. I will speak to her inside the house. If I scream, you may come to my rescue."

"I hardly think that is very funny." I pout.

Briony grins. "No, I should think not. Still, I will have my way."

"Do not bother arguing, Evelyn," Jeffrey adds. "You know as well as I, she can be stubborn as a mule."

"Indeed," I say and finish the last of the toast.

CHAPTER 44

After breakfast, Inspector Dymas arrives. Briony immediately tries her best to ply him with food and coffee. Valiantly he resists, explaining he came to tell us the investigation has been officially concluded. Jeffrey inquires as to charges Niobe may face. In answer, Dymas shrugs. Nothing can be proven. Our soon-to-be former maid has been dealt a lucky hand, in this respect at least.

Before he leaves, he turns and adds in a weary, not unkind tone, "Miss Carlisle, Mr. Harper, thank you for your assistance. I am not an advocate of civilian involvement in solving serious crimes, in this case though, it was for the best in the end. You have been very helpful."

"We were happy to be of assistance," I reply, enjoying the warm sense of validation, basking in his praise. Dymas gives me a crooked smile, puts on his hat and leaves.

"It is over now." Daniel comments as we close the door.

"I hope so."

"Of course it is!" Jeffrey shouts. "Now I must also take leave. There will be a lot of confusion at the museum today."

"Good luck, my dear," Briony plants a small kiss on his cheek.

"You will be careful when you talk to Niobe, won't you?"

"I promise."

"Good. Well then, I'm off."

Once he is gone, Briony has to perform the difficult task of dismissing Niobe. Daniel and I decide to wait in the sitting room in case our assistance is required. I rather doubt it will be. Niobe should count herself lucky indeed. All in all, coming away from it without legal repercussions is quite an achievement. I do recall that I always had a strange feeling about her. Enlightenment often arrives only belatedly.

"What are you thinking with that grin on your face?" Daniel asks, pulling me back into the moment.

"Oh, nothing. Nothing at all."

"I might go to visit Laria later and tell her. She will be at the funeral tomorrow, and I think she should know beforehand."

"I had almost forgotten. Yes, yes you must tell her."

"I want to set off once Briony comes back. Laria is probably be home preparing lunch."

"Will you be all right? Shall I go with you?"

He leans back in his chair, a faint smile pulling at his mouth. "That would be good of you. It may make her feel more comfortable to have a woman present."

"Then it is settled."

CHAPTER 45

It takes less than thirty minutes for Briony to return. "You did it?" I ask, sliding to one side of the sofa, making space for her to sit. She falls into the empty seat beside me. "I did. She will leave by noon."

"You gave her money, didn't you?" I ask, once Daniel has excused himself to fetch his hat for our walk to the village.

Briony avoids my eyes.

"Briony!"

"Just a bit! Just for the child." She gestures passively with her palms out.

"Well . . ."

"Oh come, Evie, whatever she knew, it is a sad story."

"She will marry Yannick," I say petulantly.

"Yannick, who will always know their first child isn't his. Yannick whom she doesn't love."

"But who dotes on her. She is using him!"

"Yes, she is." Briony agrees slowly, playing with the tassles on one of the cushions. "Sometimes women have to do what must be done. We do not live in a world where a woman, unmarried and with child is accepted and respected, nor in a world where she has much opportunity to change her lot in life."

I let her words sink in, their truth exposed, and admire her for finding and voicing them in opposition to my stubborness.

"You did what was right, as always."

"I hope so." She lets go of the tassle and looks at me, an earnest expression on her face.

"What is it?"

"Will you be honest with me now?"

"What on earth do you mean?" I ask, truly puzzled.

Briony rolls her eyes and tilts her head to the side.

"You know exactly what I mean. As you are acting so obtuse, I will help you. I say only: Daniel..."

"Daniel?"

Briony sighs dramatically. "Come now! You can't tell me you are indifferent. You two have been glued together nearly since you arrived!"

I am about to protest when I realize the truth of her assertion. "Well, he is a very nice—"

"Nice," Briony waves dismissively, "he is handsome, rich, and an absolute catch. What will you make of it?"

"Briony!" Heat crawls up the back of my neck.

"Well?"

"Well, nothing." I stammer, looking down as though my fingernails are suddenly terribly interesting.

"He is certainly taken with you, you have at least noticed that, haven't you?"

I shrug, feeling absurdly helpless.

"Do you like him? Come speak up, cousin dear, or must I force it out of you. I am smaller than Dymas, nonetheless, you may be certain, I shall have my confession."

This does the trick. I cast a quick glance in the direction of the door and lowering my voice admit, "I can't say I am entirely indifferent."

"Heavens, if that is all you can admit to, your courtship shall be a terribly long one. He is clearly unable to decipher your feelings, you seem blind to his. I will have to lock the two of you into a room and wait until something happens." She shakes her head in frustration, all the while maintaining a knowing smile. "You two would probably talk about books or the weather, or worse, these horrid murders. What can be done?"

"Briony, nothing needs to be done. Truly, I respect him. He is an intelligent, kind man . . . Oh, all right, he is rather handsome, but—"

"But nothing. You are perfect for each other."

Now it is my turn to roll my eyes. "We hardly know one another. How could we possibly be a perfect match?"

"You have spent a lot of time together lately. One can learn a lot about another person in the span of a few weeks. Besides, you already live together."

"Under your roof!"

"Jeffrey and I are hardly the most attentive chaperones."

"Briony! Stop these insinuations. We," I emphasize the word, "are very well behaved. Besides, there have certainly been other things to occupy our minds. Daniel was hardly in a state of mind for any wooing and neither was I."

"That can be amended now. Make the boy smile again."

My heart is suddenly beating unusually fast. I wonder whether Briony can hear it. Hopefully not, or else she would surely take it as confimation of her silly thoughts. Or are they? Maybe she isn't so far from the truth after all. There were certainly plenty of moments when I imagined . . .

"What is going through that mind of yours? You need not formulate any excuses, I understand. Frankly, if I were not entirely unavailable . . ."

"Really, you mustn't joke about such things."

"Yes," she concedes, looking chastized. "You are right. But only about this. See," she gestures at my hat on the table, "you are already planning to go off with him again."

"To help Laria," I protest weakly.

"For moral support."

"Exactly."

"To hold his trembling hand."

"Oh stop it!" I frown disapprovingly, after a moment though, we descend into a childish fit of giggles. Daniel finds us in this state, already wearing his hat, dashing as ever.

"Am I interrupting?" he asks, standing at the door.

"No, no," I get to my feet and grab my hat. "I am quite ready."

"Take your time, you two." Briony adds encouragingly.

I cringe and make for the door where I turn to give her a stern look, which she evidently finds enormously amusing.

CHAPTER 46

Daniel and I decide to walk. The bicycles are more trouble than they are worth, and I still get a faint ache in the muscles of my calves at the mere memory of the steep and winding lanes.

We set off at a pleasant pace. The day is comfortingly warm, and the sky peerless blue, not blemished by a single cloud. I think I shall never grow tired of the sight.

"Briony is much relieved by all of this coming to a close. I haven't seen her so cheerful in a while." Daniel breaks the silence while we meander around the first bend.

"She is also greatly comforted that Laria and Nikolas had nothing to do with it."

"Still, it is very sad for Rosie."

"Do you think she understands? It would almost be better, if she did not."

"We may never know. Dymas mentioned they have contacted her brother. She will return to Holland."

"They will place her in a hospital, don't you think?" I wonder sadly, kicking at a small stone, sending it skittering down the dusty road.

"It depends on her brother, whether he can afford to hire a nurse, or whether he already has a large family to provide for. Finances will play into it. Paul may have money saved. I hope she will be well cared for."

"As do I." A cloud has drifted into the horizon of my mind, though the sky above remains untainted.

"I hope Nikolas isn't home."

"It could be somewhat . . . uncomfortable," I agree.

Turning around another bend, we see the familiar façade of the village in the near distance. We walk the rest of the way in companionable silence, each doubtless rehearsing the coming conversation playing out the scene in our minds, until we find ourselves in front of the pretty house of the Zarek family.

"Well, here we are."

"Ready?"

He nods and raps the doorknocker loudly. We wait for a moment, soon hearing the sound of footsteps approaching behind the door before it swings open to reveal the lady of the house.

She looks surprised to see us and opens the door widely to let us in.

"Hello, come inside. What brings you here?" Laria's manner is friendly, but vaguely suspicious as she ushers us into her light-filled parlor. I am quick to dispell her anxiety and begin to explain.

"Inspector Dymas has arrested Caspar's murderer."

Laria gasps and brings a hand to her mouth.

"Who? Who did it? It wasn't Darius, was it? He has been arrested, but that was two days ago and—"

"No," Daniel raises a calming hand, "it wasn't Darius. It was Paul. Paul Vanderheyden."

"Paul? But why? Why would he do such a thing? What business did he have with Caspar? They barely knew one another."

"Caspar was blackmailing Paul. Paul wished to keep an event in his life private. I cannot go into the details. Needless to say, this prompted Paul's action."

"Oh, no. This is dreadful. Why did Caspar do such things?" Laria's eyes begin to swim with tears, which quickly spill down her cheeks in salty torrents.

I place a comforting arm around her shoulders and make soothing sounds. Daniel looks exceedingly uncomfortable and his expression, in other circumstances, would be rather amusing.

"This is a dreadful shock," I try to soothe. "At least we have some resolution. At least we know."

"I just don't understand," Laria sobs. I notice, with a shameful stab of envy, that she is one of those people who look even lovelier with tears staining their cheeks, no pink blotches around her nose or red-rimmed eyes.

"No one can really understand, not even Paul, I think. He seemed almost as shocked as we were by his confession."

"Tell me what happened," Laria straightens up slightly, and I remove my arm. With a nod from Daniel, I begin to tell our tale, or as much of it as I can.

"Paul and Niobe, I can understand that much at least. And of course Paul had to keep it quiet to prevent Rosie's family from discovering the truth." Laria says more to herself than us.

Daniel and I throw each other vaguely puzzled looks.

"I suppose he wanted to keep it from them. Though I doubt this was his highest priority."

Laria frowns at us. "You do not know?"

A sudden curious anxiety makes the hair on the back of my neck stand to attention, and I straighten in my chair.

"Know what?" asks Daniel, his eyes narrowed, tense body leaning forward.

"Rosie has a large fortune! Her family owns vast amounts of land. They more or less pay Paul to take care of Rosie. I should not really know this, but one evening when everyone had a lot to drink, he came out with it all."

"And if Rosie's family got wind of his infidelity—" Daniel begins cautiously.

"He would have been cut off!" I interrupt.

"It doesn't make sense," he folds his arms across his chest. "He didn't live extravagantly. He claimed he coulnd't pay Caspar's demands . . ."

"Maybe he used most of the money for Rosie's benefit. The nurse must command a decent fee, being on hand all the time. Do they own the house?" I wonder aloud.

"It should be easy to discover."

"He claimed he did it to protect Rosie?" Laria wrinkles her nose in contempt.

"He said he worried she might become aware of his affair, it would set back her recovery. Yet if your theory is accurate, it further explains why he would not leave Rosie for Niobe."

"As we suspected, he was mostly protecting himself. Perhaps he thought after a time he could amass enough money to take himself off . . . without Rosie."

"Poor woman," Laria states sadly, dabbing at her now-dry eyes with the corner of a starched white handkerchief.

"Yes, poor Rosie. At least we can be certain her family has the means to give her the care she needs. Some small comfort."

"We have to take what comfort we can. Still, nothing will bring back Caspar," Laria sighs and crushes the handkerchief in her fist.

"No," Daniel unfolds his arms and clasps his hands together in a solemn gesture, "nothing will."

CHAPTER 47

Daniel and I stay only a short while longer before taking our leave. Laria is stunned, not shattered by the news, and I hope she will be able to be happy again. She loved Caspar, and even the unveiling of his sometimes dispicable behaviour to others did not change that. He must have been very different with her as he was with Daniel. I will never truly know. My own mind is too thickly clouded with the unsavory aspects of his character, and he will never be able to disprove them by any kindness or attention.

Together side by side, we walk towards the main street. As if on tracks, we somehow find our way to Hector's Café where we slump into our usual chairs and are promptly given a basket of sweet buns and tiny cups of strong brew.

"We should tell Dymas." Daniel announces wearily. He appears well and truly unenthusiastic faced with the prospect of seeking out the inspector again, of even setting foot inside the police station, a sentiment I wholly echo.

"Later. Paul is in custody. Whatever motive he had, he made a full confession. Clarifications can be added in time." I take a sip of the scalding, fortifying brew and crumble one of the buns onto a plate.

Daniel appears relieved at the reprieve, taking a large bite of the sweet pastry. I watch him and a thought comes to my mind, no doubt brought on by the ludicrous conversation with Briony. Try as I might, I cannot push it aside.

"Daniel," I begin, faltering with hesitation.

He turns his head. "Yes?"

"What will you do now, after the funeral?" I watch his expression in response to my query, his chest rising, expanding, then collapsing again before he finds an answer.

"I haven't decided. I can't say I've given it much thought."

"You will leave?" I ask, aiming for a neutral tone to mask my disappointment at this possibility.

"Leave Crete? Perhaps. Though I have grown quite fond of this place, of the people."

The people.

"You could stay."

Again he pauses before answering, and I glance at his face to see his eyes narrowed as if in confusion. "I could. Do you plan on staying?"

"Yes, at least some time longer, as long as Briony and Jeffrey will tolerate me."

"Then you will stay forever!" Daniel smiles, and I join in.

"No, no. Jeffrey will grow tired of being outnumbered. Besides, they should have their privacy. It is only for a while. Briony still feels a bit overwhelmed, and I want to be here until that changes"

"You two are very close. I've noticed how protective you are of her, like a sister."

The comment pleases me, and a warm glow rises in my cheeks.

"We always pretended to be sisters when we were children."

"Why, if you don't mind my asking, did you not go to live with her family?"

"Oh, my aunt, well she—"I shake my head and shrug. "To be honest, for most of my life I have wondered about just that. My guardian—Aunt Agnes—and I do not have the closest of relationships. A few days ago, I received a letter, a rather unexpected one." With a surprising lack of restraint, I tell him about the contents of the letter. He does not interrupt, waiting instead, hands in his lap and eyes on mine, for me to finish.

"It is always nice to know one is wanted?" he comments with a note of curiosity turning his remark into a question.

I slowly take a sip of the cooling coffee before replying. "Of course it is."

"You are not entirely pleased, though?"

"It isn't that," I protest half-heartedly. "I just do not understand her. Even now."

"Many people struggle with showing affection. Especially people of a certain generation and upbringing who have had a stiff-upper-lip attitude instilled in them from an early age."

"That must be it. In part at least," I concede.

"And the remaining parts may always remain a mystery. Especially if you let them be."

I narrow my eyes. "What do you mean?"

"I think you understand my meaning quite well."

"I have tried," I counter defensively, aware of this being only a half-truth.

"Maybe you have. Still you are no longer a child, it may be easier now."

"I doubt it. I will not go back to live with her."

"Probably a wise decision, if you are intent on improving your relationship," he grins.

"Yes, safer for us both."

With this we get up to make our way back to the villa, and I realize he never answered my question at all.

CHAPTER 48

We decide it is only right to tell Dymas of Paul's possibly darker motives for his crime from the telephone in the Farnham home. Daniel makes the call, and I leave him to do so in private, seeking out Briony instead. On my way to the sitting room, I pass the kitchen, catching a glimpse of long and curly black hair. Niobe.

Hesitating only a moment, I open the door and step inside. She is alone and does not notice me until I make an awkward coughing sound at which she veers around skittishly like a frightened animal.

"Oh, it is you." Her tone is neither cold nor kind, wavering somewhere in the purgatory that is indifference.

"Niobe."

She regards me with dark eyes, arms crossed, a stance both defiant and disinterested. "I am leaving. You need not worry. I will be gone in an hour, before Mr. Farnham returns."

"That is for the best, do you not agree? My cousin has been very fair."

At the mention of Briony, her expression softens ever so slightly. "Mrs. Farnham is a good lady."

"She is."

"She does not hate me."

"Niobe, none of us hate you." I step nearer. "After what has happened, you must realize, we cannot trust you. Not after what you kept from us and from the police. Heavens, you would have let Darius or someone else take the blame, would you not? Did you wish to protect the man you loved? Was it money, money Paul had promised you to keep your secret? Or did he promise to run away with you?"

Niobe unfolds her arms, resting her hands on top of the gleaming counter. As if she hasn't heard my questions, she answers simply, "I loved Paul."

"Loved?" Not undying devotion after all. Probably for the best.

"I did not want him to be guilty, but if he was . . ."

"Then you weren't going to betray him?"

"He is the father of my child."

"A child he knows nothing about."

"It is best this way." She frowns and twists a strand of hair around her finger.

"Does Yannick know about Paul?"

Her answer comes with a firm resolution I did not expect. "No. Nothing. He is a good man. He would not have kept silent. Besides, he has no reason to protect Paul."

"Will you marry him?"

Niobe nods, no change in her expression, her eyes dry and unblinking. "Next weekend. On Sunday." She takes her hands from the counter and steps back to the door. "Goodbye, Miss Carlisle."

"Goodbye, Niobe."

Leaving the kitchen somewhat dazed by this encounter, I run into Daniel.

"Oh, it's you! Did you speak to Dymas?"

He shakes his head. "No, I left a message for him to ring me back or come to the house. I want it all sorted and the case truly concluded before the funeral."

"I understand. You need not talk to him, I can do it."

"No, no. It doesn't matter." The lines across his brow tell a different story, but I will not push him.

"All right. If there is anything you need . . . ?"

"Nothing, thank you."

"Evie?" I hear Briony's voice calling from above. Reflexively, both Daniel and I tilt our heads to see where her disembodied voice is coming from.

A moment later, Briony is on the stairs in a daydress of lavender cotton with a delicate lace collar. "Oh good, you're back. How did she take the news?" she descends the last step and joins us.

"Come, let us sit in the conservatory, and we will tell you." I gently take her elbow and lead her with Daniel at our heels. He appears somewhat lost at the moment. He wanted so badly to find Caspar's killer and may be confused or disappointed that true closure is much harder to come by, especially after learning of the more unsavory aspects of his friend's character.

The conservatory is bathed in sunlight, and we sit in our customary seats. In turns, Daniel and I tell Briony about our day.

"Poor Laria, though I am most troubled by the notion that Paul's motives were even more sinister than we thought."

"He led us to believe he was acting almost nobly, protecting Rosie. Doing right by Niobe and his wife, when in truth, he was probably doing it for financial gains."

". . . to protect his allowance from Rosie's family," Daniel finishes my sentence.

"Altogether tragic," is all Briony has left to say, and we can add nothing except to nod in absolute agreement.

CHAPTER 49

We stay a while longer in the gentle light of the sun as it filters through the broad glass panes. It feels as though we are trapped within a crystal. Outside the trees, small and young, sway back and forth in the mild breeze blowing in from the sea. A group of starlings, lively brown specks, make a habit of settling on the patches of grass and then, as if startled by a shotgun, lurch back into the air, turning into even smaller dots on the horizon until they disappear. The scene could be one of utter serenity, were it not for the old oak tree at the edge of the garden. A plain reminder of what it gave shade to, what I found, whom I found. One day, perhaps, this event will sink into history. Still, the past is the past. All the same, it has a far reach, warming us or burning us with an onslaught of memory.

Briony asks the cook to make us sandwiches when we realize, with rumbling bellies that we forgot all about lunch. The day's events have shaken our sense of normality and routine, and we are still trying to find our way back onto a familiar path.

When Jeffrey comes home in the evening, he is accompanied by Dymas. He towers over Briony's husband, yet both wear the same mask of tired resignation. Not to reapeat our story again and again, we let both of them sit down, fill their glasses with cool lemonade and only then inform them of Paul's likely darker motive.

Neither man is terribly shocked. Jeffrey groans, probably considering this new development just another nasty imposition on his previously peaceful life. Dymas raises his expressive brows and says little, making quick notes in a small book and soon afterwards takes his leave, reminding us he will be attending the funeral tomorrow.

"How was your day, darling?" Briony asks her husband once Dymas has departed.

"As I expected. Everyone was mystified. We do not know how to proceed. We have lost a curator and archaeologist, and with them two brilliant minds we believed to be two good friends. It will be a hard process to move forward and think about replacing them."

"Replace them . . ." Daniel repeats the words slowly.

"Daniel?"

"Is everybody replaceable?" he asks the question with neither guile nor judgement, more like a curious child waiting for an answer.

"No, of course not, I only meant—" Jeffrey stammers when Daniel interrupts.

"I know what you meant, and of course their labor and their skill must be replaced. I am thinking of the person. During the war, soldiers were taught to regard themselves as part of a greater whole, though admittedly not that this whole could function even after we were gone. Valuable, yet far from priceless; our finger on the trigger could be replaced by that of another poor, brave, foolish soul. What do we truly mean to others? In a world where murder happens every day and everywhere, where life is too often under threat not only by the elements, illness, misfortune, but by the hands of our fellow people, what hope is there for the future? What do our lives count for in the grand scheme of things?"

Jeffrey shrugs helplessly, looking at his wife and me. It is Daniel himself who comes to his rescue. Waving his hand in a dismissive gesture he says, "Oh, I am sorry. I am being morose. Let us try to talk of better things, better times ahead, yes?"

No one disagrees, though his words have taken root. We all have lost people, family, and friends and have filled their void however we could to keep ourselves from falling to pieces. I remember my parents, out of this world for many years, longer than I ever knew them. They have stayed alive in some vast pocket of my heart and mind where they will remain as long as I am here as long as I can remember or imagine. So many of my thoughts are not memories, but fantasies and imaginings, which have seen me through my blackest days.

"Will Laria attend the funeral?" asks Briony, back on the subject we cannot avoid.

"Yes, but I do not know if Nikolas will," says Daniel.

"Can't blame him," Jeffrey comments wryly. "I wonder how he found out. If he did. Maybe husbands can sense these things."

Dear Jeffrey, overly crediting the power of the husband's insight into the mind of his wife. I glance at Briony, who is mirroring my amusement.

"We will offer refreshments after the funeral for those who wish to attend." My cousin informs us, smiling kindly at Daniel, taking control of the little in this affair she can.

After some time, we disperse to perform our little chores or close our eyes for an hour before dinner. Back in my room, a nervous anxiety tugs at my insides as I think of tomorrow. My mind's eye conjures up images of a group of black-clad mourners clustered around the polished coffin; the sealed casket disappearing into the empty pit in the ground; and the lonely marker of the grave reading Caspar's name and his youthful age. I crouch down on the edge of the bed, wrapping my arms around my raised knees. Somewhere ouside the open window, I hear the cries of seagulls, shrill and keening. Closing my eyes, I imagine them flying in circles above the villa. Higher and higher they swirl and spin, gliding through the air, nearly weightless, gray and white streaks in the violet sky. To be able to fly. To drift away as one pleases . . .

Maybe one day I will experience what it is like. Men are flying aeroplanes now; even women have tried. We are competing with nature. I do not know if we can ever truly best it, or if we should. For all the energy we expend into advancing our race, an equally powerful might always looms nearby, readying to force our retreat. This is how it has always been. Humans are capable of great goodness and tremendous cruelty. To maintain a balance, we must keep one eye on each and learn from wickedness as well as wonder. One to avoid and one to aspire to. All far easier wished for than done.

Hopefully, once tomorrow's trials are behind us, we can move forward. With this thought comes my sudden need to read my aunt's letter once more. I turn to the side and fish it from the bedside drawer. After reading it, I peer at the clock. One hour till dinner. With effort, more mental than physical, I drag myself off the bed to sit on the dainty wicker chair before the oval writing desk. Taking a clean sheet of paper, simple and plain, I begin to write.

After three attempts and three crumpled pages, lying sad and discarded on the floor, I have composed a satisfying reply.

> *Dear Aunt Agnes,*
>
> *I thank you for your letter and good wishes. I have conveyed them to my kind hosts and send theirs in turn.*

This is a slight exaggeration of the truth, for neither Briony nor Jeffrey have done any such thing. Yet it is a good way to start, and I am sure my cousin and her husband will not mind me using them to ease my way into this difficult communication.

> *Crete is a lovely place and Miklos, the village near my cousin's home, very dear. Perhaps, one day you shall see for yourself.*

Too challenging, condescending . . .? I nibble the end of my pen, forcing myself to continue onto harder parts.

> *Much has happened recently, good and bad. Still, you need not worry. I am thankful for the candor you show in your last letter. We have always had our differences, you and me, have we not? I recognize my own fault in the matter and offer sincere apologies. You and Uncle Brendan gave me a home, and I do not like you to think me ungrateful, though undoubtedly I acted carelessly on many occasions. As time goes by, we move on, not forgetting the past, instead accepting it, encouraged that happier times are ahead. I have the greatest hope that our relationship, dear aunt, will much improve as we learn to understand one another better with time. At the moment I am happy to be with my cousin, to experience the ways of a different culture. Times are such that a woman of my age and position can*

do so quite freely. Thank you for the kind offer of your continued hospitality when I return to London. I will look forward to our next meeting and to a conversation long overdue.

Wishing you continued health and happiness.

Yours truly,

Evelyn

PS: Please send my regards and good wishes on to Harris and Milly and tell them, if you will, I think of them often.

There. Done. Rather exhausted from the effort, I set down the pen just as bell rings for dinner. Still wearing my dayclothes, I quickly get up, toss them aside and step into a freshly pressed blue and purple silk dress with a low waist and narrowly beaded hem. Casting a glance in the mirror I run the brush through my hair, and bolt from the room. I have a compunction not to be late. Not for anything. The curse of good manners!

CHAPTER 50

Dinner is a delightful affair of steamed white fish in lemon sauce, thick slices of aubergine roasted with goat cheese and drizzled with fruity olive oil, ripe apricots and kumquat ice cream. We speak of books, Jeffrey taunting Daniel about his writer's block; of travel, future journeys down the Nile or up Mount Kilimanjaro. Put simply, no topic is barred, none but Caspar's funeral.

It is a pleasant evening with some laughter and a deep sense of contentment to be in good company tonight. Tomorrow will doubtless be a trying day. I feel a little less afraid, a little less small and ineffectual, surrounded by people who will stand beside me, offer me a hand in friendship or a shoulder for support.

After the table has been cleared, save for our glasses of sherry or brandy, no one is able to call an end to the day, fearful, no doubt, of allowing the next one to begin. After Briony stifles her third yawn, however, and my eyes begin to droop, we grudgingly bid each other goodnight and make for our beds to toss and turn until dawn arrives.

Before I enter my room, I turn once more to Daniel, a forlorn figure in the low light of the hall.

"Tomorrow it will be over," I know it isn't true, but hope he believes me.

He shrugs sadly, not deceived. "Until tomorrow. Goodnight, Evelyn."

"Goodnight, Daniel." So much more should be said, yet I can find no words to say it.

My room is dark and instead of turning on the light, I wander over to the window. The waning moon sends silver light through the translucent curtains, and a soft breeze drifts in through an opening in the delicate fabric. The air is fresh against my skin as it felt on the first night I was here. The night before the murder, before I ever could have known what awaited us all. Not much time has passed, and still much has changed. That is the way of life. Like the hungry flames eating away my childhood, so quickly can our world be turned on its head. We must learn to walk on our hands . . . or break our necks.

EPILOGUE

Despite my prediction of sleep evading me, I awake surprisingly rested. The day begins drenched in sunlight, birds chirping outside my window, oblivious to the woes befalling the humans inside. Altogether, this scene is unbefitting the day of a funeral. Hopefully, I can take it as a sign of lighter days to come. When we assemble at the gravesite, shivering with the eerie chill that accompanies all such occasions, the warm rays will be a welcome comfort in our backs.

Breakfast is a somber affair, none of us willing to mention where we are going in an hour's time. We make ill-disguised attempts to mask our anxiety with chatter, soon evolving into silence, to eating and drinking up as quickly as we can.

At a quarter to ten our congregation of dark-clad figures bundles into the car. Yannick, silently absorbed in his duty, drives us into Miklos and down an alley towards the ancient church and cemetary, which have been built a distance away from the village.

The priest is a small, stooped man of indeterminate age, who cannot speak or understand much in the way of English. He places one of his hands on Daniel's arm, the universal sign of comfort and compassion, needing no spoken words.

We join them in entering the church. Laria, Nikolas and two men I do not know have come as well. They are muscled and deeply tanned, and I realize they are the grave-diggers.

The service is performed in Greek and Latin, and I understand only small bits here and there. Yet I need not speak the language to understand what is being said. I have attended too many funerals in my lifetime already.

Afterwards, we file outside to the grave. The two burly men stand beside the coffin, around which they tie two thick ropes and begin lowering it slowly into its final resting place. Again the priest speaks, but when the casket has settled at the botttom and the ropes are pulled up, Daniel moves to the head of the opening in the ground. His face is pale even in the sunlight, which makes the blades of grass glow with late morning dew and the tops of our heads gleam. He clears his throat and looks out at us.

"Thank you for coming today to say goodbye to Caspar Ballantine, a man some of you never really knew. In the past few days, we have learned things about him, about his character that have shocked and appalled us, myself as well as you. In spite of all of this, I will remember him as the man who stood beside me in a mud-filled trench and shared his last cigarette, the boy who helped me reel in my first fish, the friend who was there beside me on my worst days and my best. We lay him to rest today, too early, far too early. He will not be forgotten." His voice, which had begun hoarse and quiet, has grown in strength, and I feel tears pricking in my eyes for the man before me and for the man in the casket he is describing, who I will never now know. Whatever his faults, he gave his friendship to Daniel, and for that he must have been, at least in part, a decent man.

"Goodbye, Caspar. Rest in peace." Daniel smiles sadly and tosses a handful of damp earth onto the wooden coffin. We leave flowers, and the priest places a candle in a blue glass jar next to the grave as we slowly take our leave. In our stead, the two men begin their task, grunting under the weight of the earth-laden shovels and the heat of the day.

Laria and Nikolas agree to follow us to the villa in their own car, to eat with us. One last commemoration for the dead. Our cook, unfazed by murder and the loss of a maid, has managed to create a lovely buffet of delicacies ranging from tea sandwiches to spanakopita and, being a favorite of the deceased, small rum cakes.

It is a pity that none of us have much of an appetite. Even the cake receives only cursory attentions. Laria told Nikolas of Paul's guilt and he mentions it, sadly shaking his head. I think he laments the loss of the murderer more than that of the victim. Perhaps understandably so.

"Do you have any idea what will happen to Rosie?" Briony asks the doctor.

"Her brother is coming to get her. He sent a telegram informing the police that he booked passage and is expected to arrive in a week's time. He has asked her nurse to stay on until then. I went to the house last night to inquire about her and the situation as it is."

I lean forward in my chair. "How is she coping?"

Nikolas twists his features into something unreadable. "To be honest, I do not notice a difference. She has asked for him, to be sure, but she seems content enough."

"Poor woman." Laria's tone reveals her distress.

It must be an ordeal for her to sit here with her husband, having just buried her lover and manage to maintain her social graces. I give her a sympathetic smile and hope she can read its intent. She returns a tiny, grateful nod.

"What will you do now, Daniel?" Nikolas asks, taking an olive from the tray.

Daniel looks uneasy, replying, "I do not really know yet."

The chatter goes on for quite a while longer until Laria and Nikolas leave for home. At the door, when Nikolas has turned his back, Laria approaches Daniel and squeezes his hand. She is probably one of the few people who recognized the Caspar Daniel spoke of at the cemetary. It is a small bond they share and one I am oddly envious of.

After the guests leave, Briony takes me aside. She is wearing a surprising expression of excitement and anxiety, and I immediately feel a pang of concern regarding the cause of this shift in her mood.

"What is it, Briony?"

"Evie, you mustn't think me callous for being a little happy right now, but I spoke to Jeffrey last night."

A light of understanding dawns. "About Areta?"

"Well, about her, about the orphanage, about us." She smiles shyly, and her cheeks turn pink.

"And? What did he say?"

"He was a bit, oh, you know, a bit awkward at first. Typical Englishman. Typical Jeffrey. Still, I was persistent." She looks proud, and I feel a rush of relief to finally see her this way.

"How did he react?"

"He is not convinced about the idea of adoption. However, I have made it quite clear that I will be a mother one way or another, and since it simply hasn't happened in the three years we have been married . . ."

"Did you ask him to go with you and visit the orphanage?"

"I did."

"And? Come now, don't make me beg!"

"He said he will come with me on Sunday. He wasn't happy about it, but I wore him down. Once he meets the children, he will be as enchanted as I am, don't you think?"

I am not at all certain, so I smile noncommittally and she is content.

"I am happy for you. Truly, I am."

"I know," Briony gives me a quick hug. "And now I must attend to finding a new maid, our cook has been a rock, but she's struggling a bit."

"You go on." I encourage, the words encompassing more than wishing her success in replacing Niobe.

She huries off with a distinctive bounce in her step entirely unfitting for a day such as this, yet lovely nonetheless. Anytime we have reason to skip, we should count ourselves lucky. Spirit has returned to her at a time of mourning through the prospect of hope.

I wander over to the conservatory, not wanting to go to my room and face my thoughts alone. Entering, I can barely trust my eyes. A tall figure is standing on the veranda, gazing out. Daniel has ventured into the garden again.

I open the door and step into the mild evening air. Daniel turns around. His expression is serene, peaceful.

"Hello." He gives me a flicker of a smile.

"May I join you?"

"Please." His smile widens. "Would you care to take a stroll around the garden with me?"

I take a small breath, my eyes reflexively darting to the oak tree at the far right. Gathering courage, we saunter onto the dry grass. The earth is so hard and baked, the heels of my sandals do not sink while we make our way around the garden. We stop at the edge, steps away from where it happened, where the nightmare began. Daniel takes a deep breath, his chest rising underneath his white shirt. He has rolled his sleeves up to the elbows and unbuttoned the top. There is an ease about him I have not seen before. It seems as if he has laid more than one ghost to rest today.

The sun, bright and orange on the horizon, bathes our surroundings in a soft, becoming light. We stand there side by side, watching its slow descent as the clouds float by, purple and pink and blue. Seagulls drift across this vivid canvas, thin streaks, their cries carried by the wind. It is Jeffrey who interrupts this tranquility, beckonging us in for dinner. I call back that we are coming, and he disappears indoors. We take one last look at the sight before us and as we turn to go, Daniel takes hold of my hand, which fits like the missing piece of a puzzle into his, and leads me back to the house.

Pandora has closed her box again, just in time. When Hades walks among us, in times of darkness and despair, we are left with the infinite gift of hope. Hope for a better tomorrow, for change, for humanity. Treading this stage that is life, we are fragile, vulnerable, flawed, human, but we are not alone. The sun falls below the horizon, and our world is dipped into darkness, until it returns, dependable and true, warming us and lighting our way.

ACKNOWLEDGEMENTS

There are many people to thank for helping this book become a reality. Before all others, my mother - first reader, editor, best friend - who was on Evelyn's journey from the very start, thank you. To my dad and sisters, too, thank you for your kind support and perpetual understanding, even when it may have seemed as though this book was just some endless project I snuck off for every evening. I am grateful for all those whose patience and support made these words a real book, and for all of those who will read it. Lady Evelyn's adventures do not end here, and I hope you will stick around to see what is around the next turn (or rather page). Thank you!

For more information or to get in touch, you can contact me at maliazaidiauthor@gmail.com, or follow me on Twitter @MaliaZaidi